The Covenant of
Marriage

BOOK TWO IN THE COVENANT SERIES

The Covenant of Marriage

GOD'S PLAN
TO PRODUCE DEEPEST LOVE, STRONGEST RELATIONSHIPS, PERSONAL GROWTH AND TRANSFORMATION

MARK JOHNSON, MD

Carpenter's Son Publishing

The Covenant of Marriage

©2020 by Mark Johnson

Published by Carpenter's Son Publishing, Franklin, Tennessee

Published in association with Larry Carpenter of Christian Book Services, LLC
www.christianbookservices.com

Interior and Cover Design by Suzanne Lawing

Edited by Robert Irvin

Printed in the United States of America

978-1-949572-52-0

This book is dedicated to my wife Holley, my best friend,
lover, teacher, and so much more.

HOLLEY'S SONG

September 1999

First but a motion, a heart in a form danced before my eyes.
A brush of emotion, a hint of a smile; I walked up and stood beside.

Like dancers sweeping across the floor, engaging and pulling away,
Our souls circled slowly, eyes softly touched, watching, day after day.

Second, a voice sweet as an angel created a comfortable place.
Growing awareness, lovely eyes, near her I wanted to stay.

Like dancers circling on the floor with carefully concealed fire,
With gentlest grasp our eyes held each other with flickerings of desire.

Third, admiration of carriage and action gave confidence to inquire.
Truth spoken plainly of mind and heart, the doors of our hearts opened wide.

Dancers now facing, fully attentive, wait for the music to start.
Eyes gently probing opening souls saw worthy lives and hearts.

An offer was issued, and offer accepted, ears strained to hear the first chord.
Anticipation changed into delight as the music carried them on.

Like dancers just paired, whose lives have prepared them for each other's every move.
Each step was joy, each move celebration, harmony, fluid and smooth.

Teaching each other life lessons of dance, passion like lightning explodes.
Hearts, minds, bodies and lives intertwined as new life is born in the soul.

Like a tango danced to thunder by passionate birds in the sky,
Love of dance, dance of love carries them on till two lives merge slowly toward One.

Contents

Foreword

Marriage is a vehicle. Two people get in and go somewhere together. They want to be transported … to a better future, to the raptures of love, to the joys of family life, to the fulfillment of their dreams. They want to be moved … to feel, to grow, to move forward in life, to build something worth having for themselves and the one they love. But what is this vehicle they have entered? What is marriage?

We know several things about marriage. It is as old as human history, and a vital integrating point for every person in every culture throughout history. And, throughout its long and important history, marriage has remained pretty much the same all over the earth, doing the things it has always done—building something important for the couple, building the next generation, and being the focal point of cultural continuity. Marriage and family are the most fundamental social unit in every culture, and many would say the most important. And we know something else about marriage. In our culture it is increasingly challenged.

Anyone picking up this book is probably interested in marriage, and anyone interested in marriage is especially interested in having a good one. But what does a good marriage look like? How does a couple come to have a good marriage? In a culture where marriage failure rates have skyrocketed during my sixty-five-year lifetime, where couples who love each other are refraining from entering marriage in unprecedented numbers, how can one approach marriage with any real confidence? Who can tell us how to take something with such a successful track record and make it a success in our own lives? Frankly, how did we manage to turn good marriages into an endangered species in a handful of decades in our culture?

The first thing we need to learn to build a good marriage is what marriage is. Then we need to realize that this vehicle we are getting into must be constructed. There has been a plan in place throughout history for building a good marriage—a vehicle that takes us where we want to go. But, in recent years, many new plans have showen up all around us. People are building a huge array of different things that are not working nearly so well. To build something that works well, one needs a working plan, the right materials, and the willingness to do a good job of building.

Our underlying assumption now is that marital success is about finding the right person and true love. The current plan used by most is a large sheet of paper with a few words written on it: "what adds to my life, and advances what I think is my self-interest." The building material most often employed is "what I feel like in the moment." And, using this guidance and this material, two people who are strongly attracted to each other and who care deeply about each other begin to build. One day one of them feels like they can fly, so a wing is added. The next day, slowing down a bit, a wheel; when slowing down more, a seat. The next day things are going sideways, so another wheel is added pointing sideways. The other person is also adding things of their own, as they like. Then these two get in this vehicle and try to go somewhere. Where is the steering wheel, or is there one? How many are there? Are people looking forward, or backward? The point being, if there is not a carefully laid plan to build something so important, if the couple just hops in and plans to figure it out as they go—meaning they have no real plan—what kind of vehicle will they build? How strong and resilient will it be? Accidents happen. Life happens. What happens then? What are the odds that this thing will take them where either wants to go? And where do they want to go?

In case you think this picture is not real, look around. A good marriage is a well-built thing. It is carefully fashioned according to a working plan. It is built of solid and resilient material. It is up to the task and will get people where they really want to go. A really good marriage is like the most beautiful, highest quality, best designed vehicle on the road. Clearly designed by an expert, carefully handcrafted, lovingly assembled, and highly capable in every situation. Except that a good marriage cannot really be compared to a car. Marriage is a vehicle that is vastly more important. So why are most cars built with more of an eye toward function and quality than most marriages? How many marriages today are frustrating struggles, going in circles, stuck beside the road, broken down, or broken apart? How many are careening toward where only one person wants to go? Instead of a huge part of the solution to the problems of living, how many marriages are the problem? Is this a problem with marriage? Or is this a problem with our understanding of marriage? Is the problem that the institution of marriage is a relic that should be discarded, or is the problem how we are attempting to build marriages?

One clue: marriage has not changed. It has been the same from the beginning, for thousands of years. What has changed in the last few decades are a lot of things about us. We, as humans, have not changed in a fundamental way. What has changed resides in our decisions—how we choose to see things, how we choose to do things, what we choose to see as important. These decisions can be revised at any time. If we can learn how to *not* do something well, we can also learn how to do it well, especially if there is still a working plan available to us and every resource we will need is still at our disposal.

Let us think for a moment about the difference between how one builds something carefully and skillfully designed, and something thrown together on the spur of the moment. One difference is a blueprint. How does a blueprint help us build correctly? First, as we look at one, we see a clear picture of what we are trying to build. Then there are detailed diagrams of each element. A blueprint gives us both the big picture and every needed detail. If the design is appropriate and effective, one can take the blueprint and build step by step to completion. You will notice the terms "covenant plan" and "God's plan" repeated throughout the book. I want you to begin thinking of marriage as something very specific that must be built. To build the best car or house, much less the best marriage, we need the best plan; then we need to carefully follow this plan and build step by step. What do you want your marriage to become? What elements must be built into marriage so that it works best? Where did your plan for marriage come from? Or, do you have a plan at all?

The most important initial understanding, as noted, is what marriage *is*. This understanding in our culture, even our Christian culture, has gone missing almost entirely. Hence this book, which looks at marriage in light of this historical understanding. The beginning point of building a marriage to its potential is being able to define marriage correctly. We must first understand what makes this type of relationship the special thing that it is.

Fortunately, we do not need to consult friends, media, or culture about this relationship. We have another source for the definition of marriage, a source that explains every aspect, every detail that makes it so unique, so special, so powerful, so beneficial. Beyond the particulars, marriage is a special kind of relationship, termed a *covenant* relationship. We may also have heard this term applied to another relationship, the one God offers each of us with Himself through Jesus. He terms this relationship the *New Covenant*.

Most people today think of marriage as a make-it-up-as-you-go-along kind of thing. It is all about love. We simply love each other as best we can. We find someone so special that we want to spend our lives together, and perhaps raise a family together. So, do we marry? Or not? Do we even need marriage after all? Isn't this just about the love of two people? Isn't this about finding the right person, finding true love? If we find this person and this love, doesn't love for a lifetime inevitably follow? Isn't marriage, with all the rules and religious overlay, about as likely to stand in our way as to help us?

> Isn't marriage, with all the rules and religious overlay, about as likely to stand in our way as to help us?

If this is what we think—and many in our culture think just this way—this means we do not understand covenant. A marriage covenant is a relationship, but more than just a relationship. First, it is a gift of God to the human race—the first gift He gave us after life itself. If you have not read the first volume in this series I strongly recommend you do so, for in this book the historic understanding of covenant is fully explained. In this first volume we also see why our culture, including the Christian community, is confused about the basic nature of covenant, most often likening it to a *contract*. A covenant is nothing like a contract. It is not an agreement between two people to behave in certain ways. If our current understanding of covenant is challenged, might this explain why marriages in our culture, including our Christian culture, have become increasingly challenged in the last few decades?

We will see in this book that marriage is all about love. But God does not just tell us to love, then leave us to figure out what this means. Nor are we just given a list of rules. Love is not about rules. At the same time, our hearts and relationships do work according to certain principles. Our hearts respond predictably to being treated well or badly. A wedding ring does not alter this equation. If the person on the other side of the relationship displays certain character qualities, love and relationship grow. If other character qualities are displayed, love cools and relationship is damaged. In covenant God defines loving actions and loving character. Once any of us sees the full spectrum of what it means to love, we realize how far we are from being able to be all of these things, or do all of these things. Not to worry. Inherent in covenant is a plan for learning, for growth, and for the transformation of each of us. In covenant we find the motivation to do and to be our best toward our beloved. But our best will still fall short of building the best relationship or fully loving our covenant partner. Again, not to worry. If we realize this, God has us right where He wants us. Our relationships cannot grow beyond a certain point if we are not growing. In order to build the best relationship we must grow and mature, and we must grow together in specific ways as a couple.

While learning and applying God's covenant plan over the last thirty-five years, I have been amazed most of all by the love and wisdom of God. The covenant of marriage is fueled by many of our deepest drives: the desire to join ourselves to someone in a lifelong relationship; to love and be loved; to find our happily-ever-after, a deeply committed relationship that endures through good times and bad; to raise children, building a family and a legacy; and, overall, to devote ourselves to something good and noble that is larger than ourselves. God's plan also draws from the ways our mind works, the ways our heart works, and the ways that relationships work. He knows all about these because He created them. He combines every element together to create a certain outcome—the growth of love between two people. Aside from just doing what we know we are supposed to do in marriage, God's plan transforms us so we want to do these things. We understand the reasons behind these things and enjoy doing them because they are the most beneficial in the long run for everyone, including ourselves.

If we *understand and follow God's plan* for marriage, we are given everything we need to build love for a lifetime. Two people in love can come together in a way that uniquely joins and merges their natures and identities—a covenant. It is from this merger—the defining characteristic of covenant—that everything else flows. This alteration and joining of nature and identity logically changes the ways we treat each other. Because our nature and identity change—our true selves change—our true self-interest changes, and thus our priorities, values, goals, and many other things shift dramatically. But we must realize and embrace this transformation. We must learn to live out these details. Everything we do in covenant according to God's plan builds love, builds relationship, and authentically expresses who we now are. This is the perfect combination with which to build love for a lifetime.

We will predictably express these new selves imperfectly. We must grow into living out these new selves. This is not a simple process, nor is it inevitable. We must choose to conform our lives to this new reality, or we may hang on to our old status quo and try to be someone who no longer exists. Growth is slow and messy; it was when we grew up the first time, from infants to children, to teens, and to adulthood. It will be messy as we begin to grow up the second time within our marriages. But the outcome is worth the effort and aggravation.

In God's plan for growth one of the most important things we can do is rid ourselves of things in our minds and hearts carried forward from our single lives. These patterns—actions, beliefs, values, habits, and character—no longer reflect who we are, and they will predictably

> But these problems are not a terrible thing. They are not even bad things; such "problems" actually identity opportunities for learning, growth, development, and transformation.

create problems in our life together. But these problems are not a terrible thing. They are not even bad things; such "problems" actually identity opportunities for learning, growth, development, and transformation. If we deal with these issues according to God's plan, we are on the path to maturity, the path to learning to truly love across the spectrum of life.

God's plan is larger than a relationship between two people. It equips us to handle the challenges of living. Marriage is not always easy; neither is life. If we follow God's plan we will build a strong and deep relationship with our covenant partner and with God. With these resources to draw from as well as God's plan to guide us, every circumstance we encounter along the way—even adversity and tragedy—can become the ground from which grows even greater strength and maturity and a deeper capacity to love. Jesus summed up God's desire for each of us: we are to love God and love each other. We have all heard this. But have you heard His plan for developing us into people who can actually do this consistently and well, and enjoy doing so? *His plan is covenant.*

There is nothing complicated and significant we humans learn that does not involve an exacting, disciplined, and challenging training process—surgeon, professional athlete, artist, pilot, and many, many more professions. Building a great marriage and family, and becoming a good covenant partner or a good parent, these are among the highest-skill jobs of all. Do we think any less would be required if we are to do something so complex and important—and so greatly rewarded? Marriage is a much more complex and wonderful plan than most of us realize, but in order for us to benefit from this wonderful plan we must be devoted to it. To choose to devote ourselves to this plan we must see and understand this plan. Then we must have sufficient reasons to choose such devotion. That is the purpose of this book: to gain this understanding so we may reasonably choose to devote ourselves to the plan of the Author of marriage, and the Author of ourselves.

What if you had a direct and clear communication that was undoubtedly from God? There is simply no question that the God of the universe is speaking directly to you. He asks you to do something very important, something that will impact many people in partnership with Him. He provides the resources, power, overall plan, and moment-by-moment directions as needed.

How would it feel to be working with God to build something significant—learning from Him, drawing from His resources, watching His power work in and through you to have a significant impact? What would this be like for you? Would you want to do this? Would this situation not, in fact, be one of the high points of your life? Maybe the most important thing that ever happened to you? Achieving something significant as you fulfilling the purposes of the Creator of the universe?

Guess what? God is making precisely this offer to you in your marriage. See if this does not become clear as you read these pages.

CHAPTER ONE

The Real Questions

If you are picking up a book on the Covenant of Marriage, odds are you are looking for ways to improve an existing marriage or looking forward to building a new one. If you ask around in the Christian community or in the culture at large, you will hear a huge array of advice and approaches. Underlying this variety are various views of marriage and goals for marriage.

If I want to get from my home to a location on the other side of town, and I ask a half-dozen people how to get from point A to point B, I will get a half-dozen potential routes. And this is fine, because any path I choose will get me where I want to go.

On the other hand, if I, as a surgeon (my profession for decades) consult with the nation's leading expert on a complex, technically difficult operation, there will be one way to get the job done—an extremely exacting approach involving a huge number of specific details. Each detail matters, and beyond this, strict adherence to the principles of surgery is imperative if one is to deal successfully with the unexpected things inevitably encountered during an operation. Especially in an operation with no margin for error.

On the surface, marriage appears more like getting across town than a complicated operation; any way we feel like choosing will do. Many people just wing it, with no plan whatever. "We love each other; we'll figure it out." Since two people thinking about marriage or already married have already built a strong love relationship by doing whatever they have been doing, the idea of a specific plan does not seem at first glance to even make sense.

However, God knows something about marriage that we may not. He created it and conveyed it to humanity. He created us to desire a certain quality of relationship—to love and be loved—and not only for a while. Those of us who are married yearn for a certain outcome for our marriages: happily ever after. Are we aware that God also wants this for us? And that He knows how to make it happen?

What we do not realize in the midst of our head-over-heels, this-is-the-one experience is how hard it is to sustain and grow love for a lifetime as we wade through all the challenges and changes of life. But God knows. He sees all of this coming. He has fashioned a plan with us in mind, and I am convinced that He fashioned us with this plan in mind. His plan is to teach us how to love for a lifetime. The multi-tool He uses to do this is called the *Covenant of Marriage*.

My wife and I are living out a decades-long, very intense, extremely close, deeply intimate love affair. We have learned much. We have built many things together. We have grown in many ways together, and therefore we have grown together in many ways. We have been transformed in many ways since our journeys and lives were joined. And we are far more passionately in love with each other than when we each decided we had found "the one." Throughout our marriage, about once a month we have been asked by perfect strangers how long we have been together. People are always shocked to hear the answer: decades. Or someone mentions our palpable love, a connection they see from across a room that is unusual enough to merit comment. I am often not sure exactly what they notice, but a large number of people over many years have seen something between us that is apparently uncommon. What do they see? I believe they see something God wants to build for every married couple—a relationship in which the joining and merger of identities is manifested so strongly that it becomes visible, palpable. Love, chosen and built into the relationship per God's plan for decades, is formed into a power that can be felt across a room.

Did we just pick the winning number? Simply choose right? Were we fortunate enough to find true love? All of these are partly true. Holley is wonderful; I got lucky. We made good choices, both

> Did we just pick the winning number? Simply choose right? Were we fortunate enough to find true love?

in our objects of affection and in how we built a strong love relationship from the beginning. But luck changes, people drift, and love fades. There is much more to this story. Holley and I have been following God's plan for marriage enthusiastically and wholeheartedly throughout our relationship. That has made all the difference.

The more marriages I see over the decades, the more convinced I become that the quality of a marriage directly reflects how closely that relationship corresponds with, or does not correspond with, God's plan for marriage. Holley and I started marriage where everyone else begins. We cared about each other and we had a strong relationship, but we also had no idea how *different* we were. We thought differently about many things, felt differently, wanted different things, and had different ways of dealing with issues. Though we felt this amazing oneness, this did not translate into a unanimous approach to nearly anything in our lives. We had our agendas and viewpoints, and each thought we should steer the ship. We all start there. The question is, how will we handle these differences? What happens next? God's plan outlines certain approaches to these differences, while the world's plan commends an entirely different set of approaches. The plan each couple chooses, selected from these two options—because these are the only two available to us—makes all the difference.

Few people realize that God has a well-defined plan to build a marriage. Those who think God might have a plan usually think this plan is about *following a set of rules*, rules that war against our inclinations and may not even be good ideas. But God's plan is something altogether different.

Is a marriage more similar to a drive across town, or does someone having your heart and mind and future in his or her hands call for a more careful approach? Do you want to be handled with the care of a passing stranger who offers you a ride—placing your very life in his or her trembling and inattentive hands—or would you prefer someone who knows how to love in every situation, someone with high-level relationship skills, and someone who is totally committed to your well-being? When the storms of life descend on you, who do you want by your side? A mature adult and careful surgeon, or a wing-it, self-absorbed overgrown adolescent?

God's plan is designed to offer us every possible motivation to do what we want to do anyway. At least on a good day, which is to consistently love our covenant partner. And it is designed to do one other very important thing: *to change us*. To change us from the inside out, to grow us up, to tap into every potential within us to become the best person we can be. God knows how to tap into our ideas, beliefs, priorities, senses of self-interest, ideals, goals, motivations, feelings, and even our identity (and our understanding of our identity, which may be a different thing), to shape us into people who can actually do what we most want to do. We want to be loved for a lifetime, and we want to give love for a lifetime—and not just the superficial thing the world calls love, but love in action, love from the core of our being.

God's plan is extensive and detailed. Marriages are extensive and detailed, so His plan is scaled for the size of the task. As we examine the entirety of this plan, it becomes obvious that God intends to build more than a lifelong love between two people. This plan is about building people who are capable of new and different things; who know how to understand the needs of others and meet those needs; who are mature; who have developed their gifts, potential, and people skills to high levels. It is about taking these developed people and building families, communities, and cultures.

God's plan is doable. It is about going through daily life and making a certain set of choices that we are capable of making. It may involve learning and studying, thought and soul searching, and trying new things. Learning how to be a good covenant partner is just like learning any other skill or developing a special talent. While we often have invested a lot and gotten very little for it—say, in school or some other training process—if we are following God's plan we can be confident our efforts will be abundantly rewarded. I can certainly testify to that, as can my wife.

Before we can carry out God's plan, or even decide that we want to do so, we need to see His plan. The beginning point of His plan is to understand covenant. If you read the first volume of this three-volume series, you can already define this word. You know something about the three related forms of Covenant—marriage covenant, blood covenant, and the New Covenant. You understand the defining feature of covenant—*an exchange of identity between the parties*, which joins the two in a unique way. This new, merged identity means that the natures of the two have been joined and merged. You realize that as this new, merged identity and nature comes into being, each person's old identity and nature ceases to exist. The two literally become new and different creatures by entering covenant, by becoming, as the Scriptures term it, "one flesh" (Genesis 3).

In covenant people are to regard each other and treat each other in specific ways. The sum of these things is an excellent definition of love in action. But the most important insight of all about covenant is *why* we are called to do these things. We are told to treat each other in every way as well as we would treat ourselves … because in a very real sense, the other person now is myself. Every consequence of this sharing and merger of identity is illustrated by the duties, responsibilities, obligations, and opportunities of a covenant relationship. All of these behaviors are simply the logical response to this new reality—these new, merged identities. This reality and its many implications was the subject of Volume One, in addition to examining the historic basis for this understanding. We will retrace some of this information in this volume, but the first book covers this topic in a way we will simply not have space to repeat in this volume or the next. This more complete explanation is vital if one is to derive the most benefit from either marriage or a relationship with God.

Why, then, does everyone not simply follow God's plan? We covered this extensively in Volume One and will speak to this question a bit more in this volume. It is vital that we understand and cut through the confusion surrounding this question. And the confusion surrounding marriage. A clear understanding will inform better individual choices about following God's plan. One thing we will clearly see: following God's plan is a choice, a choice each of us faces in a global sense, then at every step, in every detail. In order to follow this plan we must choose to do so. And we must reaffirm this choice on a daily basis. We must find compelling reasons if we are to make these choices.

In this volume, in addition to laying out God's plan, I hope to provide sufficient reasons to follow that plan. Keep in mind that to not make a choice about this issue is, in fact, to make a choice. As you read this volume, please do not merely seek information. Keep asking yourself what you want most in your marriage, how you are most likely to get what you want, and what you are willing to do to have the best possible marriage.

In Volume One we discussed an important reality: alternative ideas about marriage throughout history appear, on the surface, to be exercises in human creativity or practicality or preference. But there is something more going on. Throughout history people have been deceived about the path to the best marriage, just as they have been deceived about the path to the best life and many other things. Our world is awash in deception and confusion. This confusion will find its way into every person's initial approach to marriage. Where did this confusion come from?

Since the first couple, covenant has been the heart of God's plan for individuals and for humanity. At the same time, humans inhabit a spiritual battleground. This was first noted in Scripture in Genesis 3 in the conversation between Eve and Satan. An excellent case can be made that this worldwide, history-long confusion about marriage comes from precisely the same source as Eve's confusion about the path to her best life. We can make this inference because confusion ever since follows the same pattern. This war of ideas is not just about true versus false, but about truth versus deception. Deceptions are false ideas made to look true, but they are more. These are ideas that promise great benefit if embraced. When we are faced with such an idea, our focus shifts from discerning truth from falsehood to desire for an outcome. If we are persuaded to want the outcome badly enough, we become willing to bend the truth or make other compromises to pursue this outcome. Promised benefits of this type always have a specific price tag: to obtain the promised benefit we must somehow depart from the plan of God. Thus, we offend Him in the process of seeking something He does not offer us. We are told that we need something different from the life God offers, then sold on the idea that this new offering is a crucial thing if we are to live our best lives. We are invited to brush past the One who truly loves us and is trying to lead us to our best lives, and reach out for . . . However, just as in Satan's initial interaction with the human race, these promised benefits never materialize—for that was never the point. But in obeying these ideas, we are now obeying the ones behind these ideas, enemies of God who have been engaging with humanity throughout history. We join them in their rebellion even if we are not aware such a rebellion exists. This is the point. These ideas are offered to do damage to us and our relationship with God. And in the process to wreak havoc in our own lives, even as we are now convinced we are on the path to our best life.

Thus, in marriage there are not many paths we might take to get from here to there. There are literally *two* paths: God's plan and "other." The reason God is so insistent on fidelity to His plan and only His plan is the ultimate source of competing ideas that we might try to synthesize with His. Thus, part of our journey is learning to distinguish the plan of God from competing ideas. We need to recognize the sources of various ideas, to spot the fingerprints on one idea or another.

> The reason God is so insistent on fidelity to His plan and only His plan is the ultimate source of competing ideas that we might try to synthesize with His.

This we can do *if* we understand the underlying principles of God's plan and those of the plan of His enemy.

In order to fully appreciate God's plan we need to look at the alternative, at the way our world teaches us to do relationship. We must examine these ideas in practice, and we must look at the outcome of these ideas with false optimism stripped away. Only if we understand the world's plan, and the predictable outcomes of this strategy, will we properly appreciate the plan of God. Then we must see the plan of God in action, and look at the kind of relationships this plan will build, and the kind of *us* this plan will build. Then we need to look at this plan as it builds families, communities, and culture.

GOD'S PLAN FOR THE COVENANT OF MARRIAGE

1. Recognize the Author of the Covenant of Marriage, and therefore His authority.

2. Understand the unity of identity and the union that occurs between covenant partners: *what God has joined together.*

3. Understand the personal transformation that occurs as one enters covenant.

4. Understand within covenant the imperative of loving one's partner in every sense of this word, and the reason we are able to do so—the transformation and unity of identity created by covenant.

5. Understand God's functional definition of love as seen in the principles, priorities, obligations, and responsibilities of covenant, which correspond perfectly with the definition of loving, virtuous behaviors in Scripture versus our various definitions of love.

6. Understand the role that choice plays in the growth of our relationships—loving, faithful, obedient choices versus everything else. Understand the motivational system in covenant that aids us in choosing loving behaviors toward our covenant partner. Understand that faithfulness to our covenant is synonymous with perfectly loving our partner. Understand that faithfulness to our covenant—our partner and our obligations—is our highest duty.

7. Understand God's plan for dealing with predictable failures to love: learning, personal growth, and personal transformation.

8. Understand God's use of issues in the relationship to motivate growth and transformation; in God's plan these are not problems, they are opportunities.

9. Understand our roles in growth and transformation and the role played by a properly built relationship.

10. Understand that learning to love well and consistently through covenant is the path to continued growth of affection and passion over our lifetimes—our happily-ever-after.

11. Understand that learning to love our partner as covenant directs is the foundation for loving our families, for good parenting, and for playing the most constructive roles in our communities.

12. Understand the big picture of covenant: God's plan is intended to teach us to love as He loves, beginning with our beloved, then extending outward to reach the world.

QUESTIONS FOR THOUGHT

1. Why is the institution of marriage in so much trouble today?

2. Why do people what to be married? What benefits derive from this relationship?

3. What roles has marriage historically played in the lives of individuals?

4. What roles has marriage historically played in society?

5. What are the most important things you want in your marriage?

6. Are these things a part of your marriage now—occasionally, often, always?

7. What do you want from a book on marriage?

8. What would you be willing to do to have the marriage you really want?

9. Do you think it is possible to have the marriage of your dreams? Why or why not?

10. What do you think God wants for you in your marriage?

Next we will look at an outline of God's plan. This outline will not mean much at this point until we more fully understand all the terms used. Once we lay out, for instance, God's definition of love, it will be clear why His definition works so much better than ours over a lifetime of marriage, and why our hearts predictably grow toward each other when we are loved in these ways.

CHAPTER TWO

The World's Plan for Marriage

THE CONTRACTUAL MODEL

To fully appreciate the radical nature of God's covenant plan, we need to contrast it with the alternative plan we are all familiar with for human relationships: a contract. A contract is an agreement between two or more parties that defines what the parties will do and not do. It specifies acts to be done and goods to be supplied, generally in an exchange of some sort. Formal written contracts are legally binding documents that define behaviors and also limit the scope of expectations and liability.

There is an informal version of this same format that governs virtually every human relationship and interaction. This encompasses our understanding of what we can reasonably expect people to do and what we can reasonably expect people to not do. If someone accepts a dinner invitation at our home, we expect that they will arrive at our home, hungry, at more or less the appointed time. We do not expect that they will bring fifteen other people with them without alerting us beforehand. Some things represent general social expectations. Then there are things in every relationship that are the result of an informal negotiation that defines what each person can expect from the other. Who pays for dinner? Is it a welcomed act of courtesy for the guy to open a door for the girl, or would he never dare offend her in this way?

When one is entering into a formal or informal contract the general approach is to offer something to the other party. Both parties bring something to the table. The ideal is a situation where both parties feel what was received has more perceived value than what was offered, a "win-win" situation. Then there are all manner of scenarios where people misrepresent the value of what is offered or otherwise manipulate the situation to take advantage of the other party.

When two are building a romance that may be moving toward marriage a much more detailed negotiation occurs. Both parties are seeing if they enjoy each other's company, find each other attractive, have a strong heart response toward the other, and like being seen in each other's company. The initial heart response is termed a crush or infatuation; as feelings grow the two begin to talk of "falling in love." At the same time, though, both parties are doing calculations. How much is this relationship going to cost me and how much am I going to get out of it? If the overall package looks like a good deal, people move forward in the relationship. In the past this meant getting married in one's teens or twenties. Today it may mean either getting married or moving in together and possibly getting married at some point before the biological clock runs down.

The thing to note here is the essence of a contract: agreed-upon expectations—or at least expectations we thought we had agreed upon. "What do you mean, 'You want us to move to Colorado?' My job and my family and all my friends are here!" We must understand the fundamental reason people enter and remain in a contract: an overall estimation of personal gain. Which is strongly linked to their original expectations and the extent to which those are actually being met. Contracts are easily ended. People walk away from them every day if they believe the other party has already breached the agreement— in this case by failing to meet their expectations. What else, after all, brought them into this arrangement in the first place? Entering and continuing a contractual romantic relationship is a function of how we see that relationship affecting our self-interest at every point. If it is working for us, we stay in it. If it is not working for us, we exercise our out clause.

THE WORLD'S CONTRACTUAL VIEW OF MARRIAGE

Based on this description of contractual relationships, I want to pose a few questions for your consideration. Would you agree that virtually all the marriages and romantic relationships you are aware of are conducted on this type of foundation? Is this a fair description of the way our world does relationship? We are informed that, "The best marriages are 50-50 kinds of things." It is commonly assumed that if mutual feelings are strong enough—therefore true love—this benefit to our existence will make everything else fall into place. True love is supposedly sufficient motivation to ensure that the other party will continue to offer us a good deal "till death do us part." Feelings of love for another person certainly bring out the best in us—they transport us to a new and delightful experience of living—and they motivate us to extremes of good behavior toward each other. But if the things we most value from a relationship are our own loving feelings toward another person, and the blessings they offer us are motivated by their own new, deep feelings for us, how stable and enduring a foundation are we basing our happily-ever-after upon? Might we want to think more deeply about this approach?

If people are actually in a covenant, why are most marriages conducted as if they are a contractual arrangement? One of the themes of this series is that one can be in a relationship that is actually one thing, but conduct the relationship as if it is something else altogether. In other words, what we build more reflects what we *think* marriage is than what it *actually is*. And we can actually *be* one thing but persist in acting as if *we are something else*. Everyone who is married is in a covenant. One does not need to understand this relationship to enter one—obviously. However, one does need to understand this relationship and all it involves to conduct the relationship in a way that realizes its potential. This is true with marriage

> We can actually *be* one thing but persist in acting as if we are something else. Everyone who is married is in a covenant.

and it is true regarding our relationship with God. If the enemy cannot stop people from entering covenants, fine. If people become confused about what these relationships represent, they will fail to accomplish some of the things, or perhaps any of the things, that God intends for individuals, families, and communities. Who wins in this case? Who loses? This is why we are emphasizing God's plan for implementing these relationships in whole and in each detail, for only via this path will these relationships produce the results He desires, and we desire.

Let's look more closely at the relationship produced by superimposing the world's mind-set on a marriage.

THE CONTRACTUAL MODEL CREATES THE 'COMPETING KINGDOMS' MODEL

If most marriages are based on a contract model, contracts are made between two separate and distinct entities. People do not enter contracts with themselves. If we are going to have a contractual model of marriage, this necessarily means that we will have two separate lives held together only by a *bond of agreement*. This and this alone—in our minds—becomes our basis for marriage. I refer to this as the "competing kingdoms model of marriage." If one is not consciously living out a covenant model of marriage, this is literally the only other option.

If we are not aware of our identity change as we enter marriage, how do we view ourselves? In the same way we always have. We have spent our lives building . . . what? *Our own lives.* We want marriage to be what? Value added to our lives. How do we build the life we want according to our culture? By getting our way: having things the way we want them, pursuing our preferences, satisfying our needs, and gratifying our desires. Our life is very much a kingdom—or queendom—and we are the monarch, the head of our lives, deeply desiring to be in charge of as much as possible because enlarging our influence equates with having a better life. We think. Thanks to many cultural influences we have come to believe that this is our path to true happiness. Whether this is actually true is another question. But this is the starting point in marriage for almost everyone, even if they are head over heels in love.

Even if we love the other person, they are still *the other person*. So now we have the dilemma of balancing our good intentions toward this other person with our perception of our best interest—at every point in our lives together. In practice, this leads to two often sharply competing sets of priorities within each party as they try to juggle good intentions and personal interests. It also results in sharply competing priorities between the parties. Why? Because the other person is on the other side of this relationship doing the same juggling act, calculating how much they want to give, or are willing to give up, to get what they ultimately want most, which will always reflect their perception of self-interest. The root of the conflict in this model is between two things that are often completely opposite in practice: perceived self-interest, with a willingness to sacrifice relationship to get the "win," versus goodwill and the desire to build the relationship, which will involve some degree of self-sacrifice if one genuinely cares about the other party. The rest of this dance is the two figuring out who is going to do the sacrificing and who gets their way in each scenario. To the extent that people pursue self-interest at the expense of the relationship, what happens to the relationship? Will it inevitably sustain damage? The quality of these kinds of relationships are determined by the way the parties strike the balance between these imperatives. Kind, considerate, and good-natured people often do a pretty good job of building more relationship and inflicting less damage, which is why marriages founded upon this model often "work." But if our relationship is ultimately at the mercy of what each of us feels like doing, and if our sense of self-interest diverges enough from the interests of the other party of or the relationship, what happens? You'll get something like this: "You must understand how much my career means to me!"

So as this plays forward we have two people negotiating and jousting, at points going at each other as hard as possible, all for the sake of protecting and promoting self-interest. Even if these people genuinely like each other and have warm feelings toward each other, you still see people undercutting each other in many ways. Why? They are trying to neuter each other's strengths to alter the balance of power. Why would two people who love each other do this? Because the more power the other person has, the less apt one is to get one's own way. And, after all, isn't this really the path to our own happiness?

> *But I am afraid that just as Eve was deceived by the serpent's cunning, your minds may somehow be led astray from your sincere and pure devotion to Christ.*
> 2 CORINTHIANS 11:3

THE 'COMPETING KINGDOMS' MODEL WITH A CHRISTIAN VENEER

Even when we overlay Christian principles and beliefs on this model—two individuals held together by an agreement—we still see this ongoing jousting match with the same result: ongoing relationship damage. Because of the things taught in Scripture about how we are to treat each other, Christians may have some additional relationship skills that help build these marriages, and they may pursue their own interests somewhat less aggressively (or not). There are principles in marriage-help books that dampen some of the conflict. And there is a train of thought in the Christian community that we are supposed to be sacrificial, to lay down our own desires, feelings, agenda, and will for the sake of God and for each other. But all of this only partially mitigates the relationship damage inflicted over time by two people who still fundamentally view themselves as separate and distinct individuals, who are agreeing to pursue their separate and distinct lives side by side. Whenever Jesus spoke about marriage He always pointed directly toward the original intent and plan:

Veneering the world's plan with a layer of Christian "niceness" does not yield the results produced by God's actual plan.

a one-flesh relationship. Veneering the world's plan with a layer of Christian "niceness" does not yield the results produced by God's actual plan.

MISUNDERSTANDING SELFISHNESS AND SACRIFICE

Covenant obviously creates scenarios that call for personal sacrifice. But what is this sacrifice supposed to look like? The words "selfishness" and "sacrifice" have both shifted a bit in Christian circles from what I believe to be their actual meaning. There is a correct sense in which sacrifice occurs. However, it is a very different thing to lay upon God's altar of sacrifice our misperception of our true interests, which is part of God's plan to revamp our perception of our true best interest, versus completely ignoring our own needs and priorities, acting as if our own needs do not really exist, or really matter. Two competing concepts are often discussed in Christian circles: being selfless and being selfish. Being selfless is commended; being selfish is condemned. We must be careful how we define these terms, however, to ensure that being selfless does not mean that we view only other people's needs and desires as legitimate while believing that God wants us to act as if our needs and desires exist only to be ignored.

Selfishness is correctly defined as believing and acting as if our interests are inherently more important than the interests of others. Somehow, though, selfishness has been redefined by some to mean any recognition of our own needs and

> Selfishness has been redefined by some to mean any recognition of our own needs and desires, any focus upon ourselves, as if God does not really want us to have needs and desires.

desires, any focus upon ourselves, as if God does not really want us to have needs and desires. The truth is that God wants us to equate the importance of our needs and desires with those of other people (note Philippians 2:4 as well as the context of the entire passage).

To the extent that real sacrifice is called for, there is another reality in play. Christ sacrificed something real by emptying and humbling Himself, but He offered up these things to obtain something of greater importance for Himself and for us. True godly sacrifice always offers up something of lesser importance to gain something of greater importance. The rub comes in our frequent misunderstanding of what is truly most important. We often sacrifice what is most important for things of lesser importance. Thus, God's call to us to sacrifice certain things often involves reeducating us about the true relative importance of things. In a similar way, God will allow life to strip away valuable things from us in the interest of leading us to things of greater value to which we may cling. In covenant God will certainly redirect our sense of true self-interest and invite us to rid ourselves of inadequate and incorrect views. If God asks you to lay down your earthly life for His sake, if you truly understand that you are offering up something that you cannot keep for the long term anyway, if you understand that laying down your life at this moment for His sake will gain something of great importance for you for all eternity, would you be willing to exchange something of less value for something of more value? This question has faced everyone martyred for their faith since Stephen. If you would choose to die for Him, will you also choose to really live for Him?

At no time does a loving God tell us that we, or our real needs, are unimportant. The only questions are: 1) how we will get those needs met; 2) how to balance our needs and imperatives with those of others; 3) what source will meet our needs (and this may be God instead of the person we are relying on in a given situation); and 4) which of our needs are real and truly important versus our tendency to misperceive our needs and misplace our priorities? In light of all of this, if we do not understand the realities of covenant we will never be able to chart the course God desires for us to meet our true needs, nor can He use us properly to meet the true needs of others. Covenant is the game-changer that not only alters our deepest needs but also provides the training process that allows those needs to be met.

At times in the Christian community teaching on sacrifice and submission can lead to an outcome God clearly does not intend: devoting ourselves to fulfilling someone else's selfish desires, as we tolerate or even enable misconduct or abuse. This common distortion of the meaning of love and of God's plan leads to codependency. In a misguided attempt to love, people continue to pour their lives into the lives of people who are simply using them, even as they continue to hope that their "love" will change the one for whose sake they are willing to sacrifice all. We need to think through this pattern extremely carefully and look at the example of Jesus, whose love was strategically sacrificial at some points, but confrontational at other points—when people were taking advantage of others, abusing them, misrepresenting themselves, or lying to Him.

It should be noted that all of the above misunderstandings and missteps, and most of the others seen in marriages, have as their foundation a misunderstanding of the fundamental relationship between people in a marriage covenant. If this relationship is misunderstood there is inevitable confusion at every level. God's gift to us, the model of a working relationship, is a model of interdependence and mutual support. The path to the best relationship is found in recognizing and applying the new value system inherent in covenant. Any plan that retains and defends the old value system and view of self will ultimately pit one's incorrect perception of their best interests against the incorrectly perceived competing interests of a spouse. This is the recipe for discord, discontent, and disappointment, and possibly divorce.

Since becoming a Christian certainly can, and should—but often does not for reasons we have been discussing—result in a person shifting their primary focus in life from their perception of self-interest toward faithfulness to their covenant, it is no surprise that Christian marriages would be troubled with a frequency that mirrors non-Christian marriages. In fact, it is only through embracing and living out the covenant model of marriage that we could term a marriage truly a "Christian marriage."

CHRISTIAN TEACHERS AND COMMENTATORS MISUNDERSTAND COVENANT

I recently heard a definition of covenant during a radio broadcast by a prominent teacher (who will remain unnamed because the view he voiced is not his own, but one I have heard many times from various teachers for decades). The definition this man stated is that a covenant is simply a contract like any other, with one exception: God wrote the contract. Is this view correct? And if it is not, how do you now think it is deficient? And what consequences might there be if such a definition is applied to the marriage covenant? I have on occasion heard teachers speak of a "soul tie" or a "mystical union of souls" in reference to marriage. But these descriptions do not really explain the nature of the joining or point us clearly to the implications of this joining.

If modern academicians and biblical scholars do not understand the nature of covenant, they will analyze these relationships through their own lens of current cultural expectations and practices. The first volume in this series detailed the scholarly work of H. Clay Trumbull, a highly respected Christian author and leader in the late 1800s who extensively researched the historic understanding of covenant. He found the defining characteristic of covenant to be the exchange and merger of identities. This defining characteristic is found in three closely related forms of covenant we discussed in Volume One: blood covenant; marriage—a relationship characterized by God as "one flesh"; and a special and unique form of blood covenant, the New Covenant offered to individuals by God, which was made possible by the outpoured blood, death, and resurrection of Jesus—a relationship characterized by the indwelling Holy Spirit.

Trumbull's book was widely known in its day, but it is definitely not widely circulated in academic circles today. There have been virtually no follow-up works building on the foundation of understanding laid by Trumbull. Therefore, people offering commentary on aspects of our covenant relationships—marriage or our relationship with God— will inevitably misconstrue these as contractual. This has a number of unfortunate effects. This model, misapplied to the New Covenant, results in the view that God simply offers us something that we cannot pay for. We offer nothing in return, thereby becoming recipients of "God's grace."

In this view there is little acknowledgment of the offer of our lives to God—the death of our old self and the growth and development of our new lives—or of our responsibilities in this relationship. There is only one quid pro quo recognized, which is our obligation to cease sinning. But sin is reduced in its meaning. Sin does not represent an entire course of life and way of being (created by following misperceptions and deceptions sown into our minds and hearts by our enemy), a path and life which we properly recognize as entirely flawed, which we agree to lay down in its entirety if we truly understand covenant. This is the actual definition of the word "repentance." To enter the New Covenant we offer ourselves up to death, trusting in God to raise us up—in covenant—to new life as new creatures, joined to Him, indwelled by His Spirit; and we are in Him. We lay down our previous understanding of self and life in favor of God's plan for our lives under His lordship. If we do not recognize these issues of death and life, or the presence within of part of the nature of Satan (also gained through covenant by the parents of our race), which requires our death to be rid of, and the influence of God's enemy as he and those under his command misdirect every aspect of human life, sin becomes merely a list of activities and perhaps attitudes that we believe we need to refrain from. In this way of thinking, we believe we are OK if we simply refrain from the "bad stuff." Instead, sin is turning from God's plan at any point to follow the alternative plan that is always before us.

The idea that sin and obedience are simply about individual actions falls in line with the Jewish thinking Jesus made such a point to refute: "What must we do to be in good with God?" In John 6 Jesus directed one such questioner away from a list of works to the nature and quality of one's relationship with God. He ended His discussion by inviting His hearers to "eat My flesh and drink My blood"—a clear invitation into a blood covenant, a meaning that was crystal clear to everyone who heard His words. God stood in front of these people and invited them into a relationship that is God's ultimate expression of love and His full definition of love. That day, as today, most people were not ready for such an offer and many turned and walked away. Instead, they still wanted a short list of rules that would allow them to keep "their" lives yet be in good with God. In response, God tells us that those who seek to keep "their lives" will lose them, but those who willingly lay down their lives for the sake of Jesus and a relationship with Him will save their lives (Mark 8:35). The short list of rules or even the long list is not about love; this is about checking off boxes on a list "because God said so." People continue to hope that holding up their end of this arrangement will cause God to bless them, because this is how these people want things to be. But this is not about love, is it? No list of rules can create love, or express it, or even define it. God's first and most important command is to love Him with heart, mind, soul, and strength. Rules do not build love. Covenant does. Can we see God's premier command as simply another way of inviting us into covenant with Himself, and to faithfulness to that covenant so that love grows to maturity?

In the same way, the contractual view of marriage reduces the Scriptural injunctions on marriage to a list of "thou shall nots." There is no recognition that God is offering expert advice on how to build the best marriage or the most deep and passionate lifetime love affair. I would simply suggest that the picture we will see when we over-lay, not principles of contract, but principles of covenant to these covenant relationships, will be much more rich, deep, coherent, and powerful than the "contract version." In addition to, in all likelihood, being the understanding God wants us to have. In our own mind we need to begin contrasting the world's plan—contracts and rules—with God's covenant plan. God's plan is about learning to love, growing and changing so that we can love better, and building relationships—start-ing with the most important ones—in ways that mirror God's love for us.

We are to obey God, not to satisfy some abstract construct of the "obedient life," but to build into our lives and relationships necessary elements of success which are revealed to us by a trusted and wise Mentor, one who is a loving Father as well as Lord of all creation. The reasons we do these things are vastly different in the covenant model

One model commits us to "not sinning"; the other is about building a loving relationship, but it also involves being careful how we act because we value our relationship. Which model would you prefer?

versus the contractual model. One model commits us to "not sinning"; the other is about building a loving relationship, but it also involves being careful how we act because we value our relationship. Which model would you prefer?

GOD'S PLAN BUILDS TRUE LOVE FOR A LIFETIME

We discussed in the first volume the differences between the world's views of love and God's view. We are all familiar with the world's concept of "falling in love," which is something like stepping into a hole you did not see. This is supposedly a random attraction that suddenly grips two people (or, even worse, only one of the people). A relationship ensues. The two then determine if the other is the *right* person, their soulmate, and if this is true love. The assumption is that if it is the right person, and true love, the relationship will go the distance. One has already found their happily-ever-after. The only thing that remains is to live out this delight. But we also noted that this whole picture is out of sync with reality. People who fall in love also "fall out of love." Why? Relationships that start with two people in love end in a variety of ways. Everyone starts in love with the above assumptions. But what determines how a relationship turns out? What it develops into over time? Whether the two grow together or grow apart? Is it not how the two people treat each other over time, and in what direction each person grows over time?

God's plan recognizes the realities of our hearts in every respect. He knows how our feelings for each other grow—or are damaged. He knows how we must treat each other if feelings are to grow over time, and He knows how to lead us to treat each other in ways that grow the best relationship. Inherent in this, since two people are growing and changing over the course of their lives, is His plan that the two grow together.

God knows that true love is love that grows and deepens over a lifetime. No one has this at the outset. A couple may have a good start; they may be deeply, head over heels in love. But this is just a start. What happens next will determine the course of the marriage. We must realize that God wants the same things for our marriage that we want in our deepest heart. The difference between us and God? He knows how we can have what we want, while we really do not have all the answers!

> The difference between us and God? He knows how we can have what we want, while we really do not have all the answers!

God's desires for us are bigger than we yet realize.

QUESTIONS FOR THOUGHT

1. If you are married, what foundation is your relationship built on?

2. Does the contractual foundation of marriage look familiar? In the marriages of other people? In your marriage?

3. The term "competing kingdoms" model was introduced in this chapter. How have you seen people compete in a marriage? What are they trying to win? What are they willing to do to win? What is the relative priority most people place on winning this competition versus truly loving their mate? How do you think this priority will impact their marriage long term?

4. What percentage of married people that you know have relationships that look like the competing kingdoms model? How about your marriage, or, if you are not married, your current or prior romantic relationships?

5. How many married people do you know who have a much better marriage at ten or twenty years than they had at five years? Are their marriages characterized by competition and conflict or love and collaboration? Do you think a "competing kingdoms" model of marriage can grow deeper and better over time? Why or why not?

6. What is the most important thing in a marriage: meeting needs; having needs met; being happy; making someone else happy; finding someone who completes you; completing someone else; finding true love; finding the right person? Or understanding and living out the true nature and purposes of marriage faithfully as your mate is doing the same?

7. Do you see marriage as a relationship one figures out as one goes, or do you see that inherent in marriage is a very specific plan for how it is to be conducted?

8. If there is a plan for marriage offered to us by God, would you be interested in seeing this plan?

9. Have you ever seen a plan for building a marriage in any church teaching? (If so, you are very fortunate—if you have seen the real one.)

10. How will you know the real plan when you see it?

CHAPTER THREE

A Review of the Definition of Covenant

In his book *The Blood Covenant*, first published in 1885, H. Clay Trumbull identified and defined the core principle of covenant: a transformation of identity and nature when covenant is entered with another person. Here we will summarize the key elements gleaned from his descriptions of this rite so we can firmly grasp the definition, nature, and principles of covenant.

To enter a covenant two individuals share something physical of themselves that contains their identities. That which contains the identity of one, now taken into the body of another, remains and becomes a permanent part of the second person. As this new element of identity is incorporated into the other person, his or her identity and nature are now changed by incorporating this new element—but more is involved than simple addition. Put another way, this mutual sharing of nature and identity now produces two beings who are completely different than they were before entering covenant. There is a new birth of two people whose nature and identity are now joined, shared, and merged. This mutual sharing of identity in marriage is accomplished via sexual intercourse.

In a covenant, while individual identity is maintained (the two do not become identical), there is still a new union and new unity between the two based on their now-shared identity. The best model to understand this individual/unity phenomenon is found in the Author of covenant, the Trinity. Three distinct personalities, all of which are God, share one nature and identity. The fullness of Godhood is seen in the three taken together, or in each of the three (John 14:9, 17:21). Our entry into the other covenant offered by God, the New Covenant, is specifically described as a new birth—being born again, becoming a new creature. Entry into marriage is described as two people becoming one flesh. In either covenant the defining element is entry of the nature of one's covenant partner into oneself, and self being altered by this entry—whether one's partner is a husband or wife, or God and the indwelling Holy Spirit.

Every aspect of covenant—the ways we regard each other and treat each other; the duties, responsibilities, and obligations; the alteration of other relationships, such as family relationships, friends, and enemies; the things that are shared or mutually assumed, such as assets and debts; the things offered to each other, which are anything that is needed; and the hearts that are intended to grow toward each other— all of these flow directly from the alteration of nature and identity that occurs as covenant is entered. In essence, one is to treat the other as well as they would treat themselves. One is to love the other as they love themselves. This makes perfect sense because the other person, in a very real sense, now is oneself. The two are joined and merged at the level of nature and identity. There is no more "me" and "mine," "you" and "yours." Only "we" and "ours."

No one understands exactly what happens as we enter the two covenants that are the subjects of this book series—or exactly how it happens. We are simply told that it does happen as we enter both relationships, and we are left to assemble clues left for our consideration—in the Scriptures, in the definition of the words, and in cultural practices through the ages of those deeply devoted to God in a relationship with God and in marriage. In the first volume we also considered a third covenant, one which I believe God also deposited within the human race. His ultimate offer of relationship to us takes this form—a Blood Covenant. We will not revisit the integration among these three covenants that we detailed in the first volume. (Again, I strongly recommend you read this material in its entirety if you want to fully understand this form of relationship, for all that we know about all three relationships is required to assemble the most complete understanding.)

We may not perceive the fullness of these realities, or perceive them at all. If we are looking for evidence of these transformations that evidence can be seen if we know what to look for. But we can never begin with such observations and fully understand the joining and transformation that has occurred. This must be shown to us. God's revelation speaks to us of things that we could not otherwise know, or fully understand, or make best use of, or derive greatest benefit from, based on our own perceptions. That is why God must reveal these things to us, things that are real but hidden to some degree from our eyes. This at least partly explains why these concepts have gone missing in our culture. Our cultural opinion leaders resist acknowledging anything as true and real that cannot be directly observed or measured in a laboratory or by some social science tool. Which is ironic, for as our culture moves farther from embracing the spiritual connection inherent in marriage and the deep lifetime commitment that follows from this connection, marriages on the whole have progressively become less successful. The presence of this reality resists measure, but refusing to acknowledge it causes outcomes that are glaringly evident.

WHY IS A CORRECT UNDERSTANDING OF COVENANT SO IMPORTANT?

We all know marriage is special. However, if a sampling of people in our church or our community was asked what, exactly, is special about marriage, we would get an array of answers. After reading about covenant to this point, is your answer beginning to change? And if we were asked why we are supposed to do the things we are told to do in Scripture in our marriages, what would we say? Some of these things could be tied to loving each other, but other things God says about marriage seem to threaten our sense of self-interest, and they certainly threaten our culture's concept of what relationships are supposed to look like.

So, what is marriage supposed to look like? The first implication of understanding covenant is that marriage is a *very specific thing*. All that marriage is was defined by God when He created it; all that marriage is flows from the underlying reality of covenant—a merger and transformation of the identities of the participants. God, though, did not just create something and say "here it is."

God created marriage in the context of our being: our mind, our heart, our needs, our life, and our future. We will see in this volume that a covenant relationship does a number of things simultaneously, and all of these address our deepest needs and strongest desires. God's plan for this relationship teaches us to love and offers strong and sufficient motivation to refrain from unloving things. God's plan for how people are to approach each other and treat each other is completely in sync with how loving feelings toward another are built, sustained, and strengthened in our heart.

> His plan is designed to grow and transform us into people who can face the rigors and challenges of marriage and family life. The challenges of life can crush people, leave them broken and scarred, and destroy relationships.

Part of His plan can be simply stated: we are to express the deepest love of which we are capable. But this plan is not just about a better *now*. His plan is to change us in specific ways. His plan is designed to grow and transform us into people who can face the rigors and challenges of marriage and family life. The challenges of life can crush people, leave them broken and scarred, and destroy relationships. Or these same challenges can refine and mature people and build deeper and stronger relationships. God's plan is to mature us, to teach us to love across the broad spectrum of life, and across the broad spectrum of relationships we will have throughout life—producing in us things at the outset that we are not even aware we need.

All of God's plan must be understood in light of the central reality of covenant. If one is not aware of this reality, there appears to be no reason for many of the things God says. The power of covenant relationships is in the new life that is created and lived out. Through this lens, all of God's directions make perfect sense. We must also realize that, by entering this relationship, people are *already transformed.* Almost all problems in marriage can be traced back to people trying to live as if this transformation has not occurred. The path to the best marriage, on the other hand, is to progressively learn how to act as if it has.

ACTION POINT: Take a few moments to consider what the underlying reality of covenant means in terms of your relationship with your spouse, or (if you are single) how it would affect your relationship with a spouse. What areas of your relationship would this reality impact? What difference would it make? Compare your thoughts with what follows.

FOUR OVERARCHING REALITIES OF COVENANT

Covenant has four central realities that we must understand if we are to grasp its full impact. The full impact of covenant lived out faithfully is love—in heart and in action—for those with whom we are in covenant. As you read these four realities, think of ways in which each of these elements is indispensable in building a heart and life of love toward our covenant partner (in the case of marriage) or partners (in the case of being welcomed into God's family and being called His child (John 1:12; Hebrews 2:11).

> The full impact of covenant lived out faithfully is love—in heart and in action—for those with whom we are in covenant.

NEW LIFE

First, covenant is about new life. At the time of marriage, people often have the (accurate) sense that their lives have really just begun, that everything up to this point was but a preamble. We now have new lives. Inherent in God's plan is also the possibility of creating new human beings. Yet another "life" is created as well, in the sense that an entity that has interests which may be distinct from those of either husband or wife. This entity is the family. For instance, one may acquire more life insurance than needed for a surviving spouse early in the marriage, when it is much less expensive, with an eye toward the financial needs of future children. At the time of the wedding, the family may consist of only the married couple or may include children previously born to either. A completely new relationship is formed between the non-genetic parent and children who are now part of his or her household. There is now a new relationship with the extended family of the other partner. The new household, even if consisting of only two people, nevertheless takes its place in the network of related families on both sides.

A theme we will return to throughout this volume and the next is the distinction between the reality of new life and its inherent potential versus what is actually developed of this life and potential through the choices of those who possess these lives. We can best understand this distinction by comparing it to our physical lives. At the time we each consist of one cell with the combined DNA of the parents, we are a distinct living being with every potential we will ever have embedded within. There is growth of this new life that is not specifically related to choices. Provided with proper nutrition and safety, this new being will grow to physical adulthood. But along the way many choices determine exactly what form this adult will assume. Are intellectual, sports, or musical potentials developed? Is good nutrition chosen, or does excess lead to obesity and poor health? Do we put ourselves in harm's way, leading to infections, life-changing injury, or addiction? The point being, in addition to the random physical adversities, much of our physical destiny is determined by our choices. We can develop our potential and make the most of our opportunities, or we can ignore them and fail to develop them. We can waste our lives in a single moment or through a lifetime of poor choices. In the same way, our mental, emotional, spiritual, and relational potential may be developed, ignored, or wasted, and our character may develop strongly or become twisted and dysfunctional.

If you know with certainty that you have a particular potential, and you understand that developing this potential will create the life you really want to live, would you make whatever sacrifice is necessary to develop that potential? On the other hand, if you do not recognize your potential, or have no understanding of how to develop that potential even if you recognized it, what are the chances you will make the most of that potential? Developing potential in any area of life involves commitment, effort, resolve, and endurance, all of which flow from a certain set of values and priorities. Such development is a long-term path, and along the way one must consistently make certain choices. This is also the mind-set and approach we must develop if we are to make the most of our new lives.

This new life offered by God is a gracious gift—but some assembly is definitely required!

> This new life offered by God is a gracious gift—but some assembly is definitely required!

We must realize that God's plan is not to build onto our old lives. He builds something entirely new; the old being ceases to exist. Yet we perceive such changes in the depths of our being partially, if at all. The day after a marriage we may *perceive* ourselves to be much like we were the day before the marriage. We will likely notice that something has changed, but we may not be aware that this *something* is . . . *everything*. This new life becomes apparent to us over time; true identities grow and manifest only as we go through the experiences of living. Or we may never fully realize who we are or fail to realize the potential that is within; thus, we may settle for a life that develops little of our true potential and expresses little of the life that is actually within us. Instead of embracing and developing our new life, we may try to keep building the life we had before our marriage, a life that at this point has ceased to exist.

Every marriage offers opportunity, resources, and other things not present in the old life. One's partner's resources are at your disposal. His or her highest honor is to honor you, and you are to reciprocate. He or she is to provide for you, protect you, and defend you to the death, and you are to reciprocate. There is something larger than oneself to which one's life is devoted—spouse, family, children. It is now possible to build things greater than could be built as a single person, such as a legacy of people in future generations who are trained to build good lives and impact their generations in turn.

ALTERATION AND MERGER OF IDENTITY AND NATURE

We all want to be part of something special, to be united, joined, accepted, embraced. We all want to be loved. This hunger is one of our strongest drives. It is also one of our most frustrated drives as we go through life. Why? Because being loved means being united with someone in a certain way and being viewed and treated in a certain way. The reason we experience so little love in this world is that people are not united in an actual way with most other people on the planet. We are distinct beings with decidedly different ideas about what our best lives look like, ideas that often clash, compete, and contend. And even if we do have some real connection—family ties or marriage— does this guarantee that we are viewed or treated as loved ones? What is missing here? Why can't humanity be one big happy family? Why can't the two or three or four of us even be one little happy family? If we are going to build our best lives it is vital that we understand the foundation of true love and how God's plan provides that foundation.

Covenant is unlike any other relationship in that it literally unites people at the deepest level—the level of identity and nature. This is the defining reality of covenant.

Before we consider the particulars, however, just consider the big picture for a moment. Every dream we have of being loved involves being joined and united in a forever way within a love relationship with another, with someone worth joining, worth loving. Relationships that are here today, gone tomorrow are not true love. Thus, God allows us to enter a relationship that permanently alters and joins us. But as we noted above, simply being joined is no guarantee of being loved. Therefore, God has surrounded this relationship with many elements, in the relationship itself and even within us—in our hearts and minds—that, in sum, can produce two people who regard each other and treat each other in ways that build the ultimate loving relationship. God's plan to do this is quite complex, as we will see, and quite effective if implemented.

What is the greatest force creating division and strife among people? One could fill in that blank with the name of a being who initiated and leads the rebellion against God—and this would be a correct answer—or with the element of this being's nature that was curiously deposited within the human race ever since the first humans joined in that rebellion. (By the way, by what means might this exchange of identity occur?) In terms of our own human experience, though, I think a good candidate for the force that drives people apart would be our varying perceptions of self-interest. Note, I did not say actual self-interest, but perceptions of self-interest. Humans are good at many things; one of the things they are best at is being deceived about what is truly best for themselves. We have all latched onto an idea, or a value, or an agenda, or a plan that did not turn out like we thought. The potential for miscues multiplies in a close relationship. All of this can be traced to an incorrect understanding of true self-interest.

Can you see how, if our identities change and merge, if our *self* changes and is joined, our *true self-interest* will also be changed? So now we have two problems: instead of merely having difficulty discerning what is best for us in many situations for the *self* we have always been, the one we have been trying to figure out for a couple of decades, now we have become a different self altogether, one with a whole new set of interests. How do we figure this out?

If our identity changes in this way, what does this mean about our sense of "who we are"? This must change. We must recognize and embrace this new reality as true. As we do so, and as we begin to act in accord with this new reality, our hearts will follow—our emotions shift, our priorities change, our goals are altered, and so are our values. Our task is to learn how to live out this new identity faithfully. Inherent in this is identifying things that were part of our "old" identity but not our new one. We are to refrain from living out things that are no longer real (such as continuing to live as if we are single if we are joined to another in marriage). The reason we must focus first on our identity, as opposed to merely trying to live out some list of duties from a sense of obligation, is that we will devote ourselves to being ourselves, to being *authentic*, to living from the core of our being in a way that we will not devote ourselves to doing a list of things "because someone said so." Is this difference between a covenant and contract beginning to become more clear?

Covenant also offers a new path to fulfillment and gratification. How? What is our most gratifying and fulfilling experience? Is it not living authentically, from the core of our being, and from this core building a life worth having and relationships worth having? God's plan not only identifies our new identity for us—merged with another—but shows us how to live out this identity via loving the one to whom we are joined, whether to a spouse or to Him. This is in every sense the most gratifying and fulfilling life each of us can live. We are built to love and be loved. God shows us the path to this outcome, to true authenticity. This is His plan.

JOINING AND RELATIONSHIP

Third, covenant is about joining and relationship. Every human has a wall in their life, and they place people on one side of this wall or the other. Those on the inside are friends, people we trust whether related by blood or not. Those on the outside are dangerous, worthy of suspicion, unknown, or merely different. This wall never completely goes away; we should not thoughtlessly expose ourselves to those who mean us harm, and many people in our world do mean us harm. On the other hand, God wants to reposition and redefine this wall in all of us. In covenant this wall shifts significantly. We now have a new set of people on the inside—those who are on the inside of our covenant partner's wall.

But the most significant change is where our covenant partner resides. In every previous relationship we have had the prerogative of moving people from the inside to the outside, and we were willing to do so in one situation: if our perceived self-interest diverged enough from theirs. Our best friends, our parents, our children can move from trusted allies to outside the circle if their agendas diverge enough from our own at a key point, or if they threaten our perception of our life to a certain degree. Remember what happened between Saul and Jonathan? Suddenly an enraged Saul is trying to pin his son Jonathan to the wall with his spear. What happens, by contrast, in covenant? There is no more *my life* and *your life*. There is only *our life*. Thus, this person with whom I am in covenant is *always* on the inside of my wall, for that is the only place they can be. And the interest they have in the lives of others now becomes my interest. This is true for a spouse or for one with whom we are in a blood covenant. This wall, it turns out, is formed of our perception of our self-interest. God's overall plan is to alter our perception of self-interest to correspond with His.

> What happens, by contrast, in covenant? There is no more *my life* and *your life*. There is only *our life*.

What we are going to see, when we look at the duties, responsibilities, and obligations inherent in a covenant relationship, is the same list of things we would do if we deeply loved someone and had perfect relationship skills. When we are instructed to be faithful to our marriage covenant, what is God asking of us? He is instructing us to do the things that will build the deepest and most pure love for a lifetime. Everything is about loving and building relationship. Nothing more, nothing less.

EXCHANGES BETWEEN THOSE IN COVENANT

Fourth, covenant is about exchanges. This is the logical, practical outworking of the first three realities. To enter covenant, identities and lives are first exchanged. When a blood covenant is entered, food, weapons, clothing, and other things are exchanged to symbolize the obligations and duties the two are now assuming toward each other. In a wedding ceremony there are vows enumerating some of the obligations people are assuming, then the bride and groom feed each other cake and perhaps wine to symbolize the mutual obligation for care and provision. Rings are exchanged as a reminder to the couple and the community of the covenant now entered.

There are many other real-life exchanges that have deep implications in marriage. Friends are now held in common, as are enemies. Debts are jointly assumed, and assets are jointly available. Family ties are now assumed on the part of each. In a larger sense, the efforts, potential, resources—not only material things but the entirety of each other's capabilities—are mutually available for the benefit of the other party. And the sense of covenant, of the two becoming one, suggests something even larger. Rather than being obligated to any list of duties that could be compiled, the mutual obligation is completely open-ended. Covenant is the ultimate blank check. The correct answer is always: "Whatever I have to offer, and whatever it takes."

HOW CAN WE IDENTIFY GOD'S PLAN FOR MARRIAGE?

It would be remarkably convenient if one book of the Bible was The Book of Marriage, but we are not given everything God wants us to know about marriage in such a tidy package. Verses scattered throughout the Old and New Testaments reference marriage in one way or another. In all of these verses we can learn important things. But nowhere is there an extensive list of everything we are to do, no comprehensive analysis of this relationship, no bullet points with commentary laid out so we may be sure we have the entire plan of God before us. Does this mean there is no plan? If we look around the Christian community and consider all the marriages we might exam-

Nowhere is there an extensive list of everything we are to do, no comprehensive analysis of this relationship, no bullet points with commentary laid out so we may be sure we have the entire plan of God before us.

ine, it certainly looks like variety is the rule, that there is no "one way" to do this thing. Let's think more about this for a few moments.

God certainly makes clear the distinctions between right and wrong, between obedience and rebellion, between good and evil. At the same time, He has built each of us as unique human beings; thus, each human pairing will have its own unique manner of expressing good, right, obedience. But good will always *not* be evil, right will *never* be wrong, and obedience and rebellion are polar opposites. White and black may both be chosen to some degree, become mingled with each other, and produce the appearance of gray. But the basic nature of white and black is not altered by mere proximity. They can never become each other. One can always clearly distinguish—and separate—white from black. Gray simply means one has chosen from both options.

We must never fall into the mental error, as we look at the grayness all around us, of believing that God intends it to be so or is pleased that darkness is present where He wants there to be only light. What God wants is that we express His perfect plan in accord with our individuality. While there is a definite plan, it will never produce identical people or identical relationships, nor is it intended to do so. But His plan, if followed, will produce good, pure, right, obedient relationships comprised of mature, pure, righteous, and loving people. It is only by mingling elements of God's plan with elements of the world's plan that we find gray in relationships and in people, and it is only by following God's plan that we are able to remove the blackness that we carry within, a darkness that inevitably accompanies us into our marriages.

So where do we find this plan, this grand scheme that produces such things? That's the topic we'll turn to in the next chapter.

QUESTIONS FOR THOUGHT

1. Think for a moment about two experiences. 1) You are looking at someone you are now committed to for a lifetime, someone you have come to believe is the biggest obstacle to happiness in your life because they are standing in the way of something you think is the most important thing you want in life. 2) You are looking at someone you are now committed to for a lifetime, who you now think is going to be the biggest human source of love, protection, provision, fulfillment, contentment, growth, and transformation in your life. How would you feel about your commitment in each of these situations? How would you feel about keeping your commitment in these two scenarios? Could these two situations actually be the same two people? Someone who, in the first example, is looking at marriage as many people in our culture look at marriage, while in the second scenario the same person is looking at their marriage as a covenant joining?

2. What difference would it make in your heart to look at your marriage partner as part of you and realize that within you is a part of *them*, then to realize that as you were joined together you each became a new creature with a new identity and new nature that now combines the two of you? Would this have any impact on the way you feel about the other person, on how you treat them?

3. How would this be different from looking at someone you just married and wondering what it is that actually holds you together?

4. New life implies new possibilities, new potential, new opportunities. What new things could you see becoming part of your life

by entering a Covenant of Marriage? How might this reality be part of God's overall plan for your life?

5. Are feelings of love, no matter how strong initially, capable of holding two people together through all the issues of life? Why or why not?

6. Two people agree to be together. First, why would they do so? Second, what forces might be more powerful in minds and hearts than a simple agreement? The real question is: "How is an agreement vulnerable to change in a way that a covenant, properly understood, is not?"

7. What is the difference in the joining produced by an agreement versus the joining produced by covenant?

8. What reasons would one have for loving the other person as they love themselves in covenant that would not exist because of an agreement?

9. Are all the duties, obligations, and responsibilities inherent in a covenant relationship, listed above in this chapter, simply logical next steps in light of the joining and change in nature and identity that occurred as covenant was entered? How might it help us to have such a strong and logical reason for doing all these things?

10. If the way two people treat each other over time does more to build or damage a relationship than any other factor, what kind of heart relationship would most likely exist between two people who faithfully lived out the principles of covenant toward each other over a lifetime?

CHAPTER FOUR

Where Do We Find God's Plan for Marriage?

DO WE FIND GOD'S PLAN IN THE GENERAL UNDERSTANDING WITHIN THE CHRISTIAN COMMUNITY?

If God has a plan, it would seem we could simply enter a covenant relationship with Him (that is, become a Christian), join a church, come alongside other people who are also seeking the blessed, abundant lives that are described in Scripture, draw from the teachings of our church, and go on to build the quality relationships, marriages, and families we all desire. At first glance, this certainly would appear to be the correct plan. There is no shortage of teaching on marriage in the Christian community, some of it of excellent quality and quite helpful.

If one is observant, though, one can see in the Christian community, even in solid, biblically based churches, that many marriages are struggling. More marriages are finding their way into this struggling group than one would expect if these folks possessed a working plan to build the best relationships. While the divorce rate among committed Christians is 25 to 50 percent less than for non-Christians (Shaunti Feldhahn, *The Good News About Marriage,* Multnomah, 2014)[1], the 20 to 30 percent rate noted among Christians is still many times higher than the 5 percent rate seen in the general population as recently as

1960. Clearly some of what has impacted marriage overall in our culture has found its way into the marriages of Christians.

Once one understands covenant and all its implications, it will become obvious that this view of marriage is not a part of current Christian teaching. Current teaching focuses on issues and topics: communication, forgiveness, better listening leading to better understanding, and more. I have attended a number of excellent churches, often pastored by biblical scholars, and have learned from the best Christian teachers of our generation, yet I have not heard the comprehensive view of marriage that can be gained by an understanding of covenant. Nor have I heard marriage topics presented in a way that tells me why certain things are, or are not, done, beyond the fact that God obviously says so. Even if we are trying to follow God's plan as it can be seen in these details, we end up with a list of things to do, but no real understanding of *why*—and at key points without understanding how.

God does have an answer to these questions. But we must find His answer. As with any issue in life, God's answer is there, but it often gets lost among the various approaches taught in the Christian community. This problem is not a new one. It has always been necessary to separate God's ideas from the well-intended advice of people who are supposedly teaching in the name of God, whose teachings nevertheless depart at points from God's Word. This is the heart of the problem Jesus had with the Pharisees—they claimed to be speaking for God, citing and often living many things in God's Word, but they were missing key pieces of the puzzle and therefore misleading people. Jesus took this very seriously, speaking against these ungodly teachings with some of the harshest words in Scripture. For their part, trying to obey God without truly loving Him led the Pharisees to murder the very God they thought they were serving.

Parts of the New Testament epistles were written to address false teachings that had already emerged within the Christian community in a few short years. Jesus also warned about wolves in sheep's clothing and false shepherds. On the other hand, the Christians in Berea were commended by Paul because they carefully compared everything he said to the Scriptures to ensure that the things he taught lined up with the things God had revealed in Scripture.

THREE SOURCES OF INFORMATION ABOUT GOD'S PLAN

In the first and second volumes of this series thus far we have discussed two places we can look if we want to understand God's plan. First, the Scriptures—they are God's truth, and in them we can completely rely. But we also must understand what the words used in these Scriptures actually mean. Thus, we've examined the meaning of the word covenant as this was understood by those who penned the Scriptures. This understanding then informs our understanding of words, phrases, and behaviors in Scripture related to covenant. But I think there is also a third place we can look if we are trying to understand God's plan for marriage.

If some things in Scripture are said point blank, while other things are inferred from the wording—or implied by the definition of certain words—how can we test our understanding of these inferences and implications? I believe it is valid to look at how people who were making every effort to obey God behaved in response to His injunctions as recorded in Scripture. If our understanding of the things implied and assumed is correct, then our predictions about what it would look like to be obedient would line up with the ways obedient early Christians acted, would they not? As we will see in the next volume, the first behaviors recorded among the earliest Christians in the second chapter of Acts line up perfectly with the ways these people would act if they had just entered covenant with each other. Which, in fact, they had done as they entered the New Covenant with Jesus.

If we want to look at marriage in the same way, where might we look to verify the idea that *marriage as God intends it* corresponds with faithfulness to the duties, obligations, and responsibilities of covenant according to the understanding we are developing? If this is true, where might we gain an even clearer understanding of God's plan and get a more realistic and comprehensive look at love? If God designed marriage as a covenant, and part of entering a covenant is speaking vows to one another, might we learn anything of value by studying these vows? Might these clearly reflect what God intended in these relationships, particularly if we look at a large spectrum of these vows through history among those who love God? If we wanted to most clearly understand God's plan for marriage, what would happen if we triangulated all three sources: the Scriptures, an understanding of covenant, and historic wedding vows?

> When placed side by side, a deeper and more beautiful picture emerges, very much like simultaneously viewing two images in a way that produces a three-dimensional image, a much more vivid and alive thing than either picture alone.

When placed side by side, a deeper and more beautiful picture emerges, very much like simultaneously viewing two images in a way that produces a three-dimensional image, a much more vivid and alive thing than either picture alone. The Scriptures relating to marriage are scattered throughout the Bible. Even when brought together in one place, each passage refers to only some aspect of marriage. Thus, trying to understand marriage via this collection can be like bringing a group of blind persons into a room to examine an elephant only by touching it. One person is certain that an elephant is a long, snake-like thing; another is sure the creature is like tree trunks. The third is sure it is like a large fan, while the fourth believes it is simply a wall that is breathing. It's important to see precisely how all the parts relate into a living, breathing whole to understand an elephant.

In the same way, the principles and truths of covenant, and the vows of marriage, help us understand how particular Scriptures fit together into a seamless whole. Again, this exercise does not to add to the Scriptures in any way beyond serving to fully define the terms used and to emphasize the real and practical outworking of these things.

THREE FACETS OF GOD'S PLAN: TO INFORM, CONFORM, TRANSFORM

Three things must occur for us to truly love in the way God intends. We must be *informed* about love, about all its dimensions and nuances. We must *conform* ourselves to being and doing these things if we are to follow God and be faithful to our covenant. If we find we are unable to conform in the moment, God has given us the means to be *transformed*, to become different from what we currently are in a way that will allow us to fulfill His will. Would it therefore be right to include in our definition of obeying God that we must also be transformed in the way God makes possible? We must be *informed* about what love actually is according to God (and what it is not). We then must make myriad, daily, moment-by-moment choices to *conform* to love. This series of decisions will build our relationships, and they will also build ourselves. We will form new habit patterns and treat others in new ways. To live out God's plan in all its fullness, changes must occur at levels deeper than simple choice. As we change the ways we treat other people and see the benefits of these new behaviors, our character begins to shift at deeper levels. We begin to develop new depths of integrity, willpower, and self-control. Our values shift, our priorities are changed, our goals and ideals are refashioned. As we live out these new attributes and see their benefits, we develop a hunger for more of this type of growth. God is in fact trying to persuade us to embrace a lifetime pattern of personal growth. Sacrifices, if made, will create greater benefits in the long run. Adjustments made will prove to be preparation for greater things that lie ahead. God has no problem having His ways field-tested, nor His definition of love tried and proven. For His ways will always prove beneficial in the big scheme. God knows that we need to experience noticeable benefits in the short run to become wholehearted toward following Him in the long run. He invites us to taste and see that He is good (Psalm 34:8).

God's plan is not some quick shift: *presto!*—and a whole new life. Instead it is a slow, steady, incremental process of changing thoughts, then decisions, then patterns and habits, which in turn produce growing and changing lives. The paths to spiritual growth and relationship maturity mirror the path of physical maturity in many ways, including its pace. We start as a single cell full of potential, we gradually grow physically, mentally, and emotionally; we gradually develop our character and our potential.

> God has no problem having His ways field-tested, nor His definition of love tried and proven. For His ways will always prove beneficial in the big scheme.

What is the goal of this transformation, assuming it is fully accomplished in our lives via our choices so that our lives accurately reflect what has been fully accomplished in the depths of our being? Conformity to God's specific Scriptural injunctions becomes not only possible for us, it becomes *the thing we most want to do*. His desires for us become our deepest desires. Why? Because His desires for us coincide with who we really are; His desires for us perfectly express not only our true identity but our perception of our true identity. This is the true genius of God's plan of covenant. The transformation of covenant re-creates us to love. When coupled with changes in our perception so that we accurately perceive who we are, we willingly live out our new identity and reap the rewards of both love and true, authentic living.

Now to Him who is able to do immeasurably more than all we ask or imagine, according to His power that is at work within us, to Him be glory in the church and in Christ Jesus throughout all generations, for ever and ever! Amen.

EPHESIANS 3:20, 21

Having offered us the *what* and the *why*, God's plan also must offer us the *how*. Not just "here it is, go do it," but why we should want to do it badly enough to overcome every obstacle; why we should be totally committed and devoted to His plan. There must be sufficient motivation for obedience. We have already noted that the way relationships turn out in the long run depends almost entirely on the ways we treat each other. Thus, the plan of God must end up teaching us how to treat each other, not just in the moment but consistently, for a lifetime. He also teaches us behaviors and attitudes to refrain from because they damage relationships. God's plan also highlights another reality: investing in another in these ways creates loving feelings within us in addition to our heart response to the ways we are being treated. This creates growing love, enduring love, and this deeply satisfying love creates the most profound of human experiences, our happily-ever-after.

God's plan also includes matching the opportunities and requirements of this relationship with the specific powers and capabilities He has placed within us. As we will see, some of these powers and capabilities must be developed and refined so we can live as God instructs. For instance, we may need to develop more discernment, willpower, or self-control. Therefore, we must examine not only covenant per se, but examine ourselves and the mechanisms God has placed within us so we can better understand the path to the transformation God asks of us. God also constructed our hearts and minds to integrate together in certain ways, for to successfully address certain issues in our heart we must at times change our thinking or beliefs. And He created our hearts to grow more deeply in love with each other in response to very specific things over time. God integrates the way relationships are built, the way hearts are built, the way characters are built, and His true Word, along with the specifics of covenant relationships, into a seamless whole, a structure that most promotes love.

In addition to integrating all of this, God brings circumstances and opportunities into our lives to which a married couple will respond as a couple. If we learn to grow the relationship as intended, if we learn to grow ourselves as intended, then these challenges and opportunities become the raw material from which life together is built. These obstacles are truly challenging, though, and these opportunities may or may not be recognized or developed. As we go through the process of learning how to learn, and learning how to grow, we will become better at dealing with adversity and making the most of our opportunities.

As we discuss God's plan, and all the elements He brings together in this plan, elements He created for these very purposes, see if this combination does not lead you to the conclusion that God is a master builder and supreme strategist as well as the Author of love—and its best teacher.

One thing I want to stress about God's plan: Christian teaching often stresses what we are not to do, and some leaders even repeatedly stress how defective we are as creatures, with anything good in our lives only due to the direct intervention of a merciful and gracious God. While these statements may be strictly true in particular contexts, they miss the big picture, in my opinion. Instead of focusing on what is wrong and what is wrong with us, I strongly believe that God wants us to focus on what can be built and what our lives can become if we follow Him. God has told us to do many things and to play many roles in this building process—in which He also plays an indispensable role, to be sure. But current teaching tends to suggest that God does it all while we simply wait patiently for Him to do it. I would respectfully suggest that, if God has a plan in which we play many indispensable roles as well, and if He has pointedly instructed us to do certain things, He will not build for us what He has told us to build (in partnership with Him) in the face of our refusal to play our assigned roles.

Which brings us to this question: "What roles has God assigned us?" Let's take a look at the answer.

QUESTIONS FOR THOUGHT

1. The Christian community would be the logical place to look for God's plan for marriage. And some teachers and groups do teach and live out substantial parts of God's plan. But do most? Why is there confusion about marriage within the Christian community? What is the source of this confusion? What is the outcome of this confusion?

2. If God created marriage and offered it as His first gift to the human race, if inherent in this gift is a plan for how it is to be conducted, and if God in His Word has offered extensive and detailed instruction about how marriage is to be conducted, what does this say about our human tendency to try to alter the nature or conduct of marriage? How do you feel about God's plan versus your ideas about marriage?

3. God's primary command to humans is to love—love Him, love others as we love ourselves, love our husband or wife. What does the nature of the covenant relationship, and what you know so far about how people are supposed to treat each other in covenant, have to do with love? Might this be a strategy to actually build loving hearts? Why or why not?

4. At this point in your understanding of covenant, what series of steps do you think would be required for you to move from your wedding day to being able to faithfully live out every aspect of a marriage covenant relationship with another person?

5. Would you like to be treated in the way one is supposed to be treated by a covenant partner?

6. What would your heart be like toward someone who treated you in these ways, consistently, for decades?

7. Do you think the many people getting married this week in our country understand the nature of the relationship they are entering? Did you, if you are married, understand the fundamental nature of this relationship?

8. Do you think this book might be part of God's plan to inform you about the nature of marriage, and about other aspects of this relationship?

9. What might one do if he or she wants to conform to God's plan to treat his or her marriage partner in the ways already outlined? Why might someone *not* want to do this?

10. Might the transformation that is part of God's overall plan for marriage be a necessary part of faithfully living out our covenants? What changes do you think might be necessary in us to reach the point that we want to live out these things?

CHAPTER FIVE

The Covenant of Marriage

But for Adam no suitable helper was found. So the Lord God caused the man to fall into a deep sleep; and while he was sleeping, he took one of the man's ribs and then closed up the place with flesh. Then the Lord God made a woman from the rib he had taken out of the man, and he brought her to the man.

The man said, "This is now bone of my bones and flesh of my flesh; she shall be called 'woman,' for she was taken out of man."

That is why a man leaves his father and mother and is united to his wife and they become one flesh. Adam and his wife were both naked, and they felt no shame.
GENESIS 2:20-25

You have been unfaithful to her, though she is your partner, the wife of your marriage covenant.
MALACHI 2:14

GOD'S ORIGINAL INTENT

When Jesus spoke about marriage He consistently contrasted current cultural thinking and practices with God's original intention. It is interesting to note how brief God's description of the reality of marriage is in the Genesis account. Yet this account contains every seed of understanding which, when fully developed, represents God's covenant plan for marriage. The word *marriage* is not used in this account, nor is the word covenant, yet our Lord and every other Scripture referencing this account are unanimous in deeming this the inception of the Covenant of Marriage. The Malachi verse is included to illustrate this point. We discussed the underlying four realities of covenant: new life, joined identity, new relationships, and practical exchanges. Let us briefly consider how these realities show up in God's description of the original marriage relationship between Adam and Eve.

First, what was their relationship? She was created from Adam's flesh: "bone of my bone, flesh of my flesh." As the life of one literally came from the life of the other, the first reality of covenant is reflected: this new relationship was created at the same time that a new life was created—directly in this case from the first human in a second special act of creation. Second, they were made of the same substance, literally of the same flesh, reflecting the second underlying reality of covenant. The identity of Adam—his being, his flesh—was the starting point for the creation of Eve. Her substance, her expression of this identity, was different from Adam—wonderfully so. Though different, they were nevertheless "one flesh"; though male and female the two were a model of covenant. This oneness was there in fullness from the beginning of Eve's life. As Eve was created the two were in this state of oneness, or marriage. There was no ceremony, no additional act which produced this joining, because none was necessary. God simply stated the reality that existed in their relationship from the outset.

This is the same oneness publicly proclaimed and celebrated by a wedding ceremony. The third reality of new relationships was not in play yet. There was no alternation of family relationships in this case, simply the reality that these two were the first family of humanity made in God's image. But this first married couple became the father and mother of the human race. Thus, they are related to all of us in the most special way. The fourth reality—exchanges and sharing—was inherent in their shared dominion, not only over the Garden, but dominion over the entire earth which had been conveyed to them by God (Genesis 1:27-29).

It should be noted that marriage was given to humanity before the Fall. And marriage today is God's plan to move us back toward the state of unity and harmony for which we were made, by creating in a couple the same reality that was present between Adam and Eve. The first marriage was intended to express the complete, total, and perfect unity and harmony of these perfect and sinless beings. But the Fall carried implications for marriage as well. God noted that the intended harmony and collaboration, the intended oneness, would be challenged, and procreation would be made more challenging. Obtaining food and providing for needs would now become arduous and uncertain (Genesis 3:16-20). These realities explain the both the yearnings of our hearts for the "perfect bond of unity," which is one of God's descriptions of love (Colossians 3:14), and the challenges we face in building this kind of unity. God's covenant plan offers us the reality of this unity as we enter covenant. But we must build the relationship that reflects the underlying reality of this unity, and in our confused and confusing world this is anything but a certainty. Hence the plan of God to build this unity in the realities of a relationship is offered to us.

> It should be noted that marriage was given to humanity before the Fall. And marriage today is God's plan to move us back toward the state of unity and harmony for which we were made.

In God's initial description we see an outline of this structure and intent of marriage as well as the challenges inherent in marriage and family. God has a plan, but so does Satan. Please note that every loss and change experienced by these first humans, and every additional challenge inherent in marriage, was a direct result of the influence of Satan on these two. These competing influences—God and Satan—and their respective plans have played out in the lives of individuals, families, and cultures ever since. We see this conflict graphically illustrated in the first family in, among other things, the murder of a brother.

WHY IS GOD'S PLAN FOR MARRIAGE SO BENEFICIAL AND DURABLE?

Despite millennia of human and fallen-angelic attacks on marriage, despite vastly varying cultures and conditions, marriage has survived and often thrived. How did God make marriage something so beneficial and durable? What did He make marriage that is beautiful and powerful enough to continue drawing humanity into this institution—His plan—even if the participants are unaware of its real Author? How did God keep before the human race, from the beginning until today, a picture of love that reflects Himself? What is marriage?

WHAT IS A COVENANT RELATIONSHIP?

The general principles of covenant are restated here for reference, drawn from Trumbull's work that was detailed in the first volume of this series. As we go through the details of marriage, note that each corresponds to the general principles of covenant, and note that each of these principles in turn flows directly and logically from the underlying reality of covenant—the exchange and merger of identities, which is termed in marriage becoming "one flesh."

SUMMARY OF THE PRINCIPLES OF A BLOOD COVENANT

- There is the death of prior individuals and birth of new, joined individuals.

- This conjoined identity causes the two to prefer each other over all others to the point of giving up one's life for the other if necessary.

- Covenant produces a relationship that supersedes any family tie.

- Blood Covenant is not a revocable relationship; it is permanent and lifelong because of the merger of nature and identity.

- The highest priority in one's life henceforth is to honor one's covenant and to honor the name and reputation of one's covenant partner above all else.

- Covenant imposes mutual obligations, responsibilities, and duties. In no sense is this a giver-taker relationship; it is a mutual commitment of aid in any form required.

- Each is to defend, protect, and provide for one's covenant partner as one would look to one's own protection, defense, and provision.

- Family ties and responsibilities are now assumed by both. One is to provide, protect, and defend the other's family as if it is their own, which it has now become.

- The resources of each are at the disposal of the other. There is no limit on the claim one may make on the other's resources or efforts.

- Friends of each become friends of both; enemies of each become enemies of both.

- Debts of each become the liability of both.

- Marriage between a male and female who are in blood covenant is viewed as incestuous and forbidden.

HOW DO WE ENTER THE COVENANT OF MARRIAGE?

MARRIAGE BEGINS AT A SPECIFIC POINT IN TIME

One obvious characteristic of a covenant relationship is that we either are in one or we are not. There is no merge lane into a covenant, only a sharp distinction between those who are joined by covenant and those who are not. God's plan recognizes this reality and draws a clear distinction between behaviors that are appropriate in light of covenant joining and inappropriate in the absence of this joining. He intends that unmarried people conduct themselves in one way while married people conduct themselves in an entirely different way. It is important to note this and to understand the reason why this is so.

During my childhood in the 1950s and 1960s, sexual activity between unmarried persons was generally known to be completely off limits. This was about the proper role of sexual activity exclusively within marriage, and about respecting and protecting oneself—and this was about more than venereal disease and pregnancy. There was the sense that in giving our bodies to another we were giving something very precious of ourselves, and this part of ourselves was to be carefully guarded. However, there was also a realistic fear of bringing a new life into the world in inappropriate circumstances, which was a distinct possibility in a world without contraception. And also is a distinct possibility in a world awash in contraception, which explains the "imperative" of abortion in our culture to deal with the inevitable consequence of sex thought to be merely a form of recreation—new lives created.

In our culture over the last fifty years, the distinction between married and unmarried has blurred as a significant percentage of unmarried teens and adults engage in behaviors God's plan confines to marriage. People enter "sort of married" arrangements such as living together, buying homes together, having children together, and other "married" things—and yet they have not yet wed. A recent poll shows that a substantial percentage of church-attending young adults do not believe that this is a problem from a moral or spiritual standpoint. We will discuss this in more

> People enter "sort of married" arrangements such as living together, buying homes together, having children together, and other "married" things—and yet they have not yet wed.

detail later. For now, simply note that God's plan recognizes two very distinct categories of people: single people and married people. There are reasons that the ceremony and intercourse are intended to happen one after the other in rapid succession. Once these reasons become clear we will see that God's requirements for sexual conduct (never before marriage, frequently within marriage) are not about impeding our good times and interfering with some "right" we think we have to use our own bodies as we please. Far from it. God really does have our best interests in mind.

THE PREAMBLE

An offer is extended to wed, and the offer is accepted. This generally begins a period of engagement, a time of preparation. Generally, a ring is worn to signify the intention to wed. A celebration is planned, all the necessary arrangements are made, and the big day arrives.

THE WEDDING CEREMONY—STILL A PREAMBLE

Though every wedding is unique, it is fascinating how many common elements have continued to show up in weddings through the millennia. These elements in some way illustrate, celebrate, or contribute to the covenant union that is to be created. For instance, almost all weddings are conducted by a person with recognized spiritual authority. This person acknowledges that the marriage is being conducted before the God of the Bible or before whatever beings are acknowledged in the spiritual realm by the participants.

There are rings. There are toasts. There are elements whose origins go beyond being amusing photo ops (such as the couple feeding each other cake and wine). One element rarely absent are vows, pledges made to each other and to whatever deity is acknowledged that speak to the nature of the joining and to the responsibilities of the parties as a consequence. Another element in most weddings is beauty, and along with that considerable financial sacrifice. It is very likely that one's wedding is the most expensive party one will ever throw. This is because a wedding signifies the most beautiful and significant life-changing event in which a person will ever take part. As we review the elements of a wedding, there is no doubt that this resonates with a Blood Covenant ceremony. It involves many of the same elements for exactly the same reasons.

CREATION OF A MARRIAGE COVENANT

At the conclusion of the wedding and reception the couple typically leaves with great ceremony—with rice or other things thrown at them, swords raised over their heads, or sparklers lit—to go to a private place to actually begin their lives together. All of these ceremonial aspects of a wedding, however, are not what actually create the marriage covenant. This is created by exchanging one very special thing: an identity-containing body fluid which passes from one body to the other. That this fluid contains a person's identity is obvious, as its other purpose is to create a new human being by combining the husband's unique genetic blueprint with the blueprint of the wife (an interesting corollary picture of the reality of covenant—two combining together to create an altogether new life). And if the woman is a virgin, there is often the contribution of her blood to the mixture of fluids. At the very least, she bathes and anoints the intimate part of her husband's body—immerses it, one could even say baptizes it—in her own intimate body fluid. Sexual intercourse actually creates the marriage covenant.

This has been the position of the Church throughout history. In most denominations until recent years, if intercourse can be shown not to have occurred, even though a wedding ceremony took place, even though vows were spoken and rings exchanged, church authority would nonetheless declare the marriage "annulled," or "never to have occurred." The evidence that this has occurred—blood on the nuptial sheets—is displayed publicly in some cultures, though most show more respect for the privacy of this most intimate event. The important thing to note is that it is sexual intercourse that creates covenant. Why would it be this, and only this, that could initiate covenant?

This is the most important reason why sexual intercourse has been exclusively reserved for marriage, and why the Scriptures go to such great lengths to make extremely clear the gravity of sexual sin. This is why sexual activity, especially losing one's virginity in a context other than marriage, is such a big deal. Sexual intercourse creates new life; not only potentially a new child, but new life and a covenant bond between those who participate. The Scriptures make a very interesting statement in this regard (1 Corinthians 6:18): "Flee from sexual immorality. All other sins a person commits are outside the body, but whoever sins sexually sins against their own body." When this statement is seen in light of the term "one flesh," which we know relates not just to physical tissue, but to identity and nature, this statement conveys the idea that sexual sin is against one's own identity, inflicting the most "internal" of injuries. Now we know why this would be the case.

Recently, some denominations have shifted their official opinion on the matter of when a marriage actually begins in light of the percentage of people who have already had intercourse prior to their wedding. Another element of the wedding has been selected that does the "real" joining, they now proclaim. The Church of England recently deemed that it is the vows that do the joining. Our son, married in England in an Anglican church, was not allowed to practice his vows during the rehearsal, for in the opinion of this denomination's leadership, doing so would have made the next day's wedding improperly redundant. But this is a recent innovation in reaction to the question posed by prewedding covenant creation: *Then why have a wedding?*

We will discuss this question farther down, for it is a real question. Perhaps a better question is: Why would we not listen to God on this matter? Let us see if, by the end of this volume, we can show why it is better, much better, to do so. Please recall how Jesus handled such questions.

IMPLICATIONS OF THE MARRIAGE COVENANT

What we are going to see through the rest of this book are the intricacies of God's plan for marriage. First, let us look at the most obvious changes in the lives of those newly wed. Earlier, we spoke of four overarching realities of covenant: new life, a merger of nature and identity, joining and new relationships, and exchanges and practical consequences. See if you can identify all of these elements in a marriage.

The centerpiece of God's plan is identity change. We might sum up the understanding of the identity change in marriage as follows.

The nature and identity of each party in the marriage now changes to encompass the identity and nature of the other. Individuality is maintained, but identity and nature are merged. Each person is now actually a "new being," in the sense that their identities are new and different versus their identities prior to the marriage. At the same time their old identity and nature—the "single, independent" individual—ceases to exist. From this merger of nature and identity a new entity is created that encompasses the two, and this is commonly termed a family. A family is "generative," a source of creation of new things, the most obvious being new human lives. But many other things are uniquely created through families. The family grows in its own way over time, just as the married parties do. A family develops an identity which is just as unique as the individuals who comprise it. The family extends beyond the nuclear group into an extended family, a group which continues to be united by a shared identity through generations. The family intersects with other individuals, families, and the community as a distinct entity, with each family member acting in one sense as its representative.

The joining and merger of the identities of husband and wife, from which all the rest flows, is the proper understanding of the term "one flesh."

Based on this new, merged identity the two people newly wed are to view each other as an extension of self; they are to treat each other in the favorable way each would treat themselves in terms of protection, provision, safety, security, and the meeting of needs. In addition, there are other behaviors, attitudes, and priorities about which we vow to each other either specifically or under the umbrella vow of taking each other in "holy matrimony." We will cover these in detail later, things like cherishing each other and giving the other person highest priority in certain ways. Note that these mutual obligations, and all the rest, are the same things the hearts of two people in love would drive them to do as they seek to display their love toward one another. Thus, God's plan at the outset resonates strongly with our hearts and our desires toward one another.

The general picture for those in a marriage covenant is that everything is now communal. There is no private sphere, no protected space in life where the other has no right to be; instead, lives are joined and mingled.

THE BENEFITS ARE IN THE DETAILS

Always keep in mind that God's plan is a very specific thing intended to accomplish many purposes in our lives, and through *us* to accomplish many purposes. The plan is there, and it works. But there is a variable at every point in terms of whether God's purposes are fulfilled in our lives, in our relationships, and in our impact on the world, and this is our faithfulness to God and His plan. That is, the success of God's plan in building our marriages, or ourselves, is directly determined by the choices each of us makes on a daily basis. If we follow God's plan in every detail, we reap a certain set of benefits. If we think we have sufficient reason to depart from God's plan, we also reap the consequences of these decisions—benefits are diminished, negative consequences occur. To the extent that we choose God's ways we have His assurance that we will be blessed. What I want all of us to see is how big those blessings can be.

At the same time, when looking at something as complex and multifaceted as God's plan of covenant, what are the chances we will get this all right, even if we really want to do so, and even if we set our minds and hearts to do so with all of our willpower? With all due respect, the chance is pretty much zero. This is the other picture I want to clearly paint as we go through this material. God's plan is not a list of things to get right, although it includes quite a long list. *God's plan is a process of growth and development.* What, then, does God want to see (that He can bless) if it isn't perfection? Consider what goes on between a child and a parent when the parent is trying to teach the child how to fulfill an important responsibility. For the child, this is challenging. He or she does not fully understand the big picture. The parent has merely presented the child with a sequence of tasks to accomplish. What does the parent want to see? Perfection? Or the child is punished? Of course not. The parent wants to see effort, a good and sincere heart, a teachable attitude, and progress. The parent wants the child to take the task seriously and take the lessons to heart. The parent is trying to help the child grow up, and the operative word is growth. This, by the way, is what the two newlyweds would properly expect of each other in their new relationship. Not perfection, but effort, a sincere heart, and growth. As for the child, what do they perceive through all of this? He or she will likely not understand the big picture until becoming a parent. The child just knows, for now, that they are to do their best on any given day with the tasks laid before him or her, and that this is sufficient.

> God's plan is not a list of things to get right, although it includes quite a long list. *God's plan is a process of growth and development.*

IMPLICATIONS OF THE CHANGE OF IDENTITY

It is interesting that people in general have some sense for the power of covenant, but given the misunderstanding of marriage prevalent in our culture, this power is baffling, even disconcerting. If marriage is just an agreement between two people, much like any other contract, why all the fuss? Why is it that being involved in a divorce is devastating in a way that most do not see coming, even the ones who wanted the divorce and initiated it? Why isn't it more like quitting your job, or selling your house and buying another, better one? (Or, perhaps, a worse one?) This is so because marriage is not a contractual thing but a covenant, and being unfaithful to a covenant is a very different thing from breaching a contract. Can we now better understand the role of adultery? The act breaks the old bond as it establishes a new one. Breaking such a relationship apart strikes the very core of our being, not simply tearing two people apart but tearing apart something in the core of our being. Separating what God has joined together in covenant is not just a violation of an agreement but a violation of ourselves, an attack on our very nature, even if self-inflicted. In the throes of a divorce, as one attacks a spouse they also attack themselves.

This merger of identities is designed to be immensely beneficial. Marriage, properly understood, removes any sense of competition between the covenant partners beyond perhaps playful competition. The strength of one party enhances the strength of the other. There is no place, or reason, for competition between the parties, for when one wins, the win is shared; when one is honored, the honor is shared; when one is favored or blessed, these benefits belong to both parties. There is no basis for jealousy over accomplishments, recognition, or rewards. If one partner is benefitted, the benefit belongs to both. The strength of one is not a threat to be neutralized but an asset to be harnessed for mutual good! The destiny of these two individuals is now firmly linked. The purpose of this joining is to harness the resources and capabilities of the two, and the synergy of their various potentials to better face the challenges of life.

The differences, even the weaknesses of the two, are not cause for elevating one and putting the other down, but for pooling strengths and combining abilities to offset weaknesses. Thus, in a marriage there is no hierarchy of importance, no differential of value between the two. Once this joining occurs the sharing of nature and identity equalizes and merges everything of the two. Not that they now are identical or do identical things, but what one does, the other does in them, and vice versa. Faithfulness to every aspect of one's covenant duties, obligations, and responsibilities is thought to be one's most blessed course of action, while harming one's covenant partner (or refraining from offering every aid and help) is deemed a violation of the letter and spirit of the mutual vows of marriage and of the intent of God's overall plan.

Beyond mechanical obedience to individual responsibilities, it is assumed that hearts will be wholeheartedly devoted to each other and to the relationship. The covenant pattern, if lived out, is designed to actually create and grow this wholehearted devotion in both parties. In contrast, if one partner does harm, tries to weaken or dishonor the other, what actually occurs? This harms *both*, weakens both, dishonors both. In harming our covenant partner, who else do we harm? Ourselves. Thus, we want to exercise the most extreme care in how we treat each other, and we are offered every motivation to do so. We are to love the other as we love ourselves, for in loving the other we are in fact loving ourselves.

> We are to love the other as we love ourselves, for in loving the other we are in fact loving ourselves.

IMPLICATIONS OF ACCEPTING THE OTHER'S LIFE WITHIN ONESELF

Many people spend a lifetime trying to be fully accepted. This is an integral part of being loved, is it not? To be seen and known for who one truly is, and to be accepted and embraced. If two in a marriage are unaware of the nature of covenant, if the basis of their relationship is having expectations satisfied, in such relationships dissatisfaction is often used as leverage by one to get more of what they want from the other.

What does it feel like to experience the calculated dissatisfaction of another? It feels like a lack of acceptance. Like a lack of love. What is the response? Some simply try harder to be acceptable, hoping, at some point, to be fully accepted. Others reciprocate, fold their arms, and begin to broadcast their own calculated dissatisfaction. How many spend entire marriages, entire lives searching in vain for acceptance? In covenant, by contrast, one has—from the beginning—been accepted in every respect into the very nature of the other. One has been accepted not on the basis of being acceptable in any detail, but because the other chose to accept the identity and nature of him or her in their entirety—within themselves. But both need to accept the reality of this acceptance and refrain from giving or receiving messages that convey that the other is "not enough." That decision has already been made by both.

WHAT DOES SELF-INTEREST LOOK LIKE IN COVENANT?

As we have discussed, the thing that causes most human conflict is people asserting their self-interest—or better put, their perceptions of their self-interest—against each other. The one who wins the contest of competing self-interests supposedly gets the better life while the loser . . . simply loses. But we are often tempted to embrace ideas of our own self-interest that are flawed or completely wrong. Thus we can devote our lives to advancing what we think are our best interests only to find that we end up with nothing of real value while our self-centered pursuits have wrecked everything worth having. The most prominent and important change produced by the alteration of identity and nature in covenant is related to our self-interest. True self-interest in covenant is pursued by *building the relationship, building the other party*, and *building ourselves simultaneously.* Anything that does not accomplish each of these three simultaneously is, by definition, not in our self-interest.

So what kinds of things would accomplish all three of these interests? As we will see, God has a plan to teach us.

QUESTIONS FOR THOUGHT

1. If the most fundamental relationship problem among humans is having different individuals with different interests pursuing their interests at the expense of others, how does God's plan for marriage address this problem? How does God's plan for marriage, as seen to this point, impact *your* view of marriage? How does it impact your view of your own marriage?

2. At weddings we have all heard the phrase, "What God has joined together, let man not put asunder." Does this phrase make even more sense now in light of the nature of this joining?

3. What relationship do you see between the realities of covenant, the ways a covenant is supposed to be lived out, what can be built through such a relationship, and the choices that two people make for the rest of their marriage? How important is it that people understand the nature of this relationship? How important is it that they understand their role in building the relationship? How can someone come to understand their role in building a covenant to its potential?

4. Does it surprise you that sexual intercourse creates a covenant? What other questions does this raise for you? Does this explain why the New Testament has so many warnings against engaging in sexual activity outside of marriage?

5. How might the course of a marriage be impacted if both people felt fully accepted and unconditionally loved? Does this require that the other person love them perfectly? (Hopefully not, for this will never happen.) What, instead, would be needed for each person to experience being loved and accepted in a given moment?

6. If the factor most at war with love in relationship is competing understandings of self-interest in the hearts and minds of two who are married, how does God's plan completely erase this factor? Two people will always have somewhat different views of what should happen or what should be done in any situation. How might these differences be handled in light of covenant versus the "competing kingdoms" model of marriage?

7. How much difference might covenant make in the overall level of conflict in marriage?

8. How much does God's original intent for marriage matter to you?

CHAPTER SIX

God's Plan for Marriage: Inform, Conform, Transform

INFORMING US

When is the last time you heard someone mention "keeping one's wedding vows" . . . in reference to anything other than sexual fidelity? Then why do we speak vows related to these other things?

TRADITIONAL VOWS OF MARRIAGE

Consider the compilation of historic wedding vows below. Are these things that are vowed in keeping with the logical outcomes of the change of identity? Do they coincide with the teaching of Scripture regarding love? Do these things build relationships? Do these things cause hearts to warm toward one another? Would each of these be a display of good character? Would these things work as a consistent display of love in attitude and action? Could these things be termed, in fact, an excellent functional definition of what it means to *love one another*? Above and beyond all this, do these things resonate with the heart of perfect love that God displays toward us? Through these vows, God is teaching us how to love in His way in simple and straightforward language. In fact, I would take the position that the sum of these vows corresponds perfectly, often in more approachable and practical language, with the various Scriptural commands and principles regarding love and virtue. Again, we are seeking to translate love in concept and intention to love in action. See if you agree with me after reading this collection of vows and the corresponding definitions of the words used.

Most wedding vows are but a sampling of a larger group of items which could be chosen. Thus, the things most people, even historically, speak as vows in an individual wedding do not fully and completely depict marriage. I think it is fair to assume that people making these abbreviated vows to each other know they are signing up for the entirety of God's intention for marriage because they also vow before Him to take each other in "holy matrimony." It is very instructive, therefore, to not just look at a sampling of individual, abbreviated vows, but at an extensive grouping. From these a composite may be assembled that paints the more full and complete picture God wants us to see.

THE VOWS OF MARRIAGE: WHAT WE ARE COMMITTING TO DO

Below is a synopsis of 100 Traditional Wedding Vows posted on the website Wedding Paper Divas.[2] See how many elements of covenant you can identify among these vows.

Before God and this congregation, I take you to be my husband/wife; leaving everything previous behind, giving every aspect of myself to you; from now we shall be as one until death do us part; no more I, only we; this ring symbolizes our covenant; I am your beloved and you are mine, I am your friend, and you are mine; as the Trinity represents three in one, so do we now, united in marriage, represent two joined as one; and as we are not just in covenant with each other, but both also in covenant with God, thus now three are united by covenant.

I therefore vow: to love, honor, and cherish you; unceasing faithfulness, undying devotion; protection, provision, trust and trustworthiness, perseverance, purity, honesty, charity, kindness, patience, gentleness, and self-control. Where my strength fails and growth of character is needed, I vow to seek the Lord for all that I am not, and by His grace and power grow into the man/woman He desires me to be, that I may love you more perfectly.

I further vow: to prefer you before all others and to forsake all others; to be yours and yours alone; to share all things, bear your burdens and sorrows, rejoice with you, comfort you in sickness and health, in poverty and wealth, and in all circumstances and situation to be true to my covenant vows to you before God.

These things, in fact, suffer from familiarity. We assume we understand these things, do these things, and that we are these things.

I suspect you have heard each of these items one or more times in a wedding, and upon hearing them would say, "Of course. This is how we treat someone we love." These things, in fact, suffer from familiarity. We assume we understand these things, do these things, and that we are these things. But let us examine each of these items more closely. And I would invite each of us, including myself, to examine ourselves more closely.

VOWED ATTITUDES AND BEHAVIORS AND OUR HEARTS

These things all resonate with something inside us—how we know we should treat people, and how we want to be treated by someone with whom we want to spend a lifetime. These vows are not meant to get us to do something we *do not want to do*, or *know we should not be doing*. Instead, these vows declare our intent to live in a consistently loving way with one whom we are declaring our love for this day, and pledging our lifelong love toward this person. This is a commitment our loving hearts want to make—and keep.

If this is what we desire to do, and intend to do, why do we need such vows? Because for various reasons, over time, we tend to choose *not* to treat our spouse in these very ways. One part of us wants to be loving, but other priorities, desires, reactions, imperatives, and values argue against our desire to love, and it is these imperatives that end up guiding our behaviors in other directions from time to time. Or we may simply revert to the ways we are in the habit of treating others, some of which may be very unloving. The universal experience of married people is that they do not always regard each other and treat each other in loving ways. If everyone is this way, what's the problem? Won't true love overcome these breaches of loving behavior? Isn't that what true love is supposed to do? But why would two people depart from acting like they are truly in love in the first place? And, if they do so, what happens next? A lot of things, and none of them grow the relationship in the right direction. How does God's plan help us move from where we all start in our marriages to the point where we are building life and relationship on all sides rather than unknowingly tearing down the very things we most want to build?

VOWS AND THE PLAN OF GOD

Let's pause for a moment and consider why God gave us a ceremony that incorporates vows, and why these kinds of things are vowed. First, a vow is understood historically to represent the most solemn and binding words that can come from one's mouth. If we make a vow, we are not engaging in poetry or metaphor. We are instead committing ourselves to do precisely what we have vowed to do, or to die trying. In our day virtually no spoken or written words have the same weight or binding power that is historically associated with vows. Please note that the recent cultural pattern of casually saying things with no intention of backing words with action is a huge departure from God's design (Ecclesiastes 5:4-6). By inviting us to speak such vows it is intended that we would have an additional reason, beyond in-the-moment feelings, that can highly motivate us to do precisely what we have committed ourselves to do. While there has never been a shortage of dishonesty and lack of follow-through on earth, we must realize that the almost total lack of connection between verbal commitments and actions in our current culture is a dramatic historical aberration. Let that sink in as we examine His plan in more detail.

DETAILS AND DEFINITIONS WITHIN THESE VOWS

It may be helpful to look carefully at the fullness of meaning in each of these vowed items so we can understand more clearly what we are committing ourselves to do and be, and what God desires that we do and be. Only then, as mentioned, can we really compare ourselves with these vowed items. Specific verses for each item are provided to demonstrate how well these things coincide with God's truth detailed in the Scriptures.

The following definitions were compiled with the aid of the Merriam-Webster online dictionary (m-w.com). The Scripture references are drawn from those pertaining specifically to **marriage**, or to **love** in a more general sense. If we are told to love our covenant partner, and certain Scripture verses define one aspect or another of love, then the injunction to love incorporates love as God fully defines it throughout Scripture. Therefore, these verses defining and illustrating love become part of God's plan of conducting ourselves toward each other in marriage. Anything said of love toward a brother or sister in Christ, or toward humanity in general, would be even more important in relation to our covenant partners. It is assumed that we owe each other the very highest standard of behavior in marriage.

1. Leave family of origin, friends, and everything else of the past behind, to join together with another person to become two new creatures in a new entity, a new family. *Genesis 2:24; Psalm 45:10; Malachi 2:14, 15; Ephesians 5:31; John 17*

2. This joining is a lifetime commitment, a permanent joining. *Mark 10:9; Matthew 19:6; Romans 7:2, 3; 1 Corinthians 7:39; Proverbs 2:17-19; 1 Corinthians 13:8*

3. The other party and you are now "us," with no part of life or self withheld. There is no protected personal space in which the other has no right to be. *Genesis 2:22-24; Mark 10:8; 1 Corinthians 6:19, 20; 7:2-5*

4. Love and friendship in their fullest possible definitions are pledged. *Song of Solomon, entire book; I Corinthians 13, entire*

chapter; James 2:8; Titus 2:4; Colossians 3:19; Philippians 2:1-15; Ephesians 5:25-31; Galatians 5:13-15, 22, 23; Romans 12 and 13, entire chapters; Galatians 3:14

5. These vows are made before God and to God, both as a witness and also to seek enforcement by Him for public, private, or secret breaches of these vows. *Malachi 2:14-16*

6. To honor. This means that the name, reputation, image, character, integrity, and overall person of the other party is promoted, enhanced, enlarged, improved, and praised whenever possible and appropriate. To dishonor is the opposite handling of this person and their reputation. This may also involve helping a person develop their own integrity, or to address other personal issues that might cause them to dishonor themselves. Honor speaks of the overall regard one has for another. *Romans 12:10; I Corinthians 12:23, 24, 13:5; 1 Peter 3:7; Proverbs 26:1, 31:10-31; 1 Thessalonians 4:4; Galatians 3:28; Hebrews 13:4*

7. To cherish. To view as of highest value, to make the highest priority, to have the greatest regard for, to adore, protect, nurture, defend, revere, esteem, admire, treasure, and prize—as well as to possess. *Song of Solomon, entire book; Proverbs 5:18, 19; Ephesians 5:25-29*

8. To be faithful. We have discussed the larger context of faithfulness, not merely physically, but faithfulness to the reality and principles of covenant, which are represented by these enumerated vows as well as faithfulness to the underlying reality of covenant—that we are now in each other. Thus the interests of one literally are the interests of the other. Faithfulness is the heartbeat of a marriage, well beyond feelings or desires. This quality represents our fixed and unchanging decision and will to live for the best interests of the other party for a lifetime regardless of how we feel, or of any other consideration. This choice, and the firm commitment to live out this choice, is the essence of true love. Love for a lifetime is not a feeling. It is first of all a choice. *Ecclesiastes 5:4; Matthew 25:23; 1 Corinthians 4:2; Luke 16:10-13;*

Proverbs 28:20; Matthew 25:14-29; 1 Timothy 3:11; 1 Corinthians 13:13

9. To be devoted. This connotes loyalty, constancy, fidelity, commitment, dedication, and adherence one to the other. There is also the sense of worship, not of the other person as a human, but recognizing the presence of the Holy Spirit within (see the section on the New Covenant) and treating this person as a vessel and temple of God. *1 Corinthians 6:19; Romans 12:10; Luke 16:13*

10. Protection. This speaks of standing against any physical risk to the person, but also includes threats in the mental, emotional, and spiritual realm. These risks may arise from outside the relationship or from within either of the parties. To protect includes speaking truth where there is lack of clarity and the obligation to search out truth if it is not initially evident. It involves emotional support as well as stepping up to defend the other party when necessary. Spiritual protection involves, among other things, defending against deception and deficient teaching of God's Word, promoting spiritual growth, and praying for one's partner. Another risk to defend against involves people's lack of recognition of, or failing to live out, their true identity and nature. Defense against this involves teaching, mentoring, and leading by example. It is never the case that one party has everything in good order while the other needs protecting. The injunction to protect, as in all things of covenant, is a mutual obligation and must be mutually exercised. At times one's partner needs protection from themselves. The vow to protect the other person provides strong motivation toward one's own spiritual growth, for spiritual immaturity in either party can cause damage. Thus, each party must be actively involved in the spiritual and character growth of the other party in addition to being involved in their own. *Ezekiel 33:4, 6; Psalm 82:3; Hebrews 12:12; Galatians 6:1, 2; 2 Corinthians 11:29; Hebrews 4:12; 1 Corinthians 13:7*

11. Provision. This speaks to any material, emotional, or spiritual need which the other party can meet. This does not, however, mean that the answer to every request is "yes." God, who loves us perfectly, does not say yes to every request. He considers every request seriously and either gives us what we request, or something better: what we actually need. This judgment involves God's superior understanding of our real needs as distinct from what we might think we need. Therefore, inherent in this commitment is the obligation to consider the deepest needs of the other party, beyond their simple requests, and to be wise, responsible, and prayerful when considering requests. With that in mind, covenant is in every sense a blank check, and it is the honor of the other party to generously and graciously meet the true needs of their covenant partner. This plan only functions to the best outcome when this is a mutual approach, with both parties literally trying to out-do each other in offering blessings. Inherent in the obligation to love the other party is that one will refrain from frivolous or selfish requests that would deplete resources without good reason. *Proverbs 31:10-31; 1 Timothy 5:8; Luke 12:33; Proverbs 12:24; Matthew 5:42; James 2:14-26; Acts 4:35; 1 Timothy 3:5*

12. Trusting in the other party, and being trustworthy. We pledge to trust this person, to believe their word and trust in their intentions unless we have unequivocal evidence to the contrary. Then, as we work through any breaches of honesty, we display confidence in the character of the other party, in their ultimate desire to get things right. We are not merely to believe this person, we are to believe in them, in their ultimate desire for our best. Here, as in several other items, there may be character work to be done to really live this out, especially when people have grown up in a culture that does not value honesty and integrity. In these cases we may be, as it was termed in my Christian life in the 1970s, "holding the crown above their head and praying that they will grow into it." (We will discuss this farther down.) The key element here is to not take the word of someone who

disparages our partner without bringing the matter before them and assuming the best about them. Also inherent in this is the development of our own integrity. One of the most important elements in a relationship is not merely truth and accuracy of speech, but transparency, or full disclosure. This is the prerequisite for intimacy, for truly knowing the other person. The opposite of this is an attempt to maintain a false image through concealing something about ourselves. Consider the distinction between actually knowing someone and simply knowing an image they are fashioning. *1 Timothy 3:11; Proverbs 31:11; Zechariah 8:16; Ephesians 4:25; Proverbs 22:21; Ephesians 4:15; Proverbs 8:7*

13. Perseverance. Life is long and challenging. This is a concept related to faithfulness, highlighting persistence, tenacity, and staying power. It is the distillation of our will, a refusal to yield in the face of difficulty, or refusal to back down when the price of faithfulness rises. It also speaks to maintaining our commitment to love when circumstances change, either externally or within our own hearts. It is from this place that we would fend off attractions to other people, and from which we continue to act in loving ways when our hearts are wounded, offended, or just weary. *Romans 5:4; 2 Peter 1:6; 2 Thessalonians 2:4, 3:5; Romans 5:4; James 1:3, 4, 5:11; Hebrews 12:1*

14. Purity. This is akin to the holiness of God: unstained, unpolluted. This is righteousness protected, honor lived out, the sum of virtues and absence of vices. This is slowly approached as one matures spiritually, though it is never fully attained in this life. Inherent in this vow is a commitment to spiritual growth and a commitment to the spiritual growth of the other party. It is also a commitment to display the best part of ourselves to the other, to give them the best of ourselves, to spare them when possible our shortcomings and character flaws while we are dealing with these things before God. The opposite of this would be acting as an agent of temptation, participating in the moral compro-

mise of our partner. *2 Corinthians 6:6; 1 Peter 3:2; Psalm 119:9; Proverbs 22:11; 1 Timothy 6:14; Ephesians 5:27; 2 Peter 3:14; 1 Peter 1:15, 16; 1 Corinthians 6:19; Leviticus 20:26*

15. Honesty. This is akin to trust/trustworthy, but with a larger meaning. Enlarging on the idea of transparency, this is a vow to reveal ourselves to the other party. This vow is in a sense the obligation to better know ourselves, just as it is to better know the other person. The close proximity of the marriage relationship is absolutely designed to reveal the hidden parts of us to ourselves as well as to the other person. Growth of personal understanding flows from mutual honesty in the context of love and acceptance. One key aspect of this is correctly identifying our own needs, feelings, and desires.

One of the most important skills of marriage is learning to ask for what we need from the other party at an appropriate time and in an appropriate way. This involves learning to determine what we really want or need in a situation, which may itself be a process. Then we ask the one who loves us to meet our need or desire. But the next step is the absolute key: we have no right in the moment to insist on this outcome or to manipulate in the face of reluctance. The key is to offer the other person the freedom to respond to our request in the moment, or to not do so. Even though the other person loves us and wants the best for us, still in this moment they may be unable to meet our needs for a variety of reasons. It is up to us to realize that the ultimate source of meeting our needs is *not our spouse, but God.* And remember, sometimes God says no in the moment as well. Our spouse is not unlimited, as God is, nor are we, thus we must make further allowances for the limitations of the other. It is vital to seek out each other's needs as well as our own, and to mutually meet

> It is up to us to realize that the ultimate source of meeting our needs is *not our spouse, but God.*

these needs when we are able. The more we engage in this back and forth, this arms race of mutual blessing, the more delightful our relationships become. The path to satisfaction in marriage is graciously receiving whatever gift our spouse is capable of offering in the moment, even if it is this: "Duly noted. I'll get back to you on that." If someone loves us, they will generally come back to this area, knowing that they can offer something that matters to us. *Ephesians 4:15, 25; Proverbs 4:24; James 5:12; Matthew 5:37; Colossians 3:9; 1 Corinthians 13:6*

16. Charity. The idea of charity, in contrast to mutual giving and receiving, involves asymmetric giving. This is about giving to one who cannot reciprocate, or offering grace and mercy to one who does not appear to deserve it. The larger sense of charity is benevolence and goodwill, the desire for the best for the other. We are to be conduits of God's grace to each other, offering kindness when condemnation or harshness would be an option. The sense of this would be to reframe situations and wording to be as gracious as possible in a situation while still being real and honest. But the essence of this vow is the reality that our spouse may not at points be capable of reciprocating—the "worse, sicker, or poorer" part of the wedding vows. We are to be generous even if this can only be a one-sided transaction, and to do so indefinitely in the case of long-term illness or incapacity. *Luke 14:12-14; Colossians 3:12,19; 1 Peter 3:7; Romans 14:1, 15:7*

17. Kindness. Similar to the above, and the opposite of unkindness, this connotes a sincere concern for the feelings of the other party. Also, this involves attention to feelings in situations where feelings might be overlooked as we pay attention to other things. Inherent in this word is an appropriate use of anger, avoiding collateral damage that occurs when anger spills beyond a specific, energetic response to a significant threat to the relationship or to the character of the other party. *Romans 11:22, 14:13-20; Colossians 3:12; 2 Corinthians 6:6; 1 Corinthians 13:4*

18. Patience. We all have things we would like to see resolved yesterday, things that chafe more deeply because of repetition. We weary of recurring problems that seem easy to solve—to us. This vow acknowledges that life is long, some issues take time, and often today's issue is not as vital or important as we believe it to be. Though we are joined, the other person is also on their own journey, and he/she brings a different set of tools and capacities to the table—and their own set of issues. People learn in different ways. It helps over time to develop an understanding of what a bad day actually looks like. As a surgeon, seeing someone die from trauma, or cancer, or seeing someone's life change in permanent, significant ways helps put more minor irritants in perspective. Crises really do come in small, medium, and large, and small ones often provoke large emotions. The common advice is, "Don't sweat the small stuff." Another lesson from surgery is the understanding that the best response to a crisis comes from a cool head and a steady hand. Thus, there is no place in life for losing control because we are upset. Patience is an important form of self-control. It is also about managing expectations. *Ephesians 4:2; Romans 14:1-12; Colossians 3:12; 1 Corinthians 13:4*

19. Gentleness. This is akin to kindness, but has to do with more than emotions. This is the soft and careful way we deal with each other on most issues. This is about finding the most constructive way to say something, the least disruptive path to deal with an issue. This is about being careful with each other. It is also about the pleasure of a soft touch. Subtlety is often more powerful than

stridor. A gentle word can be extremely powerful (Proverbs 15:1). At times I observe people in marriages trying to work through issues, and it can be difficult to tell whether the two are friends or enemies. With a gentle approach, we know we are dealing with a friend. *Colossians 3:12; 1 Timothy 6:11; Galatians 5:23, 6:1; Philippians 4:5; Ephesians 4:2*

20. Self-control. Parallel to the several previous items, this is a summary word that speaks to being under the control of God's Spirit rather than being carried away by one or another idea or passion that does harm. For God has not given us a spirit of fear, but of power, love, and self-control (2 Timothy 1:7). This involves our inner life of thought, emotion, values, priorities, attention, and will; and our outer life of attitude, word, and deed. It implies good moral choices, constructive relationship approaches, and involvement in any situation that is as constructive as possible. *2 Peter 1:6; Galatians 5:23; Proverbs 16:32, 25:28; 1 Corinthians 9:25; 2 Timothy 2:7*

21. To prefer you before all others, to forsake all others, to be yours and yours alone. The most straightforward rendering of this is the acknowledgment that at present the other person is one's best friend, and the commitment going forward is that they will remain one's best friend. At a deeper level it recognizes the truths we have been discussing about the Covenant of Marriage—that it is an exclusive relationship, that none of the preferences and priorities of marriage are properly extended to any party in a way that elevates them above the marriage partner, and that no person nor any consideration is more important than one's marriage partner, except God Himself. Since God is the Author of marriage, His interests coincide perfectly with living out the Covenant of Marriage faithfully and perfectly. *Proverbs 5:15-20; Malachi 2:15*

There are other things one might add to this list, like forgiveness, which are also vital elements of the best relationships. But if one develops the character and relationship skills necessary to do and be the above, these other necessary elements also will be present.

After reviewing this list, how would you like someone to treat you in these ways? And not just treat you these ways today, but to vow to always be there to consider and act toward you in these ways—until death parts you. What if you had confidence that the person offering this vow had the character, integrity, courage, and stamina to make good on their vows in consistent, significant ways? Would you like someone like this in your life? How would you feel getting up every day and looking forward to someone treating you consistently in these ways? Would you be motivated to reciprocate, to be increasingly scrupulous in fulfilling your own vows? If someone is treating you like this, would you say that they are loving you with their actions as well as their words? With their attitudes and priorities as well as their intentions? If you are loved in these ways consistently, what do you think would happen to your feelings for the other person over time? Would you be likely to "stay in love"? In fact, would you not love this person more and more year after year? Isn't this what God wants? Isn't this what we want? Does this look like the path to happily-ever-after? Isn't it wonderful that God has a plan? Of course, for this to happen God's plan must offer more than this information. And it does.

ACTION PLAN

IMPROVING YOUR MARRIAGE

If you are married you want to learn new ways to love your spouse. You want to learn what love looks like across the range of life experience. You want to know what matters most to your beloved. Some aspects of love are trial and error; a person may not know what will mean most to them in such a close relationship. Trying and assessing is the key, early in a marriage, when it comes to matters of preference. But covenant shows us many things—like honoring our beloved above all other things, and before all other people—that are crucial if the best marriage is to be built. The above list details the "always do this" ways we are to treat each other. Therefore, it will help immensely if you become very familiar with this list. Read it, study it, and perhaps memorize key elements. Then begin systematically applying this list to your relationship in some way. Take an item a week, or an item a day, and think of some way to live it out toward your beloved. The important thing is to begin building the relationship upon everything on this list over time. It will be even better if you and your spouse make this plan a joint project, and you can share your experiences being on the other end of these behaviors, and then fine-tune your understanding of what it means to honor each other in light of the other person's experience of you attempting to do so.

BECOMING THE KIND OF PERSON YOU WANT TO MARRY

If you are not married, take one of these items per week. Meditate on the meaning of this item and what this would look like in a relationship with those closest to you. Then take one or more of these applications and live them out during the week with those closest to you. This would be a wonderful way to train yourself to relate to people in a way that is very different from our current cultural training, better preparing you for the deeper and more intimate relationship of marriage.

(*If you do this, however, a warning and disclaimer*: do not expect people to necessarily reciprocate as you treat them in more virtuous ways. And do not be unguarded toward others, offering them opportunities to hurt you or manipulate you, which some of these items could offer if implemented without discretion and if not in a true reciprocal relationship. Relationships are just that: they are back-and-forth interactions with adjustments made according to responses. The general principle is that treating people in more virtuous ways will return blessing to you in the long run. However, not all people with whom you interact will have good intentions toward you. Even in these situations, though, better treatment from you will often result

> Even in these situations, though, better treatment from you will often result in better treatment *toward* you.

in better treatment *toward* you. It needs to be emphasized that the fullness of this behavior is only appropriate for those in covenant, with one to whom we are joined and linked per God's plan.)

In the same way, husbands ought to love their wives as their own bodies. He who loves his wife loves himself.
EPHESIANS 5:28

Husbands love your wives as Christ loves the church, and gave Himself up for her.
EPHESIANS 5:25

. . . and wives should respect their husbands.
EPHESIANS 5:33

ANOTHER IMPLICATION OF OUR VOWS

If we are vowing to treat each other in certain ways, and to be certain things toward each other, we are committing to do this consistently, and even lifelong. By implication, we are also committing ourselves *not* to treat our spouses in the converse of these ways. If we vow to honor our husband or wife, we are certainly also vowing, for instance, not to dishonor them. This is in fact where the issue of our obedience is focused. Therefore, it is helpful to go back through this list of items and their expanded definitions and identify the opposite of each. It might even be helpful to follow this exercise with the positive affirmations, "I will never . . . " This is the focal point of our obedience because now we cannot misunderstand the entire scope of our vows.

Note, also, that we have just vowed that our behavior toward our covenant partner will no longer be guided by an in-the-moment determination of how we feel or what we think we want. We have just committed to act in a loving way in spite of any other circumstance. All that remains is to figure out how to actually do what we have committed to do. This is challenging, to be sure. But is it also not the best thing we could possibly do for ourselves as well as for our beloved? Covenant is an "all-in" kind of thing. We can now see an increasingly clear picture of why this is so. But engaging in these behaviors, and confining ourselves only to these behaviors, would require a level of commitment that is simply beyond most of our capacities for consistency and persistence, especially in the beginning.

And there is another problem we must confront if we are to carry out God's plan.

THE APPARENT FLAW IN GOD'S PLAN

Is the above what is most likely to actually happen in the long run? Or will we not, as the flush of the most intense emotions wears off, return to treating our partner in ways we have always treated people? Let's be honest. Why would we not want to treat our covenant partner in all of these ways all the time? Because, while we love them, care about them, care about how they feel, and care about what they want, what is lining up on the other side of the ledger that would urge us toward contrary behaviors and attitudes?

Few people are self-aware enough to see these things clearly in themselves, so let us first think of this in terms of how the people around you treat people. I believe two things drive most of the ways people treat other people: first, our habits; and second, our view of our self-interest. Consider what goes on around you every day and see if you agree.

We tend to treat other people according to habits. Most of what we think, speak, and do follows habit patterns. This is wonderful, for it means we do not need to stop and think about everything we do. We also view other people according to how we are in the habit of viewing one kind of person or another—*kind* in this case defined according to the categories into which we customarily separate other people. These things are all done without thinking. We often have little conscious awareness of how we are treating other people. We are simply being ourselves.

But in situations where we are making choices about how to treat someone, what drives our behaviors more than any other force? Is it not our perception of our own best interests? Note I did not say our understanding of our true best interest, but our *perceptions* of our best interest, which may be in line with the truth or completely out of line.

When we are living as a single person we often do not see people's full reactions to us. We are insulated by distance and, to a degree, by disinterest. But in the up-close-and-personal world of marriage we get a full dose of each other at close range. We cannot help but notice someone's reaction to how we treat them, and we cannot help but care at some level about the experiences we are creating for them. But still, there is more.

> Note I did not say our understanding of our true best interest, but our *perceptions* of our best interest, which may be in line with the truth or completely out of line.

HOW WE CHOOSE THE COMPETING KINGDOMS MODEL FOR OUR MARRIAGE

What almost everyone does in marriage is engage in a balancing act. On one hand, we love our covenant partner, we care about them, and we care about what they want and need. But we balance this with our own sense of what should happen—again, informed ultimately by our sense of self-interest. And our partner is on the other side of the equation doing the same thing, figuring out what things he or she would ideally want to happen, and what he or she is willing to give up in order to get the most important items on their agenda. Relationships turn into a negotiation that pits perceptions of self-interest against each other. The only thing that remains is to see whose will and agenda wins out. Who does most of the giving and who does most of the taking? And now we find ourselves standing right in the middle of the competing kingdoms model we have previously discussed. Our lives turn into something between a cold war competition for supremacy and a yard sale, a sort of bargaining for the things we cannot take outright by force.

COVENANT, IN CONTRAST . . .

God's plan pits two things against each other very quickly if we sincerely intend to carry out this plan: God's idea of what we should be doing versus our own ideas about what is best for us based on the training process we have been engaging in our entire lives—the false training process about how to live and the habits we have acquired as we interact with others. This forces us to confront a critical question:

> Should we trust in what we feel, think, and believe
> about what is best for us, and have always done,
> or should we trust God and His plan?

As we noted in the first volume, God has an annoying habit of bringing us to this point of decision.

Does this question look familiar? And who have we already noted is loading our world, and our own minds and hearts, with "sufficient" reasons to depart from God, offering us purported benefits for doing so? We examined what happened in the Garden of Eden in the first volume of this series in great detail, for this exact pattern confronts each of us on a daily basis. And we noted the influence of the enemies of God ever since, offering one supposed benefit or another in return for departing from God's plan, benefits that never materialize, with a price tag far larger than we anticipate for falling in line with this continuing rebellion against God. These glorious offers in sum comprise humanity's flawed sense of self-interest. The apparent flaw in God's plan is that it goes against human nature and human frailty.

The reality of His plan is that it highlights things within ourselves that represent golden opportunities for growth, maturity, and transformation on the way to our best lives and best relationships.

The reality is that we really must decide at the outset whom we are going to follow. Another reality is that we decide things with very differing levels of commitment and resolve. Some decisions we make are easily changed, and for others we will die before we yield. Some decisions fade in the face of adversity, while for others adversity only builds our resolve and strengthens our willpower. And for some of us, having never had a belief worthy of suffering for, much less dying for, we need to learn how to identify such a worthwhile belief if it is right in front of us, and we need to build the capacity to hold firmly to a belief. If we are to follow God, we must do more than simply say to ourselves this moment, "This is what I am deciding to do." We must go through the process of building a belief system so strong that it will overcome the obstacles we will predictably encounter. And we must also build ourselves—our character, our willpower, our resolve, our determination. Are these good things to have? Are they things we must have to make the most of our marriage? Or our lives?

God's plan will lead in one direction while our own guidance systems, formed as they are by our culture—a culture whose guidance systems has largely been formed by the enemies of God—will lead in an entirely different direction. We have to decide which direction we are going before we can start our journey. And if we think we have not decided, we have. To follow our own guidance is done without thinking; these decisions have already been made. We are simply living them out. On the other hand, the decision to follow God requires departing from business as usual. This will be the best single decision we will ever make.

WHAT IS GOD TRYING TO ACCOMPLISH HERE?

At times, even with the best of intentions—which we do not always have—we are our own worst enemy in relationships. At times we do not know how much damage a decision or action is going to cause. At the same time, if we are reading this book on marriage we obviously know a lot about building a relationship. We are building toward, or already have, a marriage. God's plan has a very straightforward objective: to keep us from building our relationships with one hand as we are tearing them down with the other. If we keep building, and get better at building, and subtract the damage, what can we predict about the relationship long-term?

WHY DO WE NEED GOD'S DEFINITION OF TRUE LOVE?

Earlier in this chapter we examined a lengthy list of things we are supposed to do and ways we are supposed to be. Which makes perfect sense since love is something that has as many facets and dimensions as the entirety of our lives. This is the picture God lays before us, the ideals and specific ideas we are to draw from as we decide every minute, in every situation, how we are going to live. Do we really need God's guidance here? Try this simple exercise: go to any gathering where there are married couples. Some are engaging in loving behaviors. Other are doing things different from God's definition of love, often much different. Watch what happens next, even in the moment. Watch how people react and respond to each other. Then consider the cumulative weight of the ways two people treat each other and regard each other played out over a lifetime. Also, consider that people are generally on their best behavior in public. Once we see what love is, and is not, we begin to see something else: the impact of love, or of *not-love*, on hearts and on the trajectory of lives and relationships.

I want to introduce a concept here that you can begin to observe in the relationships around you and perhaps in your own marriage relationship. That concept is how closely two people "orbit each other" in a romantic relationship. Some people are physically close to each other, often touching, often affectionate. They interact constructively. They seem to understand each other at a deep level. They share many areas of life. They share hobbies and activities; perhaps they work together. They share pleasant and constructive emotions. They look for reasons to be together. Even in the most simple activities there is deep interaction going on between them adding meaning to even simple things. These two are "orbiting closely" and spending quality time together. Orbiting closely requires many things, but these two are always present: the ability to cooperate across a wide range of situations, and creating for each other a sense of safety.

> Orbiting closely requires many things, but these two are always present: the ability to cooperate across a wide range of situations, and creating for each other a sense of safety.

Now look for people with fewer points of connection. They may be physically attracted to each other and share a small number of other things in common. But they have frequent misunderstandings. They undercut and belittle each other in social situations. They often hide things from each other. They do some things well together, but the idea of working side by side, day after day would be unfathomable to them. They would drive each other crazy. They like to be together some of the time, but they also need lots of space in the relationship. Another way of describing this needed space is that they orbit far from each other. At a deeper level, in addition to having less ability to cooperate successfully, these people do not feel safe with each other at close range. Nor should they. Why? Your next action point is to observe how they treat each other in terms of the covenant vows we've listed in this chapter. You will likely notice that couples who orbit closely, work well, play well, and do everything well together almost always treat each other in ways that reflect covenant vows. On the other hand, those who orbit far apart will act in ways out of sync with the realities of covenant. Their ways of interacting are guided by other lights. What you will begin to see is that God's ideas of love produce closeness and cooperation while contrary ideas produce discord and distance.

Humans are remarkable creatures. Each of us begins with the notion that we are supposed to be treated with perfect love, pure justice, and complete fairness. If you do not believe this, just ask any child or teenager how they think you are supposed to treat them. And what happens if these people are not treated in these ways? They do not like it, and they are often not shy about expressing their displeasure. Where do these ideas about how we are supposed to be treated come from? Could it be that concepts like fairness, justice, and the other ways we want to be treated are wired into our very being, made as we are in the image of God? All of these are imperfect shadows of His perfection, and it is His perfection for which we are longing. Specifically, His perfect love.

At the same time, we begin with the notion that we should be "free" to express whatever is within us, and we believe that others are supposed to gratefully adapt themselves to the ways we treat them—despite those ways being anything but loving, just, or fair, and despite the fact that we would be upset if someone treated us in these same ways. The rest of the game is simply becoming powerful, influential, or manipulative enough so that things end up going our way . . . at least in our own perception in the moment . . . so that what comes back continues to be better than what we are giving out. How do people reconcile the difference between their behavior and what they want from others? They expect to be unconditionally loved even if they offer nothing resembling unconditional love to others. One thing people who engage in this curious hypocrisy simply do not see is the cumulative long-term effect of this strategy. The best relationships are reciprocal, where both parties treat the other in the ways they want to be treated, are they not? One of the most important revelations we can experience is beginning to realize what it is like to be on the other end of our behaviors. In spite of our actual behaviors and attitudes, we are also adept at maintaining an overly optimistic view of ourselves, aren't we? God has perfectly designed the intimate confines of marriage to cut through this overestimation of ourselves, to show us the true impact of our behaviors through the wounded eyes of someone whose feelings we care deeply about. God has designed marriage to show us very clearly what it is like to be *on the other end of us.*

God presents us with a clear definition of love. Our commitment before God is to love consistently, wholeheartedly, faithfully. What a game-changer, or what an unparalleled opportunity that is completely ignored. Have you seen both outcomes? The next thing to note is the role of choice—our choices—as they are made on an ongoing basis. If offered the opportunity to love, and shown what love looks like in action, we would like to assume from this point forward that we will do and be these things toward our beloved. But is this assumption realistic? God defines love for us, but the challenge is for us to choose this path, and then that we choose to do what is necessary to learn to love and, finally, to truly love.

At the same time, God offers us the freedom that true love requires. True love is ultimately an expression of choice, of choosing to fully support the best interests of another with our mind, heart, and life; of choosing to believe in another person and to offer up our own lives to them. Or we can withhold ourselves from them and direct our best efforts elsewhere. God tells us clearly how we are to display love toward Him (John Chapter 14): through obeying Him. But He wants us to obey Him and to commit ourselves to His plan from love, not from compulsion or coercion. He lays out very clearly the benefits, short-term and long-term, of following Him, and He spells out clearly the unforeseen costs of turning from Him to follow the guidance of His adversary. He wants us to respond to His love by desiring a relationship with Him more than anything else. If He is, as He says, the definition of love and truth, and we fully understand this, we will have sufficient reason to turn from distracting voices to follow Him even when His path, such as His plan for marriage, seems difficult to follow. In sum, in order to truly love God, we must realize two simple truths: His way actually is the only one truly in our best interest, the only way to the life we want; and, beyond this, He is the source of life. Remember what Peter said in a passage quoted in the first volume of this series? "Where else can we go? You have the words of life." Peter was correct. Jesus said, "I am the way, and the truth, and the *life*" (John 14:6). What is the alternative to life?

IS LOVE REALLY JUST A LIST OF THINGS TO DO AND NOT DO?

There is one more thing we need to emphasize about a marriage covenant. Though God has provided an extensive list outlining our obligations, as with all covenants the things we are obligated to do for each other may be listed only to a point. We are fully obligated to offer our very best in every way to our covenant partners. Our responsibilities are illustrated by, but not limited to, the items on God's list. Covenant, as we noted, is the ultimate blank check. The correct answer to any need, any situation, is, "Whatever it takes. If I have it, it is yours. If I do not have it at the moment, I will find it, grow it, develop it—I will trust God to show me how to meet this need, to work in me and through me. And I will trust in Him to provide beyond anything I can provide to meet your deepest needs in fullness." We give, we do, we grow, we build, we pray. Does this look like real love?

My command is this: love each other as I have loved you. Greater love has no one than this: to lay down one's life for one's friends. You are my friends if you do what I command.
JOHN 15:12-14

God offers us an extensive list of actions and attitudes that are right or wrong in both the Old and New Testaments. From the Ten Commandments to the principles and precepts of Deuteronomy, from the lessons of Proverbs to the principles and object lessons in the Prophets, from the teachings of Jesus to the expansions on His life and teachings in the rest of the New Testament, what is God doing? Throughout, He is showing us how to love. Love consists of building relationship on the one hand while refraining from doing harm on the other. Coincidentally, doing right things and displaying right attitudes will build relationship, while doing wrong things, or having wrong priorities or attitudes, will damage people and thus damage relationships. If we approach God with an attitude of wholehearted love and worship, we will learn more about His love, which in turn will better equip us to love. Everything we are told to do is not simply about "right and wrong," in some abstract or spiritual sense, but about building and sustaining relationship—with God and with other people. Thus, all of God's rules are designed to do only one thing: to equip us to fulfill the two commandments that are, according to Jesus, His greatest: to love God with all our heart, mind, soul, and strength, and to love our neighbors as we love ourselves. But there is one asterisk: we must be taught what love is from God's point of view. In fact, we must receive true love from God before we can display true love.

Love in marriage is a subset of loving overall; marriage is a very special, exclusive relationship with many specific purposes. Thus, marriage comes with a broad array of specific ways in which love is to be shown. There is huge overlap between loving in general and loving a husband or wife; however, God's plan for marriage is designed to build the most deep, broad, and loving human relationship we will ever experience, which is intended to meet our deepest needs for human love. It is from this relationship more than any other that we learn, and are shaped and formed, to love in more general ways as God commands. The other major loving and shaping influence is intended to be the Body of Christ, a topic we will cover in the next book in this series.

WHY IS COVENANT A PLAN INSTEAD OF JUST A RELATIONSHIP?

Let's think for a moment about what is required for us to move from the common community understanding of marriage all the way to building all the things inherent in covenant. Many things must change. Most do not change by simply saying, "I will

> There is a process by which our understanding of love shifts from the one we have when we enter the relationship to the one God wants us to have.

now do this." Most of these things, instead, are built in the way most important things are built—by a process. There is a process by which our understanding of love shifts from the one we have when we enter the relationship to the one God wants us to have. There is a process by which the relationship is built, by which we grow into the various roles we need to play in each other's lives and in family life. There is process by which our hearts grow toward each other—growing in trust, respect, and mutual reliance so that love continues to grow over a lifetime together. There is a process by which our characters grow, by which we mature, by which we trim off qualities inconsistent with our new lives and build and strengthen qualities that will help us, our mate, and our family reach our highest potential. Each of these processes interlock; each is aided by all the others. All of these processes occur within our covenant relationship if we simply make every possible effort to faithfully live out every aspect of this relationship.

Each of these processes involves starting at one point, moving through a series of steps, and building what should be built. If we simply list these steps, what does this represent? A plan. Since these processes interlock, or feed off each other, many of the steps that promote growth in one area will also promote growth in others. This sounds more complicated than it actually is in practice. We will walk through the overall process so we can see what is required.

The steps, in fact, are simple. The most challenging thing is to maintain our focus and commitment over a lifetime in the face of a world that is trying to lead us in other directions on a moment-by-moment basis. What I also want to show is the superiority of this plan versus anything the world has to offer, to prepare us to properly handle the inevitable challenges to God's plan within our mind and heart.

CONFORMING TO GOD'S PLAN

THE BASIC ELEMENTS

God's plan is that we love our husband or wife. He is catching us at a good time to get us to sign on to His plan because our hearts are already aflame with love and looking for ways to show it. We understand that marriage is a turning point, the momentous beginning of a new life. When God fills in some of the blanks regarding what love and marriage are supposed to look like, we are good with that step. We all have our vision for a great marriage, a strong family, for what our happily-ever-after should look like, and we have a lot of energy ready to go toward this building process inside our hearts. We also understand at some level that unloving, uncaring things oppose our dreams and goals and that being unloving jeopardizes something important. So in our hearts there are already powerful forces in sync with God's plan.

At the same time, let's just say that God's working definition of love probably goes a bit beyond our own, and His plan to confine our behavior will run cross-grain with things inside us. What we will see next are an array of factors God has put in place, in the relationship, in our hearts, in our covenant partner, and in certain capacities He has placed within us. These capacities can grow and develop, which will in turn allow us to successfully implement His plan.

What is the bottom line of God's plan? How do we know success when we see it? There are two points of measurement. First, God wants us to love another person as we love ourselves. Jesus' injunction to His followers on this point even has a name: the "Golden Rule." God made it easy for us to begin to learn how to do this by instructing us to love our other self—our spouse. But some of us do not love ourselves very well either. So God enlarges our definition of love, teaching us to love ourselves, our covenant partner, and Himself in the process in accord with His definition. The second measure is what we build in life and relationship as a result of God's process of growth and development.

The rest of this volume will highlight some of the things that reflect life and relationship built according to God's plan.

WE WILL ONLY CONFORM FOR GOOD REASONS

We need a reason, a fully sufficient reason, to do each of these things. And we need strongly compelling reasons to do all of these things consistently, now and forever, especially if we must swim against our cultural currents to do so. It is easy to do things that come naturally to us. We did fall in love, and we have built a strong and solid relationship by doing things our way, by following our feelings up to this point. Our life has never been better, in fact. Why should we even consider turning over complete control of the situation to God and doing things His way? The question occurs naturally in all of our hearts when we are asked to treat another person in a way that is unnatural for us, or seems to put us in a vulnerable position, or that might not make sense based on everything we have learned about life up to this point. Situations in which we may be tempted to say things like . . . "What is that again about how I am supposed to treat someone who is so . . . irritating! And doing this stuff on purpose! Are they trying to drive me insane? It's working! Fine! If that's the way things are, this is what they are going to get back . . . " Or say to ourselves, "But if we are nothing but nice to them, won't they run all over us?" Put another way, consistently loving another person goes against the grain at the outset, and it will continue to do so indefinitely unless certain things happen inside us. And, by the way, love does not preclude us from challenging another's misbehavior. "Nice" and "love" are not synonyms. "Spouse" does not mean "doormat" or "dumping ground." But how do we deal with a situation when someone has not yet learned how to protect us from themselves? When the first reasons that come to mind are reasons to protect ourselves?

God, who built our minds and hearts, knows how we come to believe what we believe, choose what we choose, and do what we do. We do all of these for reasons. To help us conform to His plan He gives us reasons. There are many of these. Here are five major ones.

Reason number one: We now have a reason to treat our "other self" with the same respect and deference we would like to be shown if we are way off base about something. Which we will be . . . soon. Life has a way of reversing these roles, so we do well to learn to give what we would most want to receive in these situations.

Reason number two: We all value our ability to choose. God has built this desire into us. The second reason for following God's plan is that we chose to do so. We each chose our partners, and we chose to enter the covenant of holy matrimony with that partner. Marriage is the epitome of a voluntary organization—on the way in. In marriage we have fully accepted the other person, and they have fully accepted us. We have chosen to merge and exchange lives. Having chosen, our responsibility is to make the most of our choice. Any option other than faithfulness to our choices will inevitably do harm.

Reason number three: Marriage is God's special gift to us, a package deal, a seamless whole. If we understand that marriage actually represents a plan rather than just an opportunity to figure everything out on our own, we have taken the first step in the plan. We do not want to start from scratch if the problem has already been solved by Someone much more capable. His plan for marriage has been tried and proven by countless couples for millennia. The third reason, then, is that we are presented by God with a working plan, one that will lead to our greatest benefit *if implemented per His instructions.*

> If we understand that marriage actually represents a plan rather than just an opportunity to figure everything out on our own, we have taken the first step in the plan.

God wants us to realize there are many facets of love—thoughts, feelings, actions, dreams, hopes, aspirations, and many more. Things like feelings of attraction are simply responses. But one of the most important and least emphasized aspects of love is that love is a choice, a decision, and one followed by a lifetime of decisions to continue loving. Attraction is but a doorway; decisions are the steps on the path to true love. One may act on attraction and build, or choose not to do so. What most do not know is that intense attraction is not necessary as a starting point for true love. Much more important elements of love for a lifetime are decisions and character. Loving actions over time will build love into a flame that started with but a flicker. On the other hand, the hottest initial flame will sputter and possibly die in the face of wrong decisions. Once we realize that God's plan teaches us the very things we need to know, helps us become the things we need to be, and develops the things we need to develop to make the best decisions about relationship-building—and live them out—we should have no problem embracing His plan.

Reason number four: We want a relationship that works, not a relationship that is a lot of work. Our idea of marriage centers on good times and making memories, delights and pleasures, sharing and loving. Isn't this huge "God's plan" thing going to stifle, or bury, the joy and spontaneity we all know is part of the best relationships? An excellent and important question! One vital to understand when we are trying to decide whether to wholeheartedly embrace God's training process. (Not that we can avoid this process; by trying to avoid it we simply choose a much harder road in the long run that does not build nearly as many good things.) But why should we voluntarily submit to such a process if we see love as something that flows spontaneously from our hearts?

Here is a little-known but vital truth: the greatest creativity and spontaneity are actually found at the end of a lengthy process of training and development. Elite athletes, artists, musicians, surgeons—pick any realm of human activity that requires training—and note that the very best in any discipline are capable of creating the most amazing things in the moment based upon a foundation of learning, development, and preparation. Absent this process of training and preparation, one's creative urges would likely do as much harm as good. It is the same with the most complex human task of all: marriage. Marriage at its best, as it is intended to be, is far more than an exercise in learning to cooperate and have a good time together. It is intended to be a process of growth and development that enables us to successfully meet future challenges and maintain a certain quality of life in the process. The fourth reason, then, is that marriage is a training process adequate to the task of building great marriages, and great marriage partners in the process, partners whose spontaneity and creativity are now effectively directed toward loving.

Reason number five: We vowed in our wedding ceremony that we will view and treat our covenant partner in particular ways. In fact, we vowed that we will implement God's plan for relationship in its entirety. As mentioned, vows in our day are not viewed as having the same binding power as in past years, but this is not because God has ceased holding us accountable for the things we vow. If we want to please God, faithfulness is one way to do so.

Throughout the centuries it has been understood that living the best life involves being honorable. This term involves many elements—being trustworthy; honoring one's commitments; being a faithful spouse, friend, or relative—all of which involve making good on one's word. If one made a commitment, one was thereafter bound by this commitment. Many business deals have been conducted on only a handshake. A verbal commitment, until roughly a hundred years ago, was termed a "duty" one had assumed that was entirely enforceable by law. Far more binding until recent times was an oath or a vow. A vow was counted the most solemn obligation a person could make, a commitment made not just to another human—a serious enough matter—but to God. In other cultures the spiritual arbitrator and enforcer might be another deity. But whichever supernatural being was involved, it was counted the height of foolishness to incur a divine enemy, even by those who might be willing to incur the wrath of humans for breaching a vow. In the ancient world many stories were told of people who went to great lengths to fulfill vowed obligations. This was counted the height of heroism and good character.

> In the ancient world many stories were told of people who went to great lengths to fulfill vowed obligations. This was counted the height of heroism and good character.

It is worth considering that God wants us to be truthful and keep our word. Dishonesty is not blessed. Lies incur bad consequences. If we make vows, even if our sensibilities are not trained as in years past, it is helpful to realize that anything other than the most sincere effort to make good on our vows makes us a liar. This course of action dishonors us. Is this the foundation for the best marriage? God wants us to sign on for His plan, and go all in.

Truthful lips endure forever, but a lying
tongue lasts only a moment.
PROVERBS 12:19

THE REALITY OF CONFORMING

How would you rate God's plan so far in terms of actually getting people to love each other consistently in any and every situation for a lifetime? What we have of this plan so far makes it quite a bit more likely that people will understand more about what love looks like in action, and will do and be more of these good things toward each other. But let one person be consistently careless, thoughtless, or seriously hurt your feelings; let their agenda square off with yours on something that matters; let your idea of the good life seriously clash with theirs; let your expectations for each other be let down often enough . . . and what happens? Do our behaviors turn unloving fairly quickly? Even if we want this not to be so? And this does not even take into account the times we simply do not care how the other person feels or what they think.

We quickly run into a deeper issue. Some things in the other person really do need to change, and some things in us need to change at levels deeper than in-the-moment choices. These issues are often revealed in small, daily conflicts. Do we choke down our reactions and play nice? Is this love? Or do we come in with guns blazing, determined to "help" the other person become a better person as we continue to pursue our own agenda, which, as we all know, is really what's best for both of us?

When there is a serious difference of opinion on any matter or a serious character issue in play, what does love look like? It is not just to be nice; it is not that one sacrifices their agenda, or desires, or needs for the sake of the other; it is not that the guy gets the last word because the Bible tells me so (which is far from the whole counsel of God on the husband's role in marriage, as we will see); it is not that the woman gets her way because she is entitled to whatever she thinks she is entitled to; it is not that the most skilled debater or the one with the strongest will or even the one with the deepest insight

> Instead, these little issues and squabbles are doorways. These are the doorways to God's classroom of growth and transformation.

prevails, at least according to God's plan. Instead, these little issues and squabbles are doorways. These are the doorways to God's classroom of growth and transformation.

QUESTIONS FOR THOUGHT

1. True or false: The list of vowed behaviors above corresponds to ways we are instructed to treat each other in Scripture, which can be described as "loving."

2. What other ways of treating someone would you add to this list? Can you think of a place in Scripture where your addition is commended? While we can think of many ways to be thoughtful, kind, and loving toward each other, what difference does it make whether God tells us to treat someone in certain ways? Might God know things about how hearts and relationships work that we have not yet learned?

3. We have all learned much from our culture about how to treat people. How does this training process impact our ability to love other people? Might we have some things we need to *un*learn? Some habits we need to amputate? Some viewpoints we need to adjust? How can we know for sure what real love looks like?

4. What happens if we draw from God's plan when it makes sense to us, but then follow our own ideas when these make more sense? Where did our ideas come from, and why might we think these ideas make more sense than God's ideas? Is this likely to be true?

5. We have already mentioned perceptions of self-interest and the various effects these perceptions have on relationships. First, can you see that there might be a difference between what someone thinks is in their best interest and what actually *is* in their best interest? Have you ever been in a relationship where someone put their interests ahead of you and your relationship? What was this like? Was this really their best move in the long run?

6. Is covenant just a list of things to do in a relationship, or is it more than just a list? Please explain.

7. Even if we know what we should do, do we always do it? Why do we not do things we know we should? Is it because we have reasons why we want to do other things more? Is it because we think the benefits of doing what we think we should do are less

than the benefits of doing something else? If we think we should do something, why do we think in that way? Is it because we were told by someone that this is what we are supposed to do? What if, at the same time, they did not give us an extremely good reason for doing what they said? What if we are not sure the promised benefit is real? If God knows our hearts better than we do, what is the chance He can offer us every motivation we need to do what we need to do? What is the chance that the benefits He promises will be real? What are the chances that the things He tells us to do will work out better in the long run than whatever else we might come up with? If we differ with God about an approach to something, what is the chance that He is right? What is the chance that the situation matters more than we think it does? What is the chance that God has our back more than we realize, that He wants the best for us even more than we want it for ourselves? Would it make sense for us to really explore God's reasons for doing some things, and not doing others, so that we might even begin to think like He thinks?

8. What reasons does God offer us for being faithful to our covenant in every detail? In this chapter we noted five, but are there more?

9. What things within us will oppose obeying God's plan in every detail? If we see these things clearly ahead of time, and understand the sources of the internal opposition we feel, if we realize that sources of opposition come from ideas and habits that will not lead to the best outcome, will we not have an easier time overcoming our own resistance to being faithful to our covenant?

10. In a conflict situation with another person, what does it mean to love? This is an extremely complicated question with no simple, one-size-fits-all answer. At this point, though, can we agree that the most important thing is not necessarily getting our way?

CHAPTER SEVEN

Personal Growth in Marriage

Even for the most self-aware, we only see about 15 percent of ourselves. The rest are parts we do not notice, ruled by habits and patterns we made peace with long ago, our bundle of compromises and accommodations with life. God blesses us with a mirror to see these things, a mirror called a husband or wife. He or she has not made peace with any of this, nor should they.

CONFLICT, THE DOORWAY TO GROWTH

You are newly married and having your first fight. Don't worry, everyone has their first fight. This does not mean love has left the building. Let's say the dishwasher did not get emptied, or filled, or dishes did not even get dirty because no one cooked anything, despite everyone's expectation that all of the above would be handled. By the other person. If you have already had your first marital fight, just fill in the blank with your details.

As long as people are in an arms race of blessing, trying to outdo each other at being all the things on the covenant to-do list, conflict seems to not happen. Which is a point to carefully note. Conflict does not happen until . . . what? Until an expectation is not met, or a commitment is not kept, or a responsibility remains undone, or an unkind word is spoken, or any of a million other things happen, to which the response is anger and accusation. Such conflict is inevitable as two people enter the intimate confines of marriage. But how we handle this conflict makes all the difference. And how we understand conflict will determine how we approach it. Thus, what is conflict? Somewhere, somehow, the standard for love is not being met. Early on, this is likely on the part of both people in a variety of ways.

> Holley and I have a long history of conflict because we have a long history of marriage.

Holley and I have a long history of conflict because we have a long history of marriage. In the beginning, we approached this much like anyone else. I was right, she was out of line, I was the policeman who needed to pull her over and write a ticket, meting out appropriate consequences even if I was the one who had forgotten to do something or had made the mistake in the first place. A conflict about an issue often turns into a conflict about the conflict, doesn't it? But I also had in mind covenant realities and principles. I realized this pattern for conflict was out of sync with how things should look. I was also convinced that the typical advice about simply apologizing for everything in every situation did not truly reflect reality. "Of course, you are always right, dear . . . " An appropriate apology is vital, to be sure, but it began to dawn on me that the issues on the surface that most people tie up over are only part of the story. And merely getting someone to empty the dishwasher on a regular basis, while important enough, was just the tip of the iceberg of . . . what?

What happens in a conflict? An expectation on one hand and a behavior on the other. But there is often more—much more—to this picture. There is history that formed the expectations. There is history that drove the "problem" behavior. There are a thousand assumptions about what life is supposed to look like in every conflict. What I began to see is that conflict situations tell us more about ourselves than almost any other situation. Why? Because the mask comes off. What we want to think we are, or will do, is shown to be wishful thinking to some degree as we listen to ourselves saying things we regret and justifying things for which there is no justification. What is this all about? It is about every belief, value, priority, habit, and emotion that we've accumulated during our lives and carried into our marriage. Some people term this "baggage," but this term suggests that these are things we carry around that we can simply drop and walk away from. It's usually not that simple. We can deal with these issues, but how?

God's covenant plan actually offers us a way to be rid of these unwanted, unhelpful things within, things that drive behaviors and attitudes away from love and toward . . . the very things we do not want in relationship—hurt feelings, disrespect, loss of trust, and more. What I saw with increasing clarity is that conflict is the doorway to growth and transformation. In covenant, if we are in fact one instead of two separate individuals, such conflicts make no sense. People pay to watch two people fight, to see who is stronger, faster, better trained, more determined. But no one would pay to watch someone injure themselves for half an hour. This is not interesting. This is somewhere between pathetic and insanity. So it is when two people in marriage square off and fight till only one is standing.

Conflict is a symptom of a much more important disease, one quite curable if a person knows how the cure works and how to apply it. For any cure, one first needs to know the nature of the disease. One needs to know what healthy function looks like so one can realize if there is a disease process at work, and so they will know when health has been restored. We will therefore look at our internal processes, how God intends they be used, and how these processes are misused to produce ideas, feelings, values, expectations, and priorities that are harmful.

If a person assumes he or she would benefit from growth and trans-formation, they first need to know what needs to grow and what needs to be transformed, and then how growth and transformation take place. This will be our focus in this section. Conflict is one doorway to needed growth. The other doorway is the circumstances of life. In the latter, the two may be apparent allies instead of apparent adversaries. Once we learn that, in covenant, we are actually allies even when apparently in conflict, and learn how to learn together through these situations, we will be equipped to face what life will bring us. And we will be equipped to face it together.

We also need to consider the larger question of how we learn to do things, things like play tennis or have a girlfriend or boyfriend. We take lessons to learn to play tennis well. With relationships, however, we just figure it out, right? Actually, think of all the conversations you have had, all the media you have seen, all the songs you have heard, all the philosophical concepts that float through school hallways, and every imagination you ever had that relates to relationships. No, you've had decades of extensive training in relationship courtesy of our culture. You just did not realize it. You thought all of this stuff is just you and how you relate to others. Perhaps, just perhaps, some of this education might be worth unlearning and revising.

We do more than learn things from the world's educational process. We build deeper things into ourselves. As we grow, we build character. Character could be defined as everything about ourselves we expect ourselves to be, and every way we expect ourselves to act. This is the part of ourselves about which we no longer decide. Those decisions have been made, but they were made long ago. And there is an even deeper level to us, the level of identity. What is our true identity? We spend a lifetime trying to figure this out because we want to be "authentic," to live out our true identity. This is correctly thought to be the path to fulfillment in life. But what if our character has been misformed; what if what we expect of ourselves is not always good, and we fulfill those expectations? What if we're confused about who and what we really are? Would any of this impact a marriage? Might any of this be fertile ground for growth and transformation? Might God's plan in fact take into account every misstep we have made and offer a path back to the life He always intended for us? I strongly believe this is so based upon watching what has happened in my own life and heart through the plan He offers us in covenant.

Do you wonder how Holley and I are doing in the octagon? What are our respective won/loss records? If you saw us having a fight, you would think we are having a corporate planning session. No heat, no harsh words. We are devoted to finding the best answer to whatever situation is out of kilter, and we take the most effective and efficient path to do so. This pattern took a while to work out in its current form, a few years in fact. But our differences of opinion now are viewed as an asset, and we are so far up the curve in treating each other in loving ways that occasional lapses are viewed with grace and humor. "Don't worry, that's just the caffeine talking . . . "

IS GOD'S PLAN MORE ABOUT ROMANCE, WORK, OR OBEDIENCE?

Yes, this is a trick question, but let's think about this one for a moment as we continue thinking about the big picture of marriage. A marriage characterized by ongoing growth of feeling for each other—a lifelong romance—is a rare and beautiful thing. Marriage is one of the most complex tasks faced by humans as well as one of the greatest opportunities of our lifetime. To understand why God has such a complex and involved training process, we must first understand this about marriages. Next, let us think for a moment about how people develop a high level of skill in any area. The process is largely the same for sports, music, scientific research—really, for any realm of life. The content is different, but the process of developing a high level of skill is remarkably similar for any of the complex and important tasks to which humans devote themselves.

But there is one difference between these other realms, where one only acquires high-level knowledge and skills, and marriage. In marriage God requires something of us expected in no other training process. For two people, learning to love wholeheartedly and consistently involves something beyond skill—the transformation of hearts and minds. If you do not already believe this, look around at the people you know. What would it take for every relationship around you to become truly loving and nothing else? Could any instruction, even any coercion,

> For two people, learning to love wholeheartedly and consistently involves something beyond skill—the transformation of hearts and minds.

produce this? No. What would it take? You can just hear someone saying: "You couldn't possibly pull that off with these people!" Precisely. We would need to change the people, swap them out for people who are very different, wouldn't we? Now, just apply this insight to your own marriage, as I did to mine.

The genius of God's plan is that everyone in marriage *is* this different person in a very real sense. If they acted in perfect accord with who and what they are now at the deepest level, there would be nothing but love. But we are also dealing with other realities in addition to this spiritual reality. We are dealing with human perceptions, choices, habits, undeveloped or poorly developed character, beliefs, values, priorities, and many other elements already in place in our minds and hearts. We are dealing with a new life that is present in the same way our new physical life was present originally—as a small spark of new life, a single cell which contains every ounce of potential we will ever have, but initially only in the form of potential. This potential, in one sense, is as real as any other reality, but in order to be expressed into the universe—or the marriage—this potential must be developed.

One must grow into one's potential; one must develop it. This is a gradual process that takes time; this process also requires decisions. Do we develop our musical talent or not? One cannot play an instrument at five years old in the same way they will be able to play it at thirty-five, nor will they ever play it well if they do not submit themselves to the process required to learn to skillfully play the instrument. If we are to fulfill God's plan for our lives and our marriage we must have this picture of potential and development in view as we walk through our daily lives, much as parents have a sense of the overall development of their child in view as they deal with an act of irresponsibility in a nine-year-old. There is an issue, but this issue is in the context of decades of development in the case of a child, or in a lifetime of development in the case of a marriage.

So how do we develop this new, inherent potential within ourselves and in our marriage? How do we harness the daily issues noted at the end of the last chapter and walk through the doorway to growth and transformation? And is it not consummately exciting that God has a plan in place to most fully develop you and your marriage? Is this future more exciting than the future most see for their marriages?

THE BASICS WE MUST FIRST UNDERSTAND

In order to understand how God's training process works and how we can most benefit from it, we need to understand four things. First, we need to understand *three special powers God placed within each of us* and how these powers are used. Second, we need to understand our *character*—what it is, how it is formed, and how it can change and grow. Third, we need to understand our *identity* in several respects. We need to understand how our sense of our own identity influences behavior. We need to grasp how we can come to understand our true identity—and how we can be misinformed about our identity. We need to learn the difference within ourselves between our true identity—the core of our being that needs to be loved and desires to love—and things about ourselves that are not the essence of our being but often thought to be so. This statement likely does not make sense now, but it will. Fourth, we need to see the *relationship between our three human powers, our character, our identity, and the truth*. It is the truth, as we will see, that sets us free from destructive beliefs and nonworking strategies, from a mis-shaped character that leads us to actions that produce accumulating negative consequences, and from misconceptions about ourselves that prevent us from finding gratification and satisfaction, among other things.

The transformation that God seeks, as we will see, is simply about living out truth in every area of life, especially in our most important human relationship: marriage. (In the next volume in this series, we will examine this transformation as it relates to the most important relationship of all—our relationship with our Creator.)

THE THREE HUMAN POWERS

I want to introduce you to three of your best friends, ones you may have never met face-to-face. These are three powers God has placed within each human that belong exclusively to each of us. These powers are, first, the power of assent and dissent; second, the power of attention; and third, the power of intention. Put simply, these are our abilities to determine if something is true or not; to determine, if true, how much it matters; and to determine, if it matters, what, if anything, we are going to do about it. All this may not sound like a world-beating combination—but it is precisely that.

There are two key things to understand about these powers: one, they do more to direct the course of one's life than almost any other factor; two, they can only be exercised by each person for themselves. No one can decide for us what we believe to be true. People can persuade us, influence us, even threaten us or kill us, but no one can make us believe something we simply do not believe to be true. In the same way, no one can make us take an action if we are willing to suffer any consequence for not doing so. Though we may be subject to persuasion, even coercion, ultimately we must agree, we must voluntarily yield, and we must decide on our own to embrace an idea or to take action. Thus, these three powers represent the focal points of influence that people try to wield over one another precisely because these powers are so . . . powerful.

To my knowledge these are the only powers God has given us over which we have sole control. Even God, omnipotent Ruler and Creator, allows us to make the choice to believe in Him and to believe Him—or to do neither. And if we believe in Him, we still must decide what priorities and what action flow from this belief. The same would be true of our willingness to enter the covenant of marriage with another person, and of how we choose to conduct ourselves within this covenant. How do these uniquely powerful powers work? In my first book, *Beware the Raised Eyebrow*, we looked at each step in the process of using each power, and at the many implications of doing so. Let's briefly review the main points.

THE POWER OF ASSENT AND DISSENT—THE TRUE POWER OF AN IDEA

Our most foundational power as a human being is deciding what we think is true. We use this power dozens of times a day without realizing the importance or implications of doing so. Using this power comes as naturally to us as breathing. We are presented every day with many ideas with which we already agree or disagree, which we quickly assign to the category of "true" or "false." But we often are not aware of why we agree or disagree with an idea. We simply do so. We make this determination about many new ideas that come before us each day. Some of these are carefully considered decisions based on a review of evidence. Most are not. Often we accept the views of others—our peers, people we respect, or apparent experts—without further review or a second thought. If we accept one belief, related beliefs are immediately welcomed while things that collide with a previously accepted belief may be quickly discarded without further consideration.

> Our most foundational power as a human being is deciding what we think is true. We use this power dozens of times a day without realizing the importance or implications of doing so.

One fascinating aspect of humanity is that rational and thoughtful people often arrive at opinions that are diametrically opposed—and on a huge range of issues. We can choose any realm as an example—politics, medicine, science, spiritual life, sports, economics, and many more. These divergent opinions create diversity among people that can be wonderful, but they also create the chasms that hopelessly divide people. Note the things that most unite or divide people: the things they hold to be truth. Typically our closest friends share many "truths" with us while those we dislike oppose many of our beliefs. One of the most important realities to grasp is the correlation between what we affirm to be true with *what is actually true*. While God created us so that we each get to make the call on what we believe to be true, please note that whether a given thing is actually true is another question altogether.

How does affirming one thing or another as true impact our marriage? Have we accepted the belief that we have a fundamental right to express ourselves as we choose, to say and do what we feel like doing? Or do we affirm and embrace the idea that our most important obligation, duty, and responsibility is to treat our covenant partner in certain ways regardless of how we feel in the moment?

THE PROCESS OF AFFIRMATION AND DISSENT

What is the process by which we assent to or dissent from an idea? There are three points in this process: information gathering, the decision itself, and the aftereffects. First, we sift through various opinions and whatever evidence is before us to see which position appears most credible. At this point we are subject to persuasion. In addition, our thought process already reflects biases we have picked up from families, advertising, peers, the educational system, media, and hopefully from God's Word and solid church teaching, plus the effect of beliefs we have previously embraced. All of this provides our frame of reference from which we agree with or disagree with new ideas. Fortunately, we do not have to completely think through every new idea, everything we do, and every word we speak. We come to a conclusion, then we move on, progressively building our lives upon the foundation of our conclusions. But we often do not realize how many things occur within us once we embrace an idea as our truth.

An opinion affirmed and embraced becomes a part of us in a special way. Rather than simply an idea, this opinion now becomes *our idea,* a settled part of our sense of reality, the embodiment, in our perception, of absolute truth. It assumes a powerful place in our mind and heart. The appliance or car we selected is obviously the best choice one could make given the options, and people who make another choice, we are sure, simply settled for second-best. Few people, one hopes, wrap their identity around a car or an appliance. But this same sense of "best possible option" applies to the groups we join, the sports team we choose, or the political, economic, or spiritual ideas we choose to embrace. Or to the husband or wife we just married. These are simply better choices than any other option because they are based squarely on truth—our truth. Such decisions may involve more than things or people; they can also involve ideas in many realms—beliefs, values, priorities, and other elements that direct the course of our lives. The key insight is that such decisions, in sum, now define *our* truth.

A second key insight is that this reality is the basis of a current cultural misread. Because different people arrive at different, often contradictory ideas as their truth, philosophers and thought leaders in the last hundred and fifty years have taken the position that there is no actual truth. Truth is "relative," or "in the eye of the beholder" only. While the diversity of purported/embraced truths makes it hard to assign the label "actual truth" to something based on human consensus—something which could not be done even if every human agreed on an item—the assertion that there is therefore "no absolute truth" is simply an opinion by a group of people that is . . . what? Absolutely true? Are you sure? Actually, this view completely ignores something vital: God's revelation of absolute truth. Any of us would be very uncomfortable having the opinion of any human or group of humans branded as absolute truth (including the above philosophical opinion), but it is rational to accept the words of God to us, His revelation, as absolute truth. God describes His Word as precisely this. And we get to choose whether or not to believe Him.

Which leads to the most important insight regarding our marriage and ourselves: our decision about truth has no bearing on whether an idea is *actually true.* This is vital because some of our accepted truths may vary from God's revelation. What happens next? Let us first consider what happens within us when we embrace any idea, then we will consider the implications of this idea being actually true or false. And consider the opportunity this presents to us.

Once we affirm and embrace an idea, other parts of us shift to harmonize with this idea. Our minds do not like internal conflict. This might not result in much internal revision if we are talking about a car, but there are ideas which have much broader and deeper impact on our mind, such as the idea that right and wrong are really in the eye of the beholder instead of value judgments revealed to us by God. Or buying into the idea that the true path to happiness is power, money, or fame. Or the idea that masculinity is inherently toxic. If affirmed and embraced, these ideas begin to influence our values, priorities, ideals, and even our vision for the future, in addition to our behavior choices.

One embraced idea makes it more likely we will embrace related ideas with far less persuasion. These ideas already fit comfortably in our frame of reference. Thus, people tend to embrace groups of ideas. If one embraces one tenet of liberalism, he or she is much more likely to embrace the others than to be half-conservative and half-liberal. If someone embraces a new idea with enough enthusiasm, competing ideas one had previously embraced less enthusiastically are often shifted to the "not true" pile. Consider what often happens when young people with weakly founded Christian beliefs show up for their freshman year in college. Beyond believing individual ideas and groups of ideas, we begin to define ourselves in terms of our accepted truths. We form our sense of identity around embraced ideas. We become, in our own mind, a liberal or a conservative, a communist, neo-Nazi, feminist, environmentalist—or whatever.

> Feelings expressed toward other people in much of the current public discourse can only be defined as hatred, disdain, and disgust. Why?

Affirmed ideas influence our emotions. We feel warmly toward ideas we agree with and toward people who hold these ideas. How do we feel toward those whose views differ significantly from our own? And often our feelings are deeper and stronger than mere warm fuzzies or a sense of distaste, aren't they? Feelings expressed toward other people in much of the current public discourse can only be defined as hatred, disdain, and disgust. Why? Because someone on a college campus voices reservations about abortion on demand, or expresses the idea that certain conduct is morally wrong? Why would such things provoke outrage?

In *Beware the Raised Eyebrow*, we trace the ways in which an affirmed idea becomes not only a part of our reality and our sense of identity but also an integral part of an internal legal system. Once an idea becomes our absolute truth, contrary ideas are not just different—these ideas are wrong, as are the people who believe them. The internal legal system brought into play when someone embraces an idea as *the* truth becomes the foundation for thought police, political correctness, and censorship in totalitarian societies, as well as a vast amount of peer-group coercion. But these mental and emotional biases do not function only in the extremes of viewpoint, like American college campuses or leftist media. We see these same mechanisms in a less toxic form in ways we have become accustomed to viewing and treating other people in general. We are all used to being disrespected, subtly or not so subtly, based on a position we hold.

Why in the world are we discussing all of this? Because ideas we have affirmed as true or rejected as false directly impact how we interact with other people. This mechanism causes emotional responses and forms habits, both of which significantly impact how we relate to others, and this predictably spills over into a marriage. Affirmed ideas, however, play an even larger role. Once embraced, some of these ideas play a key role in forming character. Some of these ideas form key parts of our perceptions of our identity. At every point, in every way, these ideas impact relationships with other people, especially in the closest and most intimate one—marriage.

THE POWER OF ATTENTION

The second tool we have is our power of attention. This power is our ability to sift through all the things that come before us in a given day—ideas, responsibilities, tasks, assignments, opportunities, requests, and more—to decide which of these are worth our time and attention and which are not. The second side of this coin is our ability to direct our attention on internal matters. We can choose to look at a situation as a disaster and a loss of something important to our lives, perhaps the fault of someone we can blame; or we can choose to look at the same situation as an opportunity to learn something from God, to grow, to become stronger, and to increase our dependence on Him. When hearing information about someone close to us, we can choose to believe disparaging words that we cannot know with certainty are true, or we can choose to rely on our own experience of this person and our assessment of his or her character and maintain a posture of loyalty until we know the truth of the matter. To illustrate this power, put your hand in front of your face, about a foot away, with your fingers spread. You can pay attention to one of two things: your fingers, or whatever is at a distance behind your fingers. You will focus on one or the other. You cannot bring both into focus simultaneously. What you are doing as you direct your physical vision you can also do with your thoughts, feelings, schedule book, and checkbook.

Many things clamor for our attention. We cannot pay attention to them all, even everything that is good, true, or a legitimate need. What things are important enough to merit our attention? Again, God allows us to make those choices. He has given us the power to decide what is actually important to us versus the things we deem not important. This power draws from our values, ideals, and goals so that we tend to pay attention to things we believe advance causes we deem important. As with the first power, though, there is a vulnerability inherent in our power of attention. We can be persuaded that something is more important than it actually is or that something truly important can be safely overlooked—like a credit card bill or someone's feelings.

Think of this power, in one sense, as a TV remote control. When an idea comes to us, once, or for the zillionth time—say, a memory of being treated poorly, or envisioning ourselves doing something we know at some level is not good for us—we can continue paying attention to this idea. We can keep watching this channel, we can begin to feel the feelings, imagine the sensations—we can stay with this idea until we are, in our mind, experiencing the situation, savoring it, or once again feeling the pain, rejection, and disrespect. Or we can make another choice: we can simply change channels. We have the power to redirect our thoughts, and this power can become stronger if we practice it. We also have the power to sift through possible interpretations of a situation. We can do something called "reframing." This means directing ourselves to think of other ways of looking at a situation that we initially interpret in one way. Someone who was acting out may not really be trying to hurt us. This situation may not be about us at all. The person may be so wrapped up in their own pain that they do not even notice us. Instead of wanting to strangle them, we might want to reach out to see what is going on in their lives.

Though we have vast power to direct ourselves, how many of us have cultivated this power? As with our ability to discern truth, this is a capacity that can be intentionally strengthened and employed wisely. Or it can remain weak and inadequate for the task, in which case our attention and efforts will be dragged all over the place by others who want to harness our time and effort for their benefit. This power has many important applications in a marriage—well beyond merely remembering anniversaries and birthdays. Many things in life are well within our ability to make happen if we understand how important it is that we do them. One of those very important things is being faithful to our covenant vows. There is one feature common to humanity. Over time attention can wander, even for the best and most mature. Thus, one of God's refrains throughout Scripture is to *remember*: who He is, who we are, and what is real and true. He knows the distracting world we live in, who is behind those distractions, and for what purpose we are being distracted. For this reason the institution of covenant is filled with things that jog our memory, that remind us of what is truly important. (If you are married, you are probably wearing one of those reminders on your left hand.)

This power shows up in myriad ways in marriage, from being sure we remember something important that we are supposed to do; to focusing our attention on things about our mate for which we are grateful instead of dwelling on that irritating fault; to deciding to do something that will build our relationship instead of immersing ourselves in entertainment that builds nothing of value.

THE POWER OF INTENTION

The third power we possess as humans is the power of intention. This power is our ability to take action, to respond, or to take initiative in a situation we deem to be important. There are many more things we might do than we have the time, energy, and resources to actually do. There are many more needs than we have the capacity to meet, even things about which we may be deeply burdened. So to which projects do we commit our time and effort? This power actually involves two decisions. First: *What do we choose to do?* And second, and the importance of this one is often underappreciated: *How much desire or commitment do we have to accomplish this?* That is, what position will this priority continue to hold in light of future things that arise? Does this continue to be our most important priority, or does this descend to "We'll get back to that at some point"? We often put things in the "want to do it" stack, but our weak commitment to follow through, or our lack of a sense of urgency about getting something done—these things often mean that the item in question never gets done. On the other hand, a deep sense of urgency about a matter and a firm and unyielding commitment to a particular outcome means that we will accomplish something—or die trying.

We play interesting games with our powers of intention in our culture. People try to get points in relationships by expressing good intentions even though they are not truly committed to carrying out those stated intentions. We often judge ourselves not by what we have done but by what we intended to do, though, again, we must not really have intended to do these things. We often come to believe that, if we had good intentions, nothing we did or did not do was really all that bad, was it? Because of all of the above, there is often a mismatch between what we say we will do and what we do.

One thing God wants to teach us is the importance of developing our power of intention to the point that we do what we have committed to do. Has your relationship with someone ever been improved when they did not follow through with a commitment they made? God wants us to learn the vital role that keeping our word, following through on our commitments, and keeping our vows play in growing important relationships, especially in marriage. It is true: we are ultimately judged by God for every action, word, thought, and intention. We are not obedient in His sight if we have the best of intentions yet fail to follow through and carry them out (James 2:14-26). Nor is anyone else delighted by this approach.

> *He who is faithful in little is faithful in much.*
> LUKE 16:10

This shows up in marriage in the difference between good intentions and effective action. We tend to judge ourselves by our intentions, while we are actually known by what we do—what we finish, and what we leave undone. To build anything worth having we must learn to not only finish a job but also to do the best we can in things large and small. The obvious use of this power in the context of this book is learning to be faithful in every detail to our Covenant of Marriage.

WILLPOWER

We rarely hear the above three powers mentioned, but we *have* heard a term applied to the sum of these powers, or to the combined use of these powers: *willpower.* This term describes overall force of personality, overall personal strength, or, if underdeveloped, weakness and the ability to be easily influenced. In a marriage we are called to develop willpower. This is the power to overcome any adversity, to engage in a process for as long as it takes to do what is necessary, to

> This term describes overall force of personality, overall personal strength, or, if underdeveloped, weakness and the ability to be easily influenced.

succeed against all odds. This is the power of follow-through that fully executes our intentions and commitments. Do you see how necessary a thing this quality is in order to fulfill our covenant vows? But this is not something we just decide we are going to have. Willpower is grown through exercise of the above three powers. We do not want to be strong and yet strongly wrong. We do not want to devote our full strength to the unimportant. We do not want a life of almost-did, should-have, and could-have. We want to stand firmly for what is real, true, and important, and to make the most of our opportunities.

In an age that values doing what we feel like doing, which can change on a moment-by-moment basis, instead of valuing commitment to our words, our plans, our priorities, and our principles, few actually develop substantial willpower. Willpower is the assertion of our will, for sufficient reason, over our own feelings, reluctance, laziness, or irresponsibility, and over any outside obstacle that is in the way of accomplishing something we deem truly important. Willpower is not stubbornness, which is usually a manifestation of doing what we feel like doing in the face of appropriate opposition. Willpower is the developed power of an adult that translates into mature reasoning, choice, and commitment to action. Willpower is what we display when we make a decision to do everything in our power to fulfill our covenant vows to treat or regard our covenant partner in a certain way even though, in the moment, we do not feel like doing so. We may refrain from saying something harsh, we may choose to be patient, we may make a more concerted effort to see an issue from the other's perspective, we may choose to listen even more carefully, or we may turn ourselves from doing the kinds of things we used to think were in our self-interest toward recognizing the different self-interests that exist because of covenant.

GROWING OUR WILLPOWER

God's plan for our marriage will require giving our powers of intention and willpower much exercise. We must determine what God's plan looks like in a particular situation—what is the truth here, and what are the highest priorities. Then we must reaffirm our decision to follow God's plan wholeheartedly rather than some alternative plan. It is interesting that *this* decision must be made over and over, on a daily, even hourly, basis for the rest of our lives. Of course, if we have not already decided that we are going to commit ourselves to God's plan, these thoughts will not even occur.

USING OUR THREE POWERS

These three powers taken together are, again, our power to determine what is true, what matters, and what, if anything, we are going to do about it. It is through the exercise of these three powers that God has deposited within us the capacity for obedience to His plan, the capacity to love as He directs, and the capacity to build the things He wants to build through us. At the same time, God allows us to choose how these powers will be used or not used. There are many who have wasted lives pursuing things they thought were important, who neglected the truly important things, who failed to follow through with important commitments and who refrained from building the things that would have blessed their lives and the lives of others, just as there have been people whose lives focused on important, high-impact things, who changed the world through well-focused efforts. If Satan cannot deceive us about truth, or about the importance of a matter, he has one remaining pressure point to exploit to prevent obedience to God and His plan: he can engineer hurdles to obedience significant enough to discourage us from following through and doing what we have determined to do. For some people, it does not take much discouragement to turn them to inactivity. Such hurdles can take many forms, and we are probably familiar with most of them. At any point in life, on any given day, we have many things we are trying to accomplish in an environment of competing priorities. The ultimate goal is to learn how to accomplish the most important ones, and this requires that we know what is important and continually refocus our attention on these most important things as we grow in our capacity to accomplish them.

What can adequately energize our efforts to do this? What produces the things within us that will lead to effective action? Another element in this equation is passion. Some things we realize beyond a shadow of doubt are true produce a vision for accomplishing something, and this becomes coupled with a clear understanding from God that this is something I'm supposed to do. This combination will produce the necessary focus of our mind, heart, and will to see matters through, to obey God, and to build as He directs. We term the energy of this combination within us our passion for a goal.

On the other hand, lack of clarity about truth, which produces confusion; lack of clarity about the goals, ideals, and purposes inherent in God's plan, from which we form a proper sense of what is important; and lack of urgency or developed willpower; combined with the natural obstacles that inevitably accompany God's plan and purposes . . . these things produce lack of passion, lack of focus, and a predictable lack of results. And notice that each of these elements is the result of previous choices we have made about identifying and embracing truth, clarifying priorities, and setting our mind and heart to do what is needed to build the life God has for us, including developing these three powers as much as we are able.

There is another building project beyond our relationships and accomplishments that is determined by these three powers. This is building ourselves—our internal guidance system, our habits, our character, even our deepest understanding of ourselves. Even more than founding our actions and directions on truth, we want to be founded on truth. We want everything about us to be real, true, and authentic instead of distorted, misdirected, and confused. How do we come to reflect truth, to embody truth, in our very being? By using these same three powers. We must understand that we become twisted and distorted simply by plugging things that are not true into these same three powers.

CHARACTER AND IDENTITY AND THEIR RELATIONSHIP TO GROWTH AND TRANSFORMATION

The three powers we just examined and the decisions that flow from their use obviously have much to do with our relationships, but is everything concerning our relationships about our choices? And if we see something about ourselves in a relationship that we want to change, is it always just about making a different choice? These are also trick questions; these do not have simple yes/no answers. The answer, and the good news—in fact very good news—is that a massive amount of who we are and what we do is ultimately the sum of our choices. What opportunity does this offer? We can choose or rechoose not only what we do but a large percentage of the ways we interact with people and situations. We can choose to grow and even choose to be transformed in deep and broad ways by remaking our decisions. To do any of this we need to understand which decisions to remake and how to do so. To do *this*, we need to understand more than the three powers just discussed. These are the construction crew, so to speak, that has built what we have become, and these same tools perform the rehab project. But we also must understand the structure and function of what has been built if we are to rebuild correctly. If we want to rehab a house, we need a clear idea of how it was constructed in the first place as well as a clear plan for the rebuild so we can ensure our changes are an improvement.

THE ROLES PLAYED BY CHARACTER AND IDENTITY

As noted, it is fortunate that we do not need to make choices about everything we think and every move we make. Our brains would quickly explode if this were the case. Instead, the vast majority of what we think, feel, and do are comfortable patterns, habits of thought, feelings, words, and actions developed over the course of our lives that work for us—at least to a point. These patterns are the tip of a much larger iceberg that can be called personality, but a better term would be character. Essentially, any term another person would use to describe anything about us other than our physical appearance would be describing one element or another of character.

The effect of *nature* versus *nurture* has been debated over the years. In other words, what elements of the expression of our being are hardwired, and what are learned behaviors, the sum of choices and influences? God clears up these questions, especially as we examine His plan of covenant. We each have a unique identity, hardwired parts that choice cannot change. Our perceptions of our identity, though, are always only partial, and these perceptions are subject to change, as well as subject to manipulation and deception. Character, on the other hand, is something that has been formed that can be reformed or transformed. The extent to which the potential inherent in our identity is developed is a function of our character. Our character determines how we choose to express ourselves and how we have been trained to express ourselves.

Covenant introduces another element into this conversation, for in covenant our identities change. Our goal in all of this is to correctly identity who we are and to authentically express ourselves. The term "identity crisis" has been used for decades to highlight the difficulty we all have in figuring out who we are as we grow to adulthood. Now, in covenant, we are all presented with a new task: figuring out who we have become as we enter a covenant relationship. And we are presented with yet another task, for to faithfully live out our covenants we must develop many new things in our character that will allow us to love well and consistently. While on one hand the nature of character is to resist change, the nature of affirmed ideas is to resist change, and we resist things that seem ou of sync with our vision of who we are, at the same time we can realize that we are offered, via covenant, literally the opportunity of a lifetime to build the things into our lives that will lead to the best outcomes for the rest of our lives. If we really understand this offer, we will overcome any obstacle to make the most of it.

Thus, in this section as we discuss how we can change the ways we live, we will divide our attention between issues of character and identity. *Character* is simply the sum of what we have already chosen to be. Character is the result of influences we have already chosen to embrace. Character is all about choice, and this is very good news, as we will see. The influence of *identity*, though it is fixed and does not involve choices on one hand, on the other hand involves a corollary influence—what we believe ourselves to be. We cannot be something we are not, though we may try to do so. But we will not try to be something we think we are not. While the reality of our being at the deepest level is not subject to our choices (with one exception: the decision to enter covenant), our belief about our identity is second in importance only to our true identity in determining the course of our lives. Therefore, if we are to live our best lives it is vital to bring our understanding of who we are in line with reality. This will all start to make sense as we look at some examples.

WHAT *IS* CHARACTER?

Character is a concept not often discussed in our culture. A person's character represents the individual parts that go together to make that person what he or she is in dealing with other people and with life. It is the outward expression of our internal processing and guidance systems. This includes our beliefs, attitudes, values, motivations, priorities, ideals, likes, dislikes, tastes, work ethic, honesty, integrity, willpower, level of consideration for others, and many other individual attributes. It includes what could best be described as our flavor as a person—are we upbeat and optimistic, or sour and negative; are we detached, or present in the moment; are we happy, or angry and bitter? The term character also extends to our typical expressions, gestures, and figures of speech. Overall, it helps us and others figure out where we fit in the overall scheme of things.

> Character is a concept not often discussed in our culture. A person's character represents the individual parts that go together to make that person what he or she is in dealing with other people and with life.

Our world suggests that character is not something that grows, or is formed and influenced, but is instead simply *what we are,* as if this is some fixed and immutable thing. We are hearing this idea when we are told that we should accept everyone and not judge anyone. While we are to love everyone, not everything done by everyone is acceptable, nor should we accept those things, though this lack of acceptance is deemed judgmental. This nonjudgmental approach plays well in a sociology classroom or sitcom, but in the intimacy of marriage there will be some elements of our character that will not be accepted by our spouse, nor should they be.

The idea that we are supposed to be nonjudgmental is actually designed to keep each of us from realizing the extent to which we are being formed, transformed, and perhaps misformed by our culture. If no one can be effectively criticized for dysfunctional behavior, if someone who does not like what I am doing is simply a hater—it's their problem—do you see how people can not learn some important things about how to live, and thus continue to live out really bad ideas?

As we go through our day living out our character, in our mind we are just being ourselves. But what if we find that "ourself" is creating a problem for ourselves? What if we are getting in trouble by expressing ourselves, by being ourselves? Isn't that really other people's problem? Or, is this our chance to learn something vital? Our character has been shaped at many levels by the beliefs we have embraced, which are, in turn, heavily influenced by our culture. Once we are persuaded to accept the idea that something is true, real, good, or beneficial, we see how these things become incorporated within us as a part of who we are. But these things are additions to us that came in at a point in time because *we invited them to become a part of ourselves.* This is distinct from our innate essence as a human being. We will see the importance of this distinction shortly. At the same time, elements of our true selves, our essential essence as a human—our true identity—also come through as we relate to people and navigate our way through life.

If you understand someone's character, you can predict with some accuracy what that person will do in a given situation. Do we expect someone to tell us the truth consistently, sometimes, or never? Do we expect them to look out for our interests and feelings, or do we know to stay out of their reach? The best predictor of what someone will do or be in a new situation is what they have done and been in the past. On the other hand, people are complex; many factors drive behavior and we can always be surprised. People may even surprise themselves. But whatever they do is always, in their minds, on the "acceptable in this circumstance" list. We will see how important this list is farther down.

In the first volume we detailed the relationship between reality and right and wrong. The universe we inhabit includes a system of cause-and-effect. This system, designed by God, perfectly reflects His designation of some things as "right" and other things as "wrong." Every time we act, speak, or think we set in motion various effects. These consequences are going to occur despite our beliefs or desires. These consequences can simply be termed "reality." These consequences may occur immediately or be delayed years or decades, but they will occur as a result of our choices. We cannot, from our vantage point in a given moment, know the fullness of the consequences of our actions; thus we can be deceived—or deceive ourselves—about the reality of future negative consequences.

> Right and wrong are not arbitrary assignments by a God intent on interfering with otherwise good times. Right and wrong are distinctions based on the fullness of consequences that will eventually occur.

As an example, if we devote ourselves to dishonestly enriching ourselves, we can be assured with 100 percent certainty that temporary success will be offset by long-term consequences. Thus, this behavior is wrong. Right and wrong are not arbitrary assignments by a God intent on interfering with otherwise good times. Right and wrong are distinctions based on the fullness of consequences that will eventually occur. God's intent is to protect us from unwanted consequences, to direct us instead toward behaviors that produce good outcomes. What, then, is the relationship between character and the moral universe we inhabit?

Character traits have historically been divided into good and bad, analogous to the way one would describe the good and bad behaviors that flow from these traits. And this assignment is not arbitrary any more than is the case with individual actions. This simply reflects observation of long-term outcomes, the sum of consequences of either behaviors or traits as they play out over a lifetime. God informs us of this distinction, but we can also observe them if we have a decently long period of observation.

HOW IS CHARACTER FORMED?

Character is formed slowly, over decades, one situation at a time, one decision at a time. We make a decision to act in a certain way, emulating something we have seen someone do, or trying something new to deal with a person or a situation. It works. So, we try it again; it works again. Soon this pattern becomes a habit, and before long this becomes an engrained part of our personality, something other people expect of us and something we expect of ourselves. This trial-and-error process goes on in tandem with our attempts to sort out reality—what is going work for us long-term—and to figure out what is true and real about the world and the people around us. And about us.

Suppose someone we trust betrays us. We might interpret this to mean that we need to get better at deciding who we can trust. Or, in this same situation, we might decide that we cannot trust anyone but ourselves, ever. Often character-forming decisions happen when we are very young, when our vantage point is limited and immature, but these decisions have vast power regardless of the age at which they are made. One might learn that it is best to tell the truth always, another may learn that lies provide more advantage in the moment. Can you see how character is formed? Not only by what happens to us, but also by how we interpret our life situations?

One person is not trustworthy. Nobody is trustworthy. Which is really true? People who arrive at each interpretation will proceed through life as if their belief is true. This becomes an affirmed belief, and in turn this will inform the person's emotional experience and impact other viewpoints and beliefs. One person entrusts himself or herself to trustworthy people; the other hangs back in relationships, waiting for the other shoe to fall even when dealing with people they have every reason to trust. They will remain suspicious and insecure in relationships. They will look for "evidence" to back their suspicions, even malign trustworthy people and feel completely justified in doing so, because "this person is not trustworthy." Why? Because they "know" that no one is trustworthy.

While this is an extreme example to illustrate the point, can you see how people can turn individual situations into a general approach for living, or into a general approach toward everyone around them? Can you see the problem these generalizations might cause in an intimate relationship? Such things are commonly called "trust issues" or some other kind of issue. But if we know how these issues came to be, via a decision in a single situation that is reinforced over time, does this offer us a new and useful approach when we encounter these moments . . .in ourselves? In the closeness of marriage we will from time to time misread what is going on in our covenant partner. We will think they are something that they are not, and we may be convinced we are right. But we may not be right. Or, they may not be right about us. As we sort through such misreads it is extremely helpful to keep this understanding in the back of our minds. If, in a current situation, the first thing we think is, "Wow, he/she is just like . . . " and a former traumatic situation comes to mind, and we feel the emotion of that earlier situation in this moment, we are likely dealing with the situation we just described and may be reading into this situation something that is not really in the heart and mind of our beloved.

Chosen patterns are mostly good and helpful. We often emulate successful approaches. Whether for better or worse, once these things become patterns—and then become unconscious reactions accompanied by corresponding emotions—how do we perceive these key moments? As if they are simply expressions of us. In our minds, these perceptions and feelings are simply expressions who we are. And our beliefs about people and reality, accompanied by corresponding emotions, become the reality we inhabit. This becomes our world, a world formed by interpreting events and behaviors in specific ways. Since the original decisions and situation all of this is built upon has receded into the mists of forgotten history for most of us, we do not realize the role we played in fashioning the world we inhabit, whether filled with joys, love, and opportunity, or with failures, heartache, and trolls. You might be aware of this old Chinese proverb:

> *Be careful what you see, for it will become your thoughts.*
> *Be careful of your thoughts, for they will become your habits.*
> *Be careful of your habits, for they will become your character.*
> *Be careful of your character, for it will become your destiny.*

Some of our character elements are formed by affirmations after careful consideration as we grow to adulthood, and hopefully these elements are based on truth and reality. One vital role that should be played by parents and the church is to help our young properly interpret life experiences so that character-forming conclusions are built on truth. But parents and the church, often valuing entertainment over character formation, may not make the most of the opportunity to direct young lives. Our culture specializes in leading people, young and old, toward conclusions about self, others, and life overall that are either one-off or way off views based on God's truth. Affirmations are picked up from family, peers, school, media, or general culture without further review. We simply accept most of the ideas that are propagated by those around us, especially when people make an effort to instill those ideas in us, such as progressive ideas and values instilled in the public education system. Given the various influences, motives, and personal variants of "truth" that go together to form the character of each of us, is it any wonder that some revision might be of benefit if we are to actually base our character, and therefore our life, on actual truth?

Some elements come directly from life experience. If we grew up with strong discipline, if it was required that we fulfill responsibilities well and consistently, a strong work ethic will be engrained in our character. If we were part of household productivity early in life, if our families relied on us to fulfill certain responsibilities because failure to do so would have serious consequences, our character will reflect an even stronger sense of responsibility and work ethic. On the other hand, if we were handed everything from food to clean clothes to ample spending money, if no one ever said "no" to us, if someone bailed us out of every difficulty and we had a do-over for every academic or personal failure, what kind of work ethic will be formed? In fact, dozens of character elements are misformed by such indulgence and lack of discipline. The good news, though, is that even badly misformed character can be reformed; the more sobering news is that no one can do this for us. Each of us will only change to the extent that we are determined to do so. In the close quarters of marriage, we will find ample opportunities for such improvement.

Proper discipline in home and school is a critical issue, now more than ever. One purpose for God's covenant plan of character review and revision is that those entering marriage may soon be given responsibility for shepherding the character development of one or more young lives. If we learn the realities of character growth and revision for ourselves as we troubleshoot our marriages, we will be much better equipped for this role. A vast amount of one's character is formed in the home in the first five years, and even more through the teenage years. Proper discipline recognizes that lying, stealing, failure to fulfill assignments, laziness, arrogance, contempt for authority, willingness to hurt others to advance one's own cause, and other wrongs must not only be effectively opposed with a credible deterrent to these behaviors—a punishment significant enough to convince the child that it is not in his or her best interest to continue these behaviors—but must also include correction. The reason these behaviors exist needs to be recognized, but the most important part of the corrective process is to lay the foundation for good character.

Things termed morally wrong by God will predictably and inevitably incur bad consequences. Punishment by authority figures that mirrors the magnitude of real-world consequences is crucial. Since the full consequences of these things may be delayed, and consequences incurred in the short run can be seen as a worthwhile price to pay for the perceived benefit of misconduct, the role of discipline is to shorten the time frame of cause-and-effect so the child can learn from experiencing the pain inherent in these behaviors. The intent is to impress upon people that such things are not in their best interest, now or ever, by artificially engineering an immediate system of cause-and-effect. This process ideally starts when the child is fifteen months old. At fifteen years parents are far behind the curve.

Proper discipline is conducted for the long-term benefit of the one being disciplined. This is truly an act of love. In the absence of such discipline, people are trained to conclude that there are no personal consequences for destructive behaviors. They are trained to conclude that there is no reality strong enough and no authority with enough resolve to stop them from doing what they feel like doing regardless of how damaging this action may be to self or others. People are taught by the lack of effective discipline that they are the only ones who get to determine what they are going to do. They are accountable to no one. Amazingly, we see parents and educators today standing between children and the real consequences of wrong

> Proper discipline is conducted for the long-term benefit of the one being disciplined. This is truly an act of love. In the absence of such discipline, people are trained to conclude that there are no personal consequences for destructive behaviors.

actions. In the absence of effective discipline and training, this also keeps them from learning the lessons actual consequences could offer.

CHARACTER FORMATION AND THE THREE POWERS

Character formation occurs via all three powers detailed above. Our guidance system is the sum of our affirmed truths. These form our values, priorities, goals, and priorities, as well as our degree of integrity and all the other qualities we exhibit as we live in the world. As noted, our interpretation of events comes into play, and here our power of attention rules. Two people may have identical circumstances—abundance, deprivation, pain and loss, successes, or challenges of various kinds. Individuals may draw a variety of character lessons from the identical circumstances.

For instance, two young people may suffer the loss of a parent at an early age. One may become bitter for life, blaming God for the loss, determining that something was stolen from him that ruined his life. The other young person may grieve the loss of her parent, and the loss of the things this parent would have provided in her life, but she may also be able to see God's provision for her needs coming from other sources. One sees painful experience as the stepping-stone to maturity, another sees it as stepping off a cliff. Can you see the different character that would result from these different vantage points? And can you see that these vantage points were built upon prior use of each of these young people's powers of assent and dissent, and attention? Each had already learned to look at challenges in a certain way, each focused their attention on certain aspects of these situations that resonated with what they already believed, and this focus led to the formation of additional elements of character. But, as we noted earlier, these powers also offer us options at every point to troubleshoot character qualities that become character issues in marriage or in life.

Our power of intention forms the remainder of our character. We may be weak and passive or become passive-aggressive in our dealings. We may be strong-willed or stubborn. Or resolute, faithful, strong, courageous, and persistent. Likely, we will be some combination of all of these as we enter marriage. The key is to refine our intentions and match these with follow-through appropriate to the situation. For vital and important things, as determined by our powers of affirmation and attention, we do well to cultivate the strength of will to ensure that important things are done and done well. For things less important in an environment of competing priorities, we should, for example, do our best at work, but not be so fixated on work tasks that we overlook even more important relationship priorities related to our covenants. Underlying these decisions are our priorities, which are based on our understanding of rewards. Will we benefit most in the long run from a promotion, money, or being salesman of the month, or from building respect, trust, and intimacy in our home life?

Our goal is to fully develop our power of intention in marriage, ultimately so that we can be fully faithful to our covenant. But this is not where anyone starts. Our culture, educational system, and families rarely produce people with highly developed powers of intention. And in the face of this weakness, much of our lives are underdeveloped, and much of our character is underdeveloped. It is easier to amuse ourselves grappling with a nonexistent enemy in a video game than to grapple with real character issues, and so much more important in the long run. Right?

CHARACTER FORMATION AND RELATIONSHIPS

We might have a few rough edges that did not impact life noticeably when people were at a comfortable distance. If no one was depending on us in the ways people depend on each other in marriage, these things were unimportant, if noticed at all. We all have weak spots in our character, and we are likely aware of some of them. But we have made peace with these compromises. We are comfortable with these things because they are *our* compromises. But to our surprise, the other person who now shares our life did not agree to these compromises. This person, to whom we are now joined in every way, may be anything from irritated to infuriated by these compromises. And we may feel the same way about their compromises. This is one reason the first year of marriage is so . . . interesting. What we are doing here is offering the understanding and tools to get you through this first year by building troubleshooting patterns that will lead to much greater benefits over time.

We have been thinking about how things go wrong, in character and then in relationships. But consider what a relationship would be like if both characters were well formed, if beliefs, priorities, values, and every other aspect of character were the best they could be? What if these same parts of us were reformed upon a foundation of truth? What effect would this have on our emotions? On our viewpoints toward other people, including our beloved? On our plans for living? And, therefore, on all our relationships? Remember, our affirmations bring our emotions into harmony with what is affirmed. We might begin to value, to appreciate, and to desire more and more things that are truly good and wholly loving. And our desires for things that damage, our willingness to express urges that tear down, our hungers that draw us from God's path? What might we begin to feel about these things that we used to think were just . . . *us*? What if we did not have to oppose wrong things within ourselves to build our marriage, but instead did things that consistently build our relationships because this is what we *most want to do*? Is this possible? Yes, if we understand the forces in play and how we can choose a very different life by forming our own character after the plan of God. There is more involved in actually doing this than just wanting it to be so. We will cover this process, step by step, shortly. But first, think what it would be like for you to be firmly committed to things for yourself and others that are only good.

Character is not a fixed thing. Our character is always growing and changing. We are continuously being shaped. We never stay the same even though character changes so gradually we often do not realize how far we have moved. We are often not aware what we have become. The question for us is this: changed into what? And an even more important question: What if we could consciously direct the growth of our character into something from which good and loving actions would flow? And from which our best lives could be built? Think for a moment about what is standing in the way of your best life and your best relationships right now. Now go stand in front of a mirror and take a really close look at yourself. Take a few minutes to think about that question again and see what answers begin to emerge. Now, think for a moment about God's plan of covenant, in which He gives you everything necessary, including a loving helper, to build that character and that life. This is God's plan for marriage.

IDENTITY

TRUE IDENTITY VERSUS ONE'S PERCEPTION OF IDENTITY

The definition of identity is the fullness of who God made us to be. Among other things, it includes our basic wiring system, our potential, and our deepest needs. Are we a visual learner or an auditory learner? How much raw intelligence do we have to develop? How much athletic ability, musical ability, artistic ability, or other creative potential do we possess?

Character grows and changes via ideas we embrace. Our identity is comprised of those things we cannot change. Our real identity is our inherent essence as a human being made in the image of God. God built a unique set of elements within each of us to enable us to fulfill a certain set of purposes over our lifetime according to His plan. When we fulfill these purposes and callings we have a profound sense of satisfaction and gratification. But living out these things means that we know who we are and live accordingly. It also requires an understanding of God's unique plan for each of our lives. God's individual plan for each of us, and our identity, uniquely created to fulfill God's plan, are actually two sides of the same coin—God's creation. At the same time, our perceptions of any aspect of our identity may be correct or incorrect, and our understanding of God's plan for our lives may be clear or we may be completely unaware that such a plan exists. One of life's major journeys is to understand who we are, who we were created to be, and the purposes for which we were created.

One's identity is a difficult thing to put into words. How would you fully define yourself? While our identity is a fixed thing, just as our DNA is a fixed thing, completely defined at conception, the visible expression of our DNA changes as we grow from a single cell to birth to adolescence to adulthood, and then to old age. One could not look at us at any point in time and know the full potential inherent in our DNA. In the same way, we come to know who we are at the deepest levels in increments across our lifetime. While we cannot fully define ourselves in the moment, we do have a sense for what is us and what is *not us*.

As we are trying to do something—from leading to playing an instrument to cooking to woodworking to writing a blog post—we sense that it is a good fit for us, or sense that it is not. It may take a while, to be sure; sometimes we feel like something is definitely not us when it really is. Bart Millard, the lead singer of MercyMe, as recounted in the recent film *I Can Only Imagine* (2018)[3], was asked to sing in a school musical after the choir director overheard him singing. He adamantly refused, saying, "This is not who I am." She persisted; he relented. It was only as he heard people enthusiastically applauding his performance that he realized: "I am a singer." His life changed, but why? Did his identity change, or was it his perception of his identity?

Over time, as we develop a sense of who we are, our understanding of self becomes the most powerful determinant of our behavior. Note that our understanding does not necessarily correspond to our true identity perfectly, or perhaps at all. Think of the self-image of a battered wife who continues in the relationship, or a long-term drug addict. We can be misled about who we are. What if we conclude early in life that we are a loser? What if we conclude that we are a bad person, someone deserving only bad things instead of blessings, and we do so because this message from a parent was repeated and reinforced throughout our childhood? Whatever our understanding, the most powerful refusal we can make to an offer is to simply say, "This is not who I am." And if we are somehow compelled to do things not in harmony with who we are, we feel it. We have to pretend, to fake it, to pose, and at the same time this pretense offends something within us. We resent being compelled to be what we are not. In contrast, when we find our true calling and begin doing the things for which we were created, the result is something like a fish being released into its home stream; one is suddenly right where one belongs.

Why is acting in harmony with our true identity, living out the true essence of our being, so important? Because the deepest sense of reward and the real gratifications in life come from authentically expressing ourselves into the world. We want

> We want to be known. We want to be significant, to matter for who we are. We want to be loved for who we are. The ideal intimate relationship involves sharing oneself at the deepest level.

to be known. We want to be significant, to matter for who we are. We want to be loved for who we are. The ideal intimate relationship involves sharing oneself at the deepest level, being received, accepted, and appreciated, and creating the same experience for someone else. And why are we discussing this? Because our identity changes when we enter covenant.

THE IMPACT OF IDENTITY AND PERCEPTION ON RELATIONSHIP

How does our identity influence our behavior? When we are acting in accord with our identity we are energized to do the things we were created to do. Entertainers love to sing in front of people, and they often begin doing so in the family room when they are children. Some people love complicated math problems, others love hiking in unspoiled terrain. Some love animals and devote their lives to caring for them. Others are allergic to cats and perhaps become Allergists. We gravitate strongly toward our callings. But how about our perception of our identity; how does this influence behavior?

Have you ever known someone who seems to continually be on the losing end of things even though they are smart and capable, with no apparent explanation for their string of failures? This pattern can be seen in work or in relationships. I have known a few such people. If you really get to know them, they will at some point relate that they are losers. If someone believes this about themselves, they will unconsciously sabotage their own success and find defeat in the midst of certain victory. They create scenarios that demonstrate the "truth" of what they believe about themselves. At the same time, these people are unaware that they are the architect of their own failure, and they will loudly blame circumstances or other people. If you watch closely, however, they are doing it to themselves. Or how about people who "always date the wrong guy/girl"? They seem unerringly attracted to people who will hurt them. If you get to know them well enough, you will find they believe at some level that they deserve to be treated poorly. Again, these are extremes, but there are many more subtle ways that misperceptions of identity impact lives and relationships. The bottom line? For better or worse, we tend to live out our view of who we are, often limiting what God wants to do in our life and relationships.

Most unfavorable things people say about us are brushed off, but on occasion, if we are really trying to look in the mirror to see who we are, someone may answer the question for us in a way that sinks deeply into our hearts. "You are stupid," "a loser," "ugly," "pathetic," or whatever. From that point forward, this becomes part of how we see ourselves. And how we expect others, if they really know us, to see us. This is the awful truth about us, we are sure. If another person truly knows us, they would not, could not, really love us. In fact, often we are told that we are not loved because of something about us. The truth, in this case, is that the person saying these things is the one with the love problem. Their own ability to love is compromised, but they blame this on you.

Fast-forward to adulthood, to the time you are falling in love with "the one." You may or may not remember what you learned about yourself many years ago, but if it became part of your sense of identity you will nevertheless have been living out this "truth" in the interim in at least some ways. And you will not be interested in revealing some shameful, even deal-killing part of who you are to the one you are so attracted to, will you? You want to hide this part of yourself, like Adam and Eve trying to cover their shame. What this feels like on the inside is a strong reluctance to "open up." You may have trouble trusting or committing. You may feel shut down, or something else, but whatever you feel it is not eagerness to know and be known. A part of you may feel like it is missing; you may even have missing periods of memory from traumas in childhood that impacted your sense of identity. You may not feel that you know yourself very well because you are hesitant to look inside, afraid of what you will discover. What of any of this would help the growth of an intimate relationship?

Picture this scene: you are laying on a blanket on a warm summer afternoon next to the person you are madly in love with. You are watching clouds, talking about one little thing or another, just enjoying being in each other's presence. When two people are deeply in love they do not need to be doing something to enjoy each other. They can simply be. Together. Why do we so enjoy simply being with the one we love? Is it not that the core of our two beings enjoy communing with each other even without words? There is something deeply satisfying about being seen and known at the deepest level of our being. The love of two people building their happily-ever-after is about seeing and knowing each other at this deepest level, the level of identity. How do you think God's covenant plan intersects with an afternoon like this?

DISCOVERING OUR IDENTITY—OR BECOMING MISINFORMED?

How do we become misinformed about who we are? Or how do we find out good information? When we were young we were continually looking into a mirror to see who we are. This mirror is in the eyes and reactions of those around us. Are we loved and appreciated, important and valuable, or are we just in the way, or worse? We look into the mirror, first, of parents and siblings, then of childhood friends, and then our adolescent peer group. What do we see? Where do we fit in the big scheme of things—or do we fit at all? It is easy to imagine the vast array of messages people receive from other people over time. But is all of this about us? People react to other people in many ways for many reasons. Often people's reactions say more about them than the person to whom they are supposedly reacting.

Then there is the mirror of experience. We try doing one thing or another and things do not go well. We then conclude that we cannot do anything well. No wonder people are insecure, even suicidal. I would say with some confidence that the reason most people do not live up to their considerable potential is because they do not see themselves as having that potential. They see themselves as something entirely different from a bundle of potential that is waiting to be developed, to live a fulfilling life waiting to be lived.

Our society views people in utilitarian ways. We are defined by what we can do well. According to society's rules, only the perfect few get the real prizes. The rest of us play catchup by honing our social media image, hoping that we too will enjoy even a glimmer of glory. Our world is a very unequal place, and 99 percent are not the 1 percent. How, then, do we not despair? Because in one very important way, a way that is not a part of most people's thinking, we are all equal. How? Because we are all made in the image of God. As His image and His creation, we are loved by Him. He waits only for us to turn to Him and receive the love He freely offers. While some may be a little taller or shorter, as we all stand before the throne of God those subtle differences are irrelevant. Further, God made us to be certain things, then matches the life He fashions around us to offer us opportunities to fulfill the purposes for which He created us. We each have

> None of the ways humans judge each other will have any role in our ultimate judgment by God. If we want to discover our true identity, we must turn first to God's revelation and learn who we are before Him.

a purpose in life that is ordained by God. None of the ways humans judge each other will have any role in our ultimate judgment by God. If we want to discover our true identity, we must turn first to God's revelation and learn who we are before Him, then seek to understand the uniqueness of our creation, then live this out, subtracting most of the things we have heard from other people along the way.

IDENTITY AND RELATIONSHIP AT A DEEPER LEVEL

The essence of intimacy is revealing and experiencing the true self of another person. There is great joy in this. In covenant there is an even greater joy: this sharing extends to exchanging and joining lives in the way we have been describing. This is the heart of the experience of being in love—being united in every sense. If we understand that a marriage is not simply two people coming together and experiencing each other, but is also a training and development process that helps us identify and express our true selves, this opens an entirely new realm of life and relationship. Of course, God's plan also changes our true self. His plan involves discovering and living out our new self. But far more than just acknowledging the joined aspect of our two identities, the environment created in a relationship by God's plan—the safety, security, support, affirmation, encouragement, and the ability to draw from the insight and strength of a loving partner who is as devoted to one's growth and development as to his or her own—produces a relationship that allows tender and sensitive things to grow.

These are parts of our identity which would never begin to grow without this wholly supportive environment, those first shoots that can turn into beautiful flowers or strong limbs. I have gained far more insight about myself and developed many more aspects of myself with my wife's loving support than I ever could have without her support. Things developed in me, and in her in the same way, and then feed back into the relationship, making it more rich and vibrant, building more things we would never have had otherwise. When God speaks of an abundant life, this is a big part of what He is describing. He certainly pours amazing things directly into our lives if we are following

Him, but He also allows us to build, to grow new things from the core of our being. We then enjoy the rewards of building such things in partnership with God under His direction. Honestly, do most marriages look like this? Why not? Because for this kind of development process to occur as intended, we must carefully build certain things into the relationship.

TRUE IDENTITY VERSUS OPTIONAL ADD-ONS

Why would it be vital to properly identify one's true identity? Our identity is the part of us that is fixed, the essence of our being. If we are truly loved, unconditionally loved, this is the part of us that is being loved, accepted, affirmed, and embraced. If a problem occurs in relationship, and we think we are simply expressing the core of our being—"being ourselves" in the most fundamental way possible—then whose problem is it? If we are unconditionally loved, doesn't this mean that someone who loves us with true love will not only endure what they are receiving on the other end of us, but even affirm and celebrate us for being ourselves? The problem with this view is twofold. First, some of the things people do in relationships are very destructive to those relationships. So, if the relationship is to flourish, these things need to change. Therefore, the belief that it is up to someone else to embrace the core of one's being, while true, depends on accurately understanding what is the core of one's being. This cannot be changed. The second problem, therefore, is determining the difference between one's core, that part to be unconditionally loved, and all of the other elements of personality and false perceptions of identity which have adhered to us along the way. As noted earlier, these things become—in our perception—a part of us because we have invited them to be a part of us. But these are not inherent, intrinsic, unchangeable parts of self. These things are optional add-ons. Please place emphasis on the word *optional*. What we need to learn, therefore, is what really needs to change in us for our marriage to be the best marriage. Then we need to understand how God's processes of growth and transformation produce these changes. Then, as the shoe company says, we "just do it."

PUTTING THIS ALL TOGETHER

And do not be conformed to this world, but be transformed by the renewing of your minds, that you may prove what the will of God is, that which is good, and acceptable, and perfect.
ROMANS 12:2

May I offer my sincere apology for the length of the preamble, but unless we understand the vital parts of us and how those parts fit together, we will not be able to play our necessary role in refashioning those parts so they will work together properly. Many Christians want to change and keenly feel the need to change things about themselves. But they have been taught that a relationship with God is about waiting on Him to transform us in such ways. Look at the above Scripture. It says, "be transformed," not "wait for Me to transform you into . . ." We are in the process of examining the process of transforming our minds, and therefore our lives, under God's guidance—just as He instructs us to do.

To recap, we looked at our three powers. The things we agree with and invite into our mind and heart then become our foundation, fashioning our viewpoints, values, priorities, and emotional responses, in addition to simply becoming our beliefs. This foundation dramatically influences the development of our character at every level, which in turn determines how we relate to life and other people. Our deepest quest as we go through life is to discover who we are and to fashion our lives in harmony with our identity. At stake in this is our sense of purpose, the meaning of our life, and the degree of fulfillment we experience.

As we are trying to discover truth so we can live by it, we must remember that things other than God's truth are not just *untrue*. We have the additional challenge of sorting out truth from artfully packaged, extremely attractive deceptions. These are ideas that purport to offer us something we are persuaded to want, which involve, at the same time, a moral compromise. Why? Because these enticements are specifically, intentionally designed to lead us away from a relationship with God that is what it could be—if we followed His plan for our lives.

> We have the additional challenge of sorting out truth from artfully packaged, extremely attractive deceptions.

If you will notice, the doorway into everything that happens afterward in our mind, heart, life, and relationships—the first step in this process— is our acceptance of an idea as truth, our affirmation of this idea. For us, then, the question must always be: *Is it really true?* Our track record for accurately determining truth based on our own perceptions is sketchy at best. Therefore, our loving Creator has gone to considerable trouble to lay down a written document over many centuries, then preserved it in intact form for millennia. He invites us to not be conformed to this world. How have we been conformed thus far to the world? By embracing as *truth* the deceptions which grip our world, a world which is largely in the grasp of the enemy of God because people have willingly followed his directions for living. ". . . you will surely not die. For God knows when you eat from it your eyes will be opened . . ." (Genesis 3:4)

God invites us to be transformed. How does He tell us we may do this? By the renewing of our minds. Note carefully that God is telling us what to do, not telling us what *He* is going to do to us or for us. He is instructing us to do something very specific, a plan and approach that will have a dramatic, transformative impact on our lives. What is He telling us to do? With the foundation we have laid, can you answer this question? I hope you now see the powerful and many-faceted impact that results from our exercising a power that God delegated to us: our ability to decide whether (or not) something is true. God is instructing us to go back through our minds and identify all the things we have embraced as truths. We are then to review these ideas and match them against the real thing.

Since we cannot be completely sure on our own what is true, nor can we trust without question the judgment of any other human, God has given us a standard against which we can measure any idea—His Word. God, as always, has an effective plan.

QUESTIONS FOR THOUGHT

1. What difference might it make to view disagreement, conflict, and other relationship issues as opportunities rather than problems? How does this shift in viewpoint alter how we view each other in these situations?

2. Marriage is always about expressing ourselves authentically to each other. Have you ever considered marriage as not only a place that this should occur but the path to growing into the person we were created to become? If God's plan is to teach us how to grow and mature in marriage, what benefits do you see for this for your own life? What benefits might this offer your beloved, and for your relationship?

3. Have you ever noticed, in yourself or in another person, how embracing or affirming a new idea can redirect one's life? Have you seen this move some people's lives in better directions, or in other people's lives move them in a worse direction?

4. What relationship do you see between the truth of one's affirmed ideas and whether these ideas move one's life in better or worse directions? Do you see the difference between someone *believing* that their idea is true versus it actually *being* true? How can we know that something is actually true versus being deceived?

5. What relationship do you see, then, between blessed lives, those well lived, and people who create a life full of problems for themselves and others? What role do affirmed ideas play in creating these different lives? What role do you think previously embraced

ideas might be playing in problems and issues in your own life? What remarkably powerful tool might this understanding place in your hands?

6. What helpful roles might your power of attention play in your life if this power was richly developed? What things do you want to focus more attention on, and what things do you want to focus less (or no!) attention on? Can you see how this power could be used to do what God tells us to do in Philippians 4:4-8? How can you strengthen this power?

7. What helpful roles might your power of intention play in your life if this power was strongly developed? What things do you want to start, do as well as you can possibly do, and finish? Has lack of development of this power ever created a problem for you? What is the relationship between reason and willpower? How, then, can our powers of intention be strengthened?

8. What would happen in your life if your three powers were strong and operating as intended? What kind of life would you have? Is this the life you have? If not, how can you develop these powers over the next year?

9. Have you ever considered how your character has been formed? Are there character qualities you would like to have, that you admire, that you do not have? How could you use your three powers to build the qualities you would like to have over the next year?

10. Why is it important to understand one's real identity versus misunderstanding it or thinking our identity includes things we have learned to be? Do you think there is important potential within you that has not yet been developed? If identity changes in covenant, what ways might this change your life? How can you discover and express the fullness of who you are over your lifetime? Is this important to you?

CHAPTER EIGHT

Transformation in Marriage

Growth is the development of something that has not yet fully developed or matured. Transformation refers to removing something previously in place—an idea, a belief, a value, a priority—and replacing what is, but should not be there, with what should be there (the correct idea or belief). Of course, growth and transformation are closely related in what is required and what is produced. God's plan will lead us to do both simultaneously on many fronts for the rest of our lives. Growth often refers to innate potential—like musical talent or willpower—while transformation always refers to ideas we embrace and all the effects of these ideas on mind, heart, and character.

When God tells us to be transformed by the renewing of our minds, what does this entail? Let us outline this process step by step.

God assigns us a key role in our own transformation. His goal is that we grow into, and change into, the kind of person who is able to love as He instructs us to love. He tells us that we love because He first loved us. We did not come up with a plan to fix our lives or a plan to go find a God who is in hiding somewhere. God has orchestrated a remarkably complex plan throughout history to lead us to a relationship with Himself and to decide to base our lives on His truth. His truth is in complete accord with the reality He created for us to inhabit. We did none of this. Our role is simply to follow His plan.

But His plan requires some definite things of us. He loves us equally, but by no means does He reward, bless, chasten, or punish us equally. He gives to us according to our love for Him, which in John chapter 14 is equated with obedience to Him (His Word, His plan). This is the point at which His Lordship of our lives is real, or is not. We reap not only earthly blessings and good things by following His plan, we alter our eternity by the degree to which we follow His instructions, commands, and principles. Why is it so vital to follow Him? Because following any lead other than His will compromise us in ways we will not see coming. His plan is something completely distinct and unique; it does not benefit from synthesis with any other guidance despite any personal belief we might have to the contrary. See Eve for details. No other plan will produce people capable of loving as God loves us.

The most intensive training ground for growth and transformation for most of us is marriage. While we are supposed to renew our minds with truth according to God, where do we start? We can certainly be involved in a systematic study of God's plan, like doing a Bible study correlating our wedding vows with the Scriptures and progressively implementing truths we discover. Or we could be doing a more general study of the Scriptures. But the other way we are offered an agenda for growth and transformation is simply by living in the close confines of marriage. We will all find ample opportunities for growth in the ways we treat people and in the ways they treat us—for the rest of our lives. Conflict, as noted, is the doorway to growth and transformation. Every day we encounter different challenges, different situations, different opportunities that cause us to express different aspects of our character, and this brings to the surface parts of our character in need of revision. The key is to understand the opportunity we are presented, and how to make the most of this opportunity.

WHY DO WE TREAT PEOPLE THE WAY WE TREAT THEM?

With all that we have covered, we can see that this is a bit more complicated equation than we probably realized—but it is an equation. That is, both the randomness we see in people's behaviors and the predictable patterns actually make sense. We see how affirmed ideas—beliefs—lead to viewpoints, motivations, values, goals, priorities, expectations, standards, ideals, and everything else we as humans look to for guidance for our behaviors. These in turn lead to emotional responses and thus to the ways people interact at every level. God has made this soundbite simple for us. If there is a problem, ultimately it is one of belief. We have chosen to believe something that is not true or failed to believe something that is true. Thus we need to experience the transformation that occurs when we compare our ideas with truth, then discard the untrue ones and embrace the true ones. Of course, the first thing we must determine is which belief is driving what misstep.

CORRECTLY DIAGNOSING THE PROBLEM

If God's plan is perfectly implemented, two people plan and execute their lives together by melding their viewpoints about what is best into a plan that is best for each person, the relationship, and the family. Of course, this also takes into account any specific guidance from God in a given situation. The two people are supporting each other, enabling and encouraging each other's growth and development into the people God created them to be. While there may be differences of opinion, these are approached as two close allies working out a successful solution to a complicated problem.

No matter how messy the situation looks, it is simply an opportunity for growth and transformation. We just need to correctly identify the problem.

SORTING OUT THE SOURCE OF CONFLICT

Often life looks a little messier, though. Our lingering perceptions of best interest, in conjunction with distortions in any of the list of personal elements noted above, become a source of conflict. Little slights become cause for harsh counterattacks or deeply experienced negative emotions. Small oversights turn into battles and ultimatums. Some days we just want to flip a switch and go back to watching the clouds float by in a state of bliss. No worries. No matter how messy the situation looks, it is simply an opportunity for growth and transformation. We just need to correctly identify the problem. In marriage a surprising number of conflicts occur from misunderstandings. Because of prior experience, we load words or actions with meaning, and we attribute motives to our spouse based on past experience that bears some resemblance to the present one.

As conflicts are developing or bad outcomes are occurring, it is helpful to go through the following list. In medicine, we call this a *differential diagnosis*. That is, these are the diagnostic possibilities based on the patient's presentation. Then, sort through the various possibilities to determine the actual problem.

The list below may help improve problem-solving in the moment. It is also possible that the in-the-moment issue may bring to your attention something to search out in your own heart. A word of caution: These questions, beyond the *first one*, are not intended for each other, but for ourselves. The real win is growth and maturity, and that is going to involve much rethinking and reaffirming over time on the part of each person. As we pointed out, though, this is in essence a private and personal matter. One person, even joined with another in covenant, cannot exercise the power of affirmation and dissent in the life of their partner. Keep in mind that every move and step that will be commended for the rest of this volume is about seeking out the truth, affirming it, embracing it, and living it. This is all that is required for success. (By the way, where does "winning the argument" fit in the list of relationship priorities? We do need to solve the problems we encounter, but it is very helpful to focus on getting things right, versus "being" right.)

SELF-ASSESSMENT FOR MARITAL CONFLICTS

1. Is this a misunderstanding? Determining this is quite easy. Simply voice to the other person what you think they are trying to say to you, and have them do the same for you. If either of you hear from the other something that is not at all what each other

is trying to communicate, dialogue until each person can accurately characterize the position of the other person. This simple move, called *reflective listening,* will end many conflicts. If there is still a difference of opinion when opinions are clear, one can move down the list.

2. Is this a covenant issue? Is the issue a question of being or giving something that I have already committed to be or to give? In this case, why do I not want to fulfill my responsibility?

3. Is this a matter of seeking what I think is my best interest, one that I feel is now being threatened? What is my best interest in this situation in light of our covenant joining?

4. Is this a matter of values, priorities, and motivation? What is the real goal in each person's position? What should the ultimate goal be? The correct answer will be some variant of building people and relationship. Individual issues are simply tools to that end. It is exceedingly rare that a decision made in one way or another on any issue will dramatically affect the course of two lives. Far more common is the situation in which people hold far too tightly to their values and priorities when those things have not been subjected to proper review. At the same time, if there are real moral issues involved, unwillingness to compromise is appropriate. By the end of these discussions we often discover a third path that is morally appropriate and acceptable to both parties—and most beneficial to all.

5. Is this situation a matter of character on my part? Is the issue one of honesty, integrity, follow-through—i.e., essentially a character issue? If so, character work is indicated.

6. Is this a matter of expectations not being met? What is the basis of these expectations? Are these reasonable, and will they spur me toward being a better person? Are they unreasonable, rooted in a desire of one to take advantage of the other or rooted in a desire that is inappropriate for other reasons?

7. Is this an issue of the integrity of the relationship? We can at times send signals to others and solicit inappropriate attention or in other ways skirt the edges of the exclusivity of the relationship. These may be old habits that a person may not intend in the way they are perceived. Great care must be taken to always honor our covenant partner. It is especially vital for both partners to maintain propriety in relation to the opposite gender.

8. Is this an issue of hurt feelings due to things said or implied? An issue that triggers insecurity? An issue related to self-image? On one hand, we need to learn sensitivity to each other's issues; we need to deal very carefully with each other's hearts under any circumstances; we need to be careful to encourage and affirm instead of undercutting our spouse. On the other hand, we perhaps need to consider our own self-image to more deeply understand why something said without intent to hurt is so painful. Almost always this pattern will relate to prior emotional wounds that overcharge words or actions which resonate with the original emotional injury. And these wounds almost always involve not only the intent of the other party to wound but a conclusion we draw about ourselves in the process. These conclusions might well become our main focus.

9. Is this an issue of identity? Does God's plan call for us to love in a way that we cannot love because we are . . . what? In this realm, it is very helpful to consider who God says we are. It is true that we love because God first loved us (1 John 4:19), but it is also true that we will not love as He tells us to unless we actually *experience His love*. We must receive it. This is yet another time when we must affirm that something is true and real and then open the door to our heart and receive what God graciously offers. Then, and only then, will we have something within that we can give.

10. Is this really the other person's problem? On the surface, this may be true. They may have any number of issues. As do we. But now their issues are our issues in more than an abstract sense. Our goal is growth, for us and for our beloved. In order to create

the environment for growth, what is most needed? I will simply say that love, encouragement, and the sense that we are in this together will do more to motivate someone to grow, and create an environment where they feel safe doing so, than a sharp word or a condemning look. Just remember, the shoe will definitely be on the other foot soon enough. This is a wonderful time to practice Jesus' most quoted advice: "Do unto others as you would have them do unto you." And the key thing to keep in mind is that our real source of supply for the things we most need for the abundant life is God, not our spouse. If our spouse is not up to being everything they might ideally be, our lives do not depend on making sure that they measure up. Our lives depend on God, and as we follow Him by loving our beloved, He will bless us in ways beyond all we ask or think. There are very few hills worth dying on. And if we think one is when it is not, guess who ends up dying?

FROM CORRECT DIAGNOSIS TO EFFECTIVE TREATMENT

Sorry, this long-time surgeon can't resist the medical allusions. The above list is only a beginning, but it will work to begin to sort out situations into misunderstandings, simple inattention, lack of knowledge, or incorrect priorities; into character issues; or into identity issues. Often more than one of these is in play, but focus on getting just one issue on track at a time. Life is long, fortunately, so we have a lifetime to deal with us. God's model for growth and transformation has already been outlined: inform, conform, transform. At every level, for every issue, the pattern is the same.

GROWING AND TRANSFORMING INTO GOOD COVENANT PARTNERS

To build the best marriage we really need a clear vision of what marriage is designed to look like and how it is designed to function. Thus, the first task in building a great marriage is becoming intimately familiar with God's plan. He has made significant effort to inform us of His plan for marriage, and we have been examining it in detail throughout this volume. There is a more deep and rich mine that you can draw from for a lifetime—the Scriptures—but this book's goal is to help get you started and pointed in the right direction. Our next task is to become very clear about why we would have a better life by conforming to God's plan than by following any other direction. Again, there are many resources that speak to this issue. The key is to reach a point where you make God's plan your own. The only path to success is to embrace the only path to success.

Much progress can be made by getting better at doing what we already know we want to do. We can practice our three powers, strengthening them in the process, and building both ourselves and our love lives. There are many techniques for keeping our attention focused, for being accountable for follow-through, for learning to deal more effectively with adversity, distraction, and competing priorities.

> **Transformation will not happen over your objections. Your doorway to transformation has a handle only on the inside.**

When we run into an issue where previous affirmations have built patterns in our character that create problems, I want to offer you a strategy that may not be found in other marriage self-help books. By now, I hope you have some sense for what this scenario will look like and feel like from your perspective. It will appear to you that you are right, and that you are simply expressing yourself. You will feel completely justified and may be offended that your covenant partner is calling you out. You will also notice that your position is a bit different from God's on the matter.

What now? Is this a matter of personal freedom, self-expression, and the need for your partner to unconditionally love you, or is this your cue to be transformed by the renewing of your mind? You will need to decide, because transformation will not happen over your objections. Your doorway to transformation has a handle only on the inside.

Let's suppose you overcome your sense that you might as well cut off a limb as give in on this issue, and you grab the handle and open the door just to see what God might have for you. And it is worth noting that you will only resist this process once. After you see the blessing of God in your life that occurs via this kind of transformation, you will begin to eagerly seek these opportunities.

A PATTERN FOR PERSONAL TRANSFORMATION

There is no single technique that is the "right" way to grow. There are many patterns and approaches to engage with God's truth that can have wonderful results. This is the pattern I have found to be of greatest personal benefit. I have used this pattern for many years to deal with issues in my own life, and I have taught it to many other people who also found it of benefit.

First, let's suppose you have become aware of something that needs to change in your approach. Let's nominate one issue for this example: at times you do not tell the truth when under pressure. You say things when questioned that make you look better in the moment, but your statements are simply not accurate. This lack of integrity is beginning to create trust issues. Your spouse is beginning to wonder about everything you say, and not sure when, or if, you are ever telling the whole truth. What now?

The goal is to renew our minds with truth, so go to the Scriptures and search for passages that deal with truthful speech. There are quite a few, and you should be able to do a search for them on one of the major Bible sites like Bible Hub, or go to the concordance at the back of most Bibles, or find a *Thompson Chain Reference Bible*, a *McArthur Study Bible*, or one of the many other excellent Scripture search aids. What you are looking for, again, is an actual list of Scriptures that deal with integrity of speech.

Why do we want to find all the Scriptures on a topic instead of just one, or a few? Because there are many aspects of truthful speech. One

Scripture might address only one of these aspects. In order to see the full picture, we must view them all. This is true regarding many issues. In reference to drinking alcohol, for instance, the Scriptures present a complex picture. In some verses drinking to the point of drunkenness is condemned, while in other verses drinking is commended in modest amounts. In some verses it appears as if alcohol is condemned outright. If one picks just one verse and holds this as "God's truth," this person might well condemn another believer for choosing other verses as his or her guide. We want to hear the *whole counsel of God* on an issue and view the entirety of His message to us. Then, among the spectrum of possible positions, prayerfully seek God's will for your own life in the situation in question.

Some want to view God's will as a path through the woods. They find this path and invite people to follow them in every respect, essentially in a single-file line. But a careful reading of Scripture shows a different picture. God's guidance is more like a playing field. There are definite boundary lines. Some things are clearly out of bounds. But within the boundaries there may be considerable latitude, which could be termed *freedom in Christ*, about things not clearly prohibited. Thus, we must view the entirety of God's instructions and get the complete picture before we assume we understand God's heart and mind, or where the real boundaries are. The balancing truth, voiced by the apostle Paul in 1 Corinthians 8, is to not allow our freedom to cause a brother to stumble, and certainly not to use our sense of freedom as a license for indulgence (Galatians 5:13).

> We must view the entirety of God's instructions and get the complete picture before we assume we understand God's heart and mind, or where the real boundaries are.

Read the collected verses, study the context, and learn as much as you can about what God says about speaking truth. By the way, why would I choose this example? Because one of the central themes of this book is the importance of basing our ideas, and from this our entire lives, on truth. Thus, it should be obvious that speaking truth is as important as believing it. And it is sadly true that in our culture the connection between speech and truth is as challenged as the connection between truth and most other things.

A FIVE-STEP PROCESS FOR TRANSFORMATION

Once we have all of God's truth on a matter, the next step is to determine, among the many aspects of integrity, exactly what God wants to see in our lives right now. What is our next step? We will confine our approach to this portion of God's truth. It is extremely helpful to write all of this down on paper or in your computer. You need to thoughtfully work over these questions, and this is aided by having the truth, the questions, and your responses in written form. You will also have access to your work in the months to come, which is extremely helpful so you can be fully accountable for what you are learning.

STEP ONE

Having collected specific Scriptures on the topic and identified one or more that speak directly to the heart of the issue, write in your own words the truth God wants to build into your life right now.

STEP TWO

Write a description of what your life is like now in relation to this truth. Stay with this one for a few minutes. When God is tapping me on the shoulder about something and I get to this point, my first response often is, "Pretty good on that one, in fact." Which raises the question of why God is taking His time to engage with me on this issue. If I simply allow God's Spirit time to search my heart and my life, a very interesting thing almost always happens. God's truths have layers, much like an onion. There are superficial applications, but also deeper and deeper layers. God's definition of truthfulness might be more exacting than the one I begin with. Even though my words might be technically true in a situation, still, I might, via words that are strictly accurate, be creating a false impression or an incomplete picture. I may have words that are right but a motive that is wrong. I may select what is said, withholding key information. I may not want to go where the truth leads and be somehow standing in the way. I will soon begin to see applications of God's truth that were not at first evident to me, to the point that I am often near tears by the time God is finished with even this several-minute review of my life and character.

This exercise always leaves me something to work on, and will for the rest of my earthly life. We never in a lifetime fully understand and fully apply even God's most straightforward commands.

STEP THREE

Now write a description of what this truth would look like lived out in the situations in question. In other words, what should my life look like? This should be written in as much detail as necessary to paint a full and complete picture.

STEP FOUR

Next, write a step-by-step plan to move your actions from Step Two to Step Three. This might include memorizing one or more pertinent Scriptures so we have God's specific Word, and even specific wording, on this topic in mind at all times. One of the most important elements of success is identifying a problem situation on the front end, as it is developing, before one is already in the middle and thoughtlessly repeating the old pattern. Thus, the plan should include awareness of the scenario that triggers these behaviors. Then undertake a series of steps that will result in correct action. Perhaps pause and think about a response before speaking or responding, perhaps praying, perhaps silently reciting a pertinent Scripture for clear guidance. Then take action that is truly appropriate.

STEP FIVE

Last, plan a checkup point. Depending on how frequently the issue occurs, you want to pick a time interval when there will have been opportunity for changed behavior one or more times. Simply note on paper or computer how things went, and perhaps schedule another checkup. It is helpful to involve a trusted friend as an accountability partner. Perhaps your spouse, but in issues directly related to your spouse, there are advantages in a third party, a same-gender friendship centered on personal and spiritual growth.

Depending on the issue, its complexity, and the strength of the hold on behaviors, it may take several repetitions for a new habit pattern to begin to form. For more challenging situations, refined approaches and more support may be required. The key is to do whatever is necessary to produce the desired behaviors on several occasions. As we engage in appropriate behaviors, what should we expect? First, they will feel unfamiliar and uncomfortable, and you will likely feel vulnerable. Then something else will occur. Good behavior yields good consequences. God is likely to bless you in ways that may be related to the situation, or in ways that seem unrelated, except that you will be aware that your faithfulness is being rewarded. The endpoint of this exercise is a new habit.

THE OUTCOME OF THIS EXERCISE

What have we just accomplished? We have affirmed and embraced a new truth, one directly from God. As we do this, as previously noted, far more than a simple behavior is at stake. Other things in our being begin to align with this truth. Other elements of our character will shift. Our frame of reference shifts. One thing that will definitely happen is an increased level of confidence in the benefits of applying God's truth to our lives. God actually invites us to reality-test His guidance: "Taste, and see that the Lord is good" (Psalms 34:8).

One such exercise does not an excellent character make, but we now have one real and true brick in place in our foundation. As we add one after another, our character grows and strengthens. After we have engaged in this process in a formal way for a year or so, we will begin to internalize this pattern of growth so we no longer need to write these things down, though this is always helpful. This pattern of growth itself can become a habit.

Earlier in my Christian life I took two Bibles (so I would have a copy of both sides of each page) and literally cut out every verse I could identify about what a Christian was supposed to do or be. I collated these topically and taped them to note cards so I would have the full counsel of God on each topic. Then I went through these cards one after another, creating pages of meditations on each topic in a large notebook. The eighteen months or so I took to get through all the notecards is perhaps the time of most rapid spiritual growth in my life. One could easily follow this same pattern regarding marriage, and you are now holding a resource for at least some of the pertinent Scriptures in your hand.

As we are looking at problem areas and identifying and implementing new ways of living, we also need to take note of another reality. Why did we have our former pattern? There's a simple reason: because we had at some point affirmed that this was our best option in a situation, and we liked the results enough to continue the pattern. So now that we have affirmed a new truth, what happened to the old idea, the untrue one upon which our way of life was based? It is still there at this point and is still capable of guiding our behavior in certain situations.

MOVING FROM AFFIRMATIONS TO CONVICTIONS

Have you ever seen someone who does some godly and good things, but also has behaviors based on other ideas, ungodly ideas? Our churches, sadly, have too many such people. Their behaviors are a curious mixture of godly obedience and behaviors far from God's truth. Why this odd mixture of obedience and disobedience? Because people have not learned how to exclusively follow God's ways. Perhaps they see no reason why they should, or they are waiting, as noted above, for God to transform their lives so they no longer want to do something they already know is wrong. In light of our discussion so far, you may already have an approach in mind for this situation.

To follow Him only partially or only at times is not in fact following Him. This approach is based on confusion and can only produce confusion. Such people have competing guidance systems vying for control. God says loving Him is synonymous with obeying Him; in contrast, those who want something from God as a mere value-add to their lives, but who do not genuinely love God or believe in Him, will not actually follow Him. This is why Jesus made the distinction between the criterion for entering covenant with Himself—believing in Him—versus any other basis for approaching Him. There is only one way to a genuine relationship with God—entering covenant with Him—and this will be evidenced by the trajectory one's life takes afterward. A covenant relationship with God is the only grounds for accessing the blessings and benefits of God.

But at times even very mature Christians, who are evidently trying to follow God wholeheartedly, will fall into serious transgression. What is happening here? Each must decide to commit such an act, and they will do so for reasons that, in the moment, seem sufficient to them. Here also it is all about decisions and reasons. In this case, an idea either was present at the time one came to Christ, or was embraced later; such behavior was enticing because of some supposed benefit. This idea remained a part of the person's operating system, though it remains lurking in the shadows in the face of contradictory guidance from God's Word. We see variants of this phenomenon all the time in the less dramatic compromises Christians make with the world. People give credence to new ungodly ideas that float through our culture, or have previously embraced such ideas.

Remember, as long as we have affirmed an idea, it becomes the basis for "acceptable" behavior, even if we also embrace contradictory ideas. Remember the name of our first human power? It is termed the power of affirmation and dissent. The second part is also very important. There is one more step we must make to reach a point where the old thing we did becomes the last thing we would do given the opportunity. This step is to disaffirm our earlier affirmed idea for a very important reason: because we now know it is a lie.

Why would we go to this trouble? Because simply embracing godly behaviors as a desired objective does not weed the potential for ungodly behaviors. What we want is not a situation where we will follow God but at the same time reserve the freedom to follow our old ways in the (rare) occasions when this still seems to us to be a good idea. What we want is a situation in which we have purposed to follow God and His plan. Period. Inherent in this, per the explicit instructions of Jesus and the Scriptures, is that we will not do things contrary to God's plan. In other words, Jesus calls on us to develop an unshakable *conviction* that we will act in a particular manner regardless of the pressures exerted to get us to do otherwise from without or within.

DEVELOPING A CONVICTION

Step one: This process in some ways mirrors the previous one, but instead of identifying the behavior we want, we seek to identify and reject a lie we previously embraced as our truth. The first step is to recall how this lie was introduced and embraced. We may remember the situation when this behavior started, or this may not be recalled. In the latter case, we may need to look at our behavior and ask ourselves: What must I believe if I am doing this? Once we articulate the idea, our memory may be jogged to remember earlier examples. We may remember a traumatic event associated with developing the pattern in question, or guidance we heard from a trusted source. Perhaps a parent was abusive, so lying to avoid provoking that parent became a reasonable option for a five-year-old. It does help to identify traumatic events because, rather than one lesson, we may have learned many false lessons, all of which merit revision. We may need to rethink and revise all of these at some point. What we are looking for is both a wrong behavior or way of being and the benefit we thought would be obtained by a course of action different from God's desire for us. We want to find more than the lie; we want to find the deception. What goal are we still trying to accomplish?

Step two: A lie is just false information, but a deception involves offering us something we are persuaded to want, in fact something we want badly enough to do something we know (at some level) is wrong in order to obtain. Almost always our goal is not the wrong act, it is the supposed benefit. Eve wasn't really that hungry for food, but she did become hungry to be like God once she was prompted to think about it.

> Eve wasn't really that hungry for food, but she did become hungry to be like God once she was prompted to think about it.

Step three: Consider why this offer is a deception. Did you really get what you want in the end? Or did you just create more trouble by lying? What you wanted probably reflects a real need: physical safety in the above example, but only in situations involving one abusive person, not the entire human race. Consider whether you now place yourself in more danger by lying or by telling the truth. Then consider how to really meet your needs in a way consistent with God's Word. If the need is legitimate, God will have a way to meet this need that is good and appropriate. In this situation the need for safety could be addressed by trusting Him for protection even when truth is spoken instead of relying on conveying a false impression. We now want to identify the reasons why the only way to really meet a particular need is via God's plan. Every other path offers great benefit but delivers only pain, even death in the end. Once we realize we have been the subject of a con job, no one wants to continue investing in the same plan. In fact, that becomes the last thing we would ever want to do. That realization is the goal of this exercise.

Step four: Formally dissent from this idea. In your mind, brand each element of the falsehood as the lie that it is. Then hold up God's truth as the true path to life, the actual way to meet your needs. It may be helpful to speak this out loud as a commitment to yourself and to God.

What just happened? You have just used your most precious and important power, the power of assent and dissent, in the most focused and direct way to impact your own mind, heart, and character. You have assented to truth and dissented from a corresponding lie. What is so important about the latter? Imagine a person with two ropes tied around their waist, the ropes being pulled in opposite directions. When the person tries to move, what happens? Not much. But we do not just have one set of competing embraced ideas; all of us start out with dozens. So now put a dozen ropes around someone's waist pulling in all directions and let them try to move in any direction. Have you seen people whose lives seemed stuck in one place? Who seemed confused? Who were not sure which way to go and end up going nowhere? Why are they stuck in place?

The scriptural term for a mind that holds competing ideas is "double-minded" (James 1:8). This verse goes on to describe this person as "unstable in all his ways." The opposite of this would be "wholehearted." A person who is wholehearted is moving with clarity, focus, and passion toward a goal. How does one become wholehearted?

All Judah rejoiced about the oath because they had sworn it wholeheartedly. They sought the Lord eagerly, and He was found by them. So the Lord gave them rest on every side.
2 Chronicles 15:15

When one ends up with only one guidance system, with a rope that is pulling in one direction—the right direction—then rapid progress can be made. Unhindered progress, in fact. This is a picture of one who is all-in to the plan of God, to a relationship with God, and to his or her marriage. We make our determinations about what is true and false, good and bad, for what we think are legitimate reasons. The above exercises invite us to really think through these things, to base our affirmations and dissents on solid observations about our lives, to see for ourselves the correlation between God's moral injunctions and the cause-and-effect universe we inhabit, and to choose to believe things based upon thoughtful consideration of the big picture of life. This is what it means to be wholehearted.

Once we are wholehearted about an issue, we can be said to have a *conviction* about this issue. That is, where we once would have followed another course on this issue, one informed by the world, now and forevermore our former approach would be the last thing we would do given the opportunity. Instead, the only choice we will make is the one we are now convinced is the only one for us. We will simply not follow a lie if we know it is a lie. We will be fiercely devoted to our truth if we understand that it is also *actual truth*, and if we understand the danger of other approaches. All our faculties will line up with truths about which we are completely convinced—our emotions, decisions, and will become devoted to living out things we are completely convinced are true. The key word here is *completely*. What this exercise is designed to do is erase the confusion that, at some level, blurs almost everything in life, that weakens our commitments and our resolve because we are not sure whether other ways might be better. If we are confused, we remain open to any seemingly better idea.

MOVING FROM A PLAN TO THE DESIRED OUTCOME

The above is an outline of steps. What does this plan look like and feel like if implemented between, say, this author and his wife? The above format does not look like we are directly addressing "real" problems, like who is going to handle some aspect of home life. We are just talking about ideas and saying certain things to ourselves about those ideas.

But why is this such a powerful move to build the marriage we all want? Well, our marriage started as an idea. And that idea had a vast impact. Not only what marriage is, but what we think it to be has vast and ongoing impact. The entire goal of this exercise is to bring what we think into line with reality about not only marriage but about every issue of self and life. How do we achieve this goal in a real relationship?

Many think that the Christian life is simply about refusing to do wrong things, but these people enter a tug of war with themselves—and frequently lose—over these wrong behaviors. Why? Because the issue is not simply whether we do something on the "bad" list. The real issue is having real needs and being presented with a false offer to meet real and legitimate needs. Or a sense of need is created for something that is substituted for a legitimate need. Someone may be sold promiscuity as a substitute for true intimacy and love, blessings found in fullness only through God and His plan. God provides the only actual path to meet our deepest needs. If we grasp this, having reasoned our way to this point, we can enthusiastically jettison alternative paths that predictably cause damage, paths whose promised benefits never materialize. This has been Satan's plan from the beginning: to misinform us about what we really need, then offer us his (rebellious) path to get there, the path leading directly away from our best lives. If, instead, we cease to be fixated on what we have been told will meet our needs and take a clear-eyed look at our actual deepest needs, then look at the paths we are being offered—God's and "other"—and consider which path is most likely to meet our actual needs, we have now turned from the path toward deception and are walking on the path toward truth. This, again, is the actual definition of "repentance" (Matthew 21:32; Acts 2:38).

When we add in a love relationship to the mix, often our misconceptions about love may be added to our misconceptions about ourselves. If we are in love, or married, we are enjoying life and relationship in ways we never have before. We want to keep the good times rolling. On occasion, we see a few storm clouds on the horizon, but for the most part life is at its best, so any thought of rocking this boat with new and different ideas about ourselves or relationship may sound more risky than helpful. There are two potential paths we can take at this point. We can keep doing more of what we have been doing or we can move toward truth. Truth can be a tricky thing in a relationship. Sometimes we do not want to hear the truth; sometimes the other person does not want to hear the truth. Sometimes what we think is true is only part of the truth, or we know that what we are hearing, that the other person is convinced is true, is at best only partly true.

Most can spot the impropriety of promiscuity, but our "normal" ways of relating are filled with unloving approaches that seem normal to us, even beneficial. These represent all the little compromises we make because they seem comfortable, useful, even to represent the truth about the best way to get along with others. But suddenly, out of nowhere, our spouse takes exception to one of these ways of being. What now?

There are two realities to keep in mind: the difference between affirmed truth in both parties and actual truth; and the difference between love and manipulation. We have noted that someone's truth may not be true, though to them it certainly feels like truth. We have noted that connection plus something untrue is ultimately manipulation at some level. People in close relationship, taught by our world how to relate, will manipulate each other frequently to get what they want and even manipulate each other in a misguided attempt to help each other. And for those who have not been in close, loving relationships, simply receiving attention, especially intense romantic attention, may be misinterpreted as love. Real romantic love is intense, but intensity may not be real love. We can superimpose God's template for love over someone's behavior to assess their heart toward us.

True love is an exercise in only truth. True love is described in God's Word, and it is built by faithfulness to our covenant. If two people share a vision for discovering and living out truth, if their life together is a journey that pursues truth, true love will be built along the way. We can settle for what we have and hope it works out—which it may, to a point—or we can devote ourselves to finding God's path for each of us and for our marriage. The difference? One is a pursuit of the status quo; the other is a pursuit of truth, through which we find God and His path. We have only to match what we believe to be true, or what feels like truth to us, with what God has revealed to us as truth. It is that simple. The challenge is sorting out truth from the pretenders. In this we are greatly aided by having two people focused on this task together instead of just one. Why? Because my wife is unlikely to be comfortable with my affirmed truths that are comfortable and familiar to me and yet not true. And vice versa. We serve as a mirror for the other, hopefully one reflecting a true image. This has been one of our greatest gifts to each other for decades. Of course, one must first get over the emotional impact of being wrong. Which is good for us to do, for one thing this discussion should have already highlighted is that we are wrong far more than we realize. And it is far, far better to realize how and when we are than to remain clueless. Truth builds life, while being clueless only builds a false sense of security, and perhaps a false sense of superiority.

> If our goal changes from being right to getting things right, what direction will our relationship take?

As we work through each issue we will encounter with and within each other in the intimacy of marriage, if we make the search for truth/love our main objective, what is not our objective? Getting our way, pursuing our advantage, winning a debate, or defending things in ourselves that need to change? If our goal changes from being right to getting things right, what direction will our relationship take?

Another problem we encounter if we get a clear look at our real needs—to give and receive love, along with intimacy, protection, security, connection, and all the other blessings of covenant—is that we may see no way that the person in the mirror can have these things. We must settle for second-best because of who and what we are. We cannot be these good things ourselves, and thus we cannot expect them from someone else. Recognizing this reality is the first step on another path it is vital we travel if we are to find our best lives. This is the path of personal growth and transformation. It is likely that the person looking back at you from the mirror does not have the character, habits, skills, perception, wisdom, and understanding to offer or to receive what is needed to have the best experiences of life and relationship: true and perfect love. And this perception may be totally accurate in this moment, spot on. But God has a plan for your life that includes changing you into precisely the person who can do these things, who can build this quality of relationship, who can have this life. God loves us where we are but does not leave us where we are.

God has a directive to us that is stated in but a few words in Romans 12. We reviewed this verse last chapter, but I want us to meditate on it again—and three others—here as well. To explain this verse in a way where one can begin to understand its point and application takes several pages. To apply this verse takes a lifetime. It is through applying this verse that our thoughts, beliefs, values, attitudes, goals, desires, dreams, aspirations, priorities, habits, feelings, character, views of ourselves, views of life, and views of God change. Applying this one verse will do more to alter the course of our lives in a good and rewarding direction than any other direction we have received from God. In fact, carrying out all the other directions we have from God, including loving Him with our whole heart, and everything else that flows from this, including loving our partners in the Covenant of Marriage and everything else that flows from that, depends on our mind being transformed as God instructs. We have just seen a road map for doing this in relation to marriage. (We will consider the same road map for a relationship with God in the next volume in this series.)

Be therefore transformed by the renewing of your minds,
that you may prove what the will of God is, that which is good,
and acceptable, and perfect.
ROMANS 12:2

This is my command, that you love one another.
JOHN 15:17

You will know the truth, and the truth will set you free.
JOHN 8:32

Anyone who sins is a slave to sin.
JOHN 8:34

From what does Jesus describe being set free? From the slavery of attachment to the plans of the enemy of God. We accept the enemy's plan through our power of affirmation and dissent. We depart from the enemy's plan and attach ourselves to God's plan by using this same power. It is true that God does many things so we may become free from the influence of Satan's plan. He provides the truth to us, and in the New Covenant He provides us with His life, new life as a new creature, which breaks the power of sin over us . . . in one respect. But sin (or executing the plan of the enemy to rebel against God) can still hold us captive if we affirm any of the ideas upon which this plan is based. From this we can see that our power of affirmation and dissent has even more impact than almost anyone realizes—anyone, that is, except God. This is why He instructs us to put on His ways like a piece of clothing, and to take off those of His enemy (Colossians 3:9). If this transition was accomplished by entering a relationship with Him, God would not have issued His written instructions to Christians. This transition, this renewing of our minds, is something we are charged to do by God. God went to considerable trouble over thousands of years to lay down and preserve His Word for use in this process.

GOD'S COMPREHENSIVE PLAN FOR CHARACTER DEVELOPMENT

We do not need a five-thousand-page curriculum for life development. We just need to get up every morning and deal with what comes to us each day, reviewing it in light of a several-thousand-year-old written collection of truth. The caveat is that best results only come to those who recognize, as they make their way through life, the imperative of growth and transformation. God has provided us a lifetime to grow. This is good, because there are myriad aspects of character to address and a rich mine of growth in the Scriptures to explore. It takes even more than a lifetime to complete this project, but in God's plan we have all of that.

The doorway to our mind, our heart, our character, and the course of our lives is *what we choose to believe is true*. We have just discussed the path by which any of these beliefs can be revised as needed. Therefore, if your life is not going in the direction you want it to go, what step might you take that will have the greatest possible impact? On your mind, heart, will, character, and life?

THESE TWO EXERCISES APPLED TO THE VOWS OF HOLY MATRIMONY

Adults often go back to school to get education that will advance a career. People make time to tackle these studies because they have a clear goal and a strong desire to meet that goal. This combination impacts one's daily schedule. If we have children, we do not forget to feed them for days at a time. Why? Because they need food several times a day. This is necessary for them, and for us to attend to as parents. So we do. What if we view our marriage as something for which continuing education is important, for which daily tasks, including learning, is crucial for advancement? God has given us wonderful curriculum material in Scripture, but in regard to marriage the points are scattered throughout a large book. What if this same curriculum was in a place more easy to access? This is how I have utilized the vows of marriage. This list of behaviors, along with the corresponding and essentially identical list of behaviors that comprise the duties, responsibilities, and obligations of covenant, are a wonderful way to build our marriage. We must only look at each element and learn to apply it in various ways in our marriage.

If we want to build the best long-term marriage, the most passionate ongoing love affair, deepest friendship, and the most intimate relationship, we must realize that our own character growth is

> We literally cannot know another person more deeply than we know ourselves. Nor can we value others in a real sense any more than we value ourselves.

the strongest move we can make to build such a relationship. Further, the more we understand and appreciate our own identity, the more we value the image of God in ourselves and develop the potential inherent in our unique identity, the more we are capable of recognizing and valuing the unique identity of another person and helping them develop their own potential. We literally cannot know another person more deeply than we know ourselves. Nor can we value others in a real sense any more than we value ourselves. People with a low self-image are afraid to honestly look at the people next to them, much less deeply value other people. Thus, as we discover and build upon the truth of who we are, we also lay the foundation for a more deep and rich relationship and a better marriage.

WHAT IS THE PATH TO A PASSIONATE LIFETIME ROMANCE?

Someone is joined to you in a covenant relationship. While romance is the heart of this relationship—the fuel, the energy that drives many of the other things that are designed to happen—there are many other moving parts. The two of you are literally holding each other's mind, heart, and very life—in the largest possible sense—in each other's hands in the same way that a surgeon with a knife in his hand, standing over your exposed brain, holds your mind and your life in his hands. The implications of things done by a surgeon to a patient are not far off from the impact two people have on each other in a covenant relationship. There are probably more accomplished surgeons in this country than people really good at marriage, only because people seem to take surgical training more seriously than people take preparation and training for their marriages—for reasons not at all clear given the role marriage plays in our lives.

Let us think for a moment about the following concepts in relationship to surgery or to a marriage: freedom, spontaneity, creativity, adaptability, skill, knowledge, responsibility, and success. The image we have of ourselves in a romantic relationship is all about expressing our deepest selves in a rapturous dance of self-revelation, self-expression, and transparency; in a delightful intimacy of mind, heart, spirit, and body, played out in the routines of day-to-day life. How does this kind of romance relate to, say, surgery?

What many do not understand is that surgery is not a cookbook, routine thing. Instead, it is a highly creative expression of the surgeon's abilities. Each operation, even the most simple, is a unique adventure. Each is a first-ever-in-history combination of factors: the individual's reason for surgery; symptoms and other factors; the patient's overall medical condition, understanding, expectations and emotional coping capacity; along with each patient's unique anatomy, physical response to surgery, capacity to heal, and other factors that may occur during or following surgery, like a stroke or an infection. Each encounter between patient and surgeon is not unlike an encounter between husband and wife over a large expenditure, a job loss, a medical issue, or myriad other challenges we face in life. Each of these adventures is unique, made of many elements, choices, viewpoints, biases, habits, and coping strategies.

> Each of these adventures is unique, made of many elements, choices, viewpoints, biases, habits, and coping strategies.

Some surgeons get good results more consistently than others. And, obviously, many people do not make it through the training process. Regardless of how talented a person is, how smart, how good with their hands, there is one thing more than any other that determines how good one will be as a surgeon. That is one's devotion to the training process, to learning every detail that might matter in someone's care. In the case of a surgeon, this means spending ten years or so pursuing this training process with single-minded devotion for one hundred hours or more per week. If you are watching an accomplished surgeon operate, it is much like watching a virtuoso musician perform or a high-level athlete in competition. It looks so creative, so spontaneous, so easy for them. And it is.

But this is only because that person has built the foundation within themselves of knowledge, character, habit, and many other things that allow this moment to happen. It is an odd paradox that the freedom to most creatively—and effectively—approach a problem comes from disciplined mastery of the fundamentals, and this is achieved only by a process of training. This is true for athletes, musicians, surgeons, scientists, and . . . for two people in love. If two people are in love, they are assured of a great experience—at least for a while. But only those who take marriage seriously enough to get really good at it achieve happily-ever-after.

GOD'S PLAN FOR MARRIAGE IN REVIEW

This is God's plan for marriage, at least in the detail this volume allows. We have seen how God joins us together and how He informs us to be toward each other. We have seen how He matches His plan of covenant to our hearts, encouraging us to express the love we feel toward each other in all the ways true love can be expressed. We see how God protects our hearts of love toward each other, how He teaches us to live with each other in ways that cause hearts to grow stronger toward each other over a lifetime. We see how God matches our rough edges, and our inappropriate tolerance for them, with a partner who can help us identify areas needing growth and transformation in the close quarters of marriage. We see how God matches the mechanisms He built within for growth with the loving influence of our partner to maximize our opportunity to grow to maturity, and to aid our partner in doing so. We see the beautiful foundation this maturity lays for raising a family.

If we are going to buy a particular vehicle, to make it a part of our family—or, in this case, to buy into building our family according to a particular plan—we want to know all about performance. What can this thing really do? We hear the sales pitches, see attractive glimpses of it skidding across our TV screen, but before we buy something even as expensive as a car we want to check the performance. Does this offering perform as promised? Much more so if we are talking about the all-in investment of life that is required by God's plan. If we want to invest our all in the very, very best . . . is this the one? Unfortunately, you cannot take a well-built covenant relationship for a test drive. You have to build your own. But I can offer an extensive description of what such a relationship is like. In the next chapter we will look at a number of the characteristics of the only marriage I have full access to that is built on this foundation: our marriage, with most of the potentially embarrassing details redacted. I hope. Maybe I should have let Holley proof this before we sent it to the printer . . .

QUESTIONS FOR THOUGHT

1. What is God's ultimate goal for our transformation?

2. When we encounter a conflict or other issue, what questions should we ask ourselves? Where does "Who is to blame for this?" fit into this list? If our primary goal is not to assign blame, what is our primary goal?

3. If I said that, in a conflict scenario, we are supposed to be a clear and loving mirror for our partner, would you agree or disagree? If I said that solving, though important, is not as important as building a *pattern of building* in each partner, would you agree or disagree? If I said that allies solve and build better than adversaries, would you agree? What, then, is God's plan to address problem areas in the relationship?

4. It is often challenging at first to connect our behavior, attitude, priority, and the like to a specific affirmed idea. Does the list of diagnostic questions in this chapter offer any help in this search? It is often helpful to ask ourselves: *What must I be thinking if I am acting this way?* Ferreting out these ideas is a skill like any other—it grows over time with use. How important might it be for you to develop this skill?

5. If we want to base our lives on truth, how important would it be to learn to use the five-step process to build truth into our lives? How do we search out actual truth for this project? Where do the Scriptures fit? How do we find the specific truth we are looking for in Scripture? What other tools might be useful? What role do prayer and a growing relationship with God play in this process of transformation? What role might a trusted friend, accountability partner, or mentor play in this process?

6. What impact in your own life might subtracting—disaffirming—certain ideas play? Can you get a sense for how branding as lies the reasons we use for counterproductive behaviors can unplug the power of these behaviors over us? Can you get a sense for how addressing our reasons for doing things we might be

tempted to do—like the online watching of people do things we should not be watching people do—can strengthen our resolve to avoid such things? Can you see how continuing to strengthen our reasons for doing good things, and our reasons for not doing destructive things (to the point that we are simply unwilling to do a particular counterproductive thing)—in essence, developing a conviction on such a matter—will offer our lives and relationships great benefit over time?

7. If I said that one of our most important roles as a follower of Christ, and as a husband or wife, is to form convictions on one issue after another about our views, attitudes, behaviors, values, priorities—about ourselves, our spouse, our marriage, and our God and our relationship with Him—would you agree or disagree? If you agree, what could you do over the next year to build this pattern into your life?

8. What is the relationship between developing convictions and becoming wholehearted about an issue, or a person, or your marriage? If this is the path to becoming wholehearted (which it is), what is the relationship between becoming wholehearted and building love-for-a-lifetime, our happily-ever-after?

9. What is the relationship between developing a pattern of convictions and growing and transforming our character—thus fully developing us and forming us into the people we were intended to become?

10. Is there any other path by which our character, life, and marriage can be built to their potential? If you believe, as I do, that building our lives on truth and weaving this truth into every fiber of our being and every aspect of our conduct is the only path to the fully transformed life that God offers us, under His guidance, what can you do over the next year to build this pattern and position it as one of your highest priorities?

CHAPTER NINE

The Kind of Marriage That Covenant Builds

Marriage is an "all-in" kind of thing. God has a comprehensive plan, but we must fully embrace this plan and live it out for best results. What happens if we do?

TO BUILD A RELATIONSHIP WE MUST FIRST BUILD OURSELVES

Before we look at specific issues of relationship, I want to reflect on how my relationship with my wife has been built. What does a really good marriage look like as it is growing? As I look at my wife and myself now, then look back through time to the beginning of our relationship, several things stand out. First, we are the same "us" as people, and as a couple, as we were when our covenant was created on our wedding night. But we have also changed and grown in many ways, some fairly striking, reflecting the growth of our character and more full development of the potential inherent in our identities. And in this we have grown together. That is, we have both been on a journey of growth and transformation, consciously and aggressively pursued. As we have been together in the process of growing, we have grown together. We thought a lot of each other while we were dating, to the point that we wanted to marry. But now, decades later, we know each other to the very depths of our souls, and we like each other and enjoy each other now more than ever. How did this happen?

From the day we met we followed God's plan of covenant in the ways we treated each other and in respecting our physical purity. Our relationship grew to the point that marriage was the desired next step. We conducted our wedding and initiated our covenant according to God's pattern. We have now consciously followed this same path for decades, not perfectly, but sincerely and consistently. And overall my relationship with Holley has been by far the most fun thing I have ever done. As well as the most exciting, rewarding, delightful—I could go on, but the point is that following God is far more delight than drudgery. Our lives have been devoted mostly to growing and developing, not to ongoing trouble-shooting, backtracking, and rebuilding. This does not mean we have skated through life on smooth ice. We have had many serious challenges and issues to confront over time and continue to have the same life issues other families face. We have seven children, so there is little we have not seen. But throughout everything in our lives, the love and the relationship built between Holley and me has provided everything we needed to weather every storm, climb every mountain, meet every challenge, make the most of every opportunity, and enjoy the quiet stillness and beauty of God's creation as we go and as we follow Him. We have extensively field-tested every concept in this book. God's plan, in sum, produces exactly what we might expect of God's plan—a remarkably blessed marriage and life.

I frankly struggle a bit as I describe our lives, because on the one hand many may find it hard to relate to something that sounds consistently wonderful in a marriage. But this is an accurate description of our marital experience. What is behind this experience is more effort, heart, focus, and persistence than anything else in life. We have made our marriage, behind our relationships with God, the center of our lives—very busy, full, and productive lives. I really do need to speak truthfully here, that if a couple devotes themselves to living out God's plan, and has an accurate understanding of that plan, in conjunction with the truth that God has graciously provided for us, while life will never be free of trouble, challenge, adversity, and disappointment, on the other hand we can face all these realities constructively, play as positive a role as we can, and be at peace in the midst of whatever comes at us. Or, we can delight in the wonders and glories of God and His creation in the middle of the Italian countryside, as we did last month while visiting a daughter and son-in-law who live in Italy. Our outer life looks good in some ways, challenged in others. But our inner lives and our experience of living seem quite different from most people around us. Realizing this, I was motivated to write this book, to explain something in life that is right there for the taking: a life planned and guided by God, provisioned by the Creator of the universe, overseen by the Omnipotent one, side-by-side with the true Lover of our souls . . . who then provided a covenant partner for each of us, a partner who has been truly amazing.

We have had adversity, challenges, and struggles. And at points, rather than an issue turning out well we ended up with the worst-case scenario, the last thing we would ever want to see. But looking back, we have noted something truly amazing. From the aftermath of these "worst" things has grown some of the greatest blessings in our lives. God was not using these things to torment or devastate us, but to prepare us or to direct us, ultimately into a place of blessing. We just had to continue to trust Him and follow Him through the process. This pattern, once recognized, has been a source of great strength and peace. For when the next threat looms on the horizon, we now know that it is not actually the threat it appears to be. Either it will fade or come full force. Either way our lives will be blessed in the end. It is extraordinarily helpful for our hearts to know this, not as some abstract slogan, but as a proven and consistent reality in our lives.

Life is a journey, and a journey is simply one step after another. On any given day we made decisions according to certain principles, rules, and priorities—all drawn from God's Word and from the other sources we have been discussing that reflect His Word. Almost never did it feel, on any given day, like something dramatic was happening to us or in our lives. We were simply living in the same world everyone else inhabits, dealing with the same stuff. And we had no shortage of problems, struggles, and pain. But slowly, gradually, sometimes reluctantly, we followed God's pattern in this way day after day. We talked about our insights, lessons learned, approaches, and outcomes. We worked hard learning how to learn. And we were always on the same page in terms of the most important priorities: obeying and pleasing God, then loving each other. We simply had to figure out how to do this day by day in the myriad issues of life. And we did not get everything right, any more than you will. But a mistake is not a failure, it is just another learning opportunity. If, that is, a couple approaches mistakes in the right way—instead of using them for leverage or hiding them to polish an image.

> We talked about our insights, lessons learned, approaches, and outcomes. We worked hard learning how to learn.

Recently, two things struck me as I thought about our journey. First, how gradual a thing is the process of change. Second, how far one moves without realizing it—until one looks back to where it all started. The things God asks of us are not heroic, painful sacrifices. They are a lifetime of practical, commonsense things that have good outcomes, all of which result from a few upfront decisions. They are bite-sized meals and a steady progression. They are far easier in the long run than doing damage control or trying to rebuild a wrecked life or marriage. Through a bit more effort on the front end, this path is progressively easier the further one goes.

Being in love, feeling the full intensity of delight, knowing that we literally cannot live without each other, these merely buy the ticket for the journey. No worthwhile journey ends without going somewhere. The key to happily-ever-after is to be on the path ordained by the One who created us, who loves us more than we can image, who walks with us each step of the way, teaching and shepherding us. He built the reward system within our hearts, and He built the reward system we will experience for eternity. One of the most surprising things to me about our life is where God's leadership has taken us. So many opportunities have come our way that I never saw coming, some of which remain huge and wonderful elements of our current life, or have been stepping-stones to other good things. When it says, "Now, to Him who is able to do immeasurably more than all we ask or imagine . . . " (Ephesians 3:20), I truly understand what Paul is saying, even in this life. We have been on quite a journey already, and seem to be just getting started.

MOVING FROM IN LOVE TO TRUE LOVE

The head-over-heels-can't-live-without-you-for-the-rest-of-my-life relationship we had when we gave ourselves to each other in marriage was characterized by a few simple things. But marriages rapidly expand and grow, expressing new functions that progressively express this joined couple into the universe. True love is built by decisions, first and foremost about how these two people relate to each other. If the flush and passion of attraction and anticipation grow into being and doing the loving things called for by covenant, feelings will continue to grow.

But one must realize that the experience of love is not the end-point of God's plan, nor should this be our focus. It is a by-product, an outcome of building the marriage in certain ways. A person does not exist purely for the purpose of feeling certain good things about life and self. A person feels these things as he or she wisely develops the potential within, building self and building what he or she is capable of building, while conducting himself or herself toward others in certain ways. A delightful experience of life comes from building a life worth feeling this way about. The thrill we first felt looking in each other's eyes we still feel in a more profound way years later as we look in each other's eyes and recount our journey or plan the next step. The delights of romantic touch are far deeper and more profound, as this now draws from decades of going and growing together. Physical intimacy, properly understood, is a reflection of the sum of the relationship, past and present; if it is this, the power and satisfaction only grow over time, in this and other realms of the relationship.

HOW DO WE FIND A GOOD COVENANT PARTNER?

This is admittedly difficult. But finding the right partner is vastly less difficult than finding the wrong partner. If you want to consciously build a relationship on covenant principles and realities, you want to be sure that someone has a similar understanding and wants to follow this course as much as you do. This likely means studying this area together extensively and growing together in this understanding well before you are on the way to the altar. And given what will be required, character obviously matters, perhaps more than some of the other criteria common in our culture. Like "hot." Physical attraction is important; being able to grow together, and to grow at all, is more important. Holley and I started these patterns in our relationship as we started getting to know each other, and were married eighteen months later, so we had already seen each other in action in a number of spheres, including relationship-building and troubleshooting. We were very much on the same page about building a relationship. How did I find someone like this? I was not planning to meet Holley. I was planning to attend a church service, and she happened to be there. There is a God. That reality is important at every step in this recruiting and decision-making process.

Initially, my wife and I checked each other out in many ways, getting each other in front of trusted friends and family members, meeting each other's friends, and asking lots of questions—all of this in addition to having a strong heart response to each other that suggested we were a good match. I actually had an encounter with God a few nights after our first date in which it was shown to me that Holley would be my wife. At this point, I knew almost nothing about her, and this revelation was a bit shocking. Nevertheless, we both did due diligence. We built our relationship slowly, addressing one issue at a time in depth.

One does not need to be married to treat someone in the loving ways God details. Holley was scrupulous to do exactly what she said she would do, like to call or be somewhere at a given time, or to take care of something. Our relationship quickly became an intense competition, but not in the usual sense. Each of us did our best to out-bless and out-love the other. We had many discussions about covenant and God's definition of love, applying these truths and encouraging each other in these things. Even so, marriage was a much more powerful thing than we anticipated, fortunately in the best way possible. We believe, because we did build so consciously and carefully upon God's plan, that He simply showered blessings upon us. We have every confidence that He will do the same for you.

I should issue a warning at this point: many people get married thinking that marriage will improve an already troubled relationship. That it will either better motivate or somehow change the other party into a good husband or wife. And the transformation that accompanies entering covenant may seem to support this hope. But if people are not willing to grow, evidenced by character that is far from that needed to be significantly faithful to a marriage covenant, a wedding is much more likely to reveal even more shortcomings than to resolve the ones already seen.

Many people confuse attention, connection, enthusiasm, and passion with love. They are enjoying more attention from someone than they have ever had, and perhaps having more fun than they've ever had. But if there are also behaviors or attitudes totally out of sync with God's definition of love, and if the other person's "right" to behave in these ways outweighs his or her heart to love and their obligation to learn to love, a marriage with this person will not sit on a foundation on which the kind of relationship we are describing can be built.

If someone wants to marry you, make sure their viewpoints on marriage mesh with yours, and that both of yours mesh with God's. Look at the major areas of responsibility in covenant and make sure that the other person's character has matured to the point that they have a good chance of fulfilling these commitments. Make sure they are willing to learn more about how to love instead of insisting that you embrace a flawed version of love. See that a person you might consider marrying is committed to God's plan for life in general. See that they are capable of dealing with their own shortcomings and problems and of dealing well with yours. Are the two of you bringing out the best in each other and supporting the best in each other?

Do behavior and attitudes toward each other already reflect covenant principles? You have now seen a comprehensive definition of love. Are both of you committed to this as your goal for the relationship, and are you (already) growing in this and growing together through this?

Here is one more vantage point on partner selection, illustrated by a pastor's comment in the Sunday school class where Holley and I met. The pastor said to write down every quality one wanted in a mate, and every deficiency we were aware of in ourselves, areas for which we would seek another's strength to offset our weakness. He instructed us to take that list and then go out and *become* that person we wanted to marry because of their strengths. Only after we have become a person we would want to marry, he said, should we seek someone to marry. We do not want or need someone to complete us, for no one can do that, and we do not want our attraction to be based on neediness. Instead, we want to see the joining of two healthy and competent lives, two people with lives that merit being shared. In other words, devote yourself to becoming the covenant partner someone has dreamed of finding.

RELATIONSHIP CHARACTERISTICS PRODUCED BY COVENANT

MEETING DEEPEST NEEDS IN COVENANT

If we are to love another in covenant, we must know their needs. This is not the same as having some sense of our own needs and doing for others what we would value. Every human has a unique set of emotional needs. There are perhaps fifteen or twenty different needs a person might have at the deepest level, depending on how one counts. From this list each individual will have three or four that are most important, their unique set of core needs. Gary Chapman has a wonderful introduction into this realm in his books on Love Languages. Some people need physical touch; some do not like to be touched. One needs quality time, another is deeply touched by a gift, one needs affirming words, and the next person may most appreciate acts of service. Some like to reveal their hearts, others prefer to listen. In marriage we have the time, access, and mandate to learn to love our spouse, not just in general terms, and not just in terms that might mean something to us. We are to get to know our covenant partner at these deeper heart levels and love them in ways that mean most to them.

How does someone know the specific things to do or not do to love someone? The first skill to develop is simply learning to ask and listen. Often, however, people have never had someone this close before. They may not know what they need or what they want; much of this process is trial and error. We observe the reaction of our beloved. The key thing to understand is that, though two are in covenant, the individuality of the deepest needs of each is maintained. What we are left with is the joy of discovery. We may not discover the things that mean the most to our beloved right away, or even for a while. But what happens to hearts when someone really makes the effort to get it right, to listen, to observe, and to more and more deeply understand?

Over time, as the two come to know each other at this level and continue to explore ways to bless each other, aside from the delights of someone doing things that really feel good to us, we begin to feel like we are truly known in the depths of our hearts, truly appreciated, truly valued.

UNCONDITIONAL ACCEPTANCE

Acceptance can be an interesting dance in a relationship, even in a marriage. How much effort have we expended in life trying to make ourselves acceptable to other people? Yet how often do we experience being fully accepted by another person? This is our most basic need in relationship, the very first step on the path to being loved. In a romantic relationship it seems, at first glance, that acceptance would be a given since this is one of the foundations of love; instead, in most relationships a foundation of insecurity forms as each is trying to decide if this is "the one," and is also awaiting this answer from the other. Once the proposal is made and accepted, though, this should settle the issue.

But in many people's minds there remains a back door in the relationship. When two are married, all uncertainty should be gone if one understands covenant, right? Instead, with the contractual basis of most marriages this evaluation and uncertainty continues indefinitely. Here God's plan for marriage and the world's (Satan's) distortion of marriage diverge most sharply. Many people have developed a style of relating to others that uses withholding acceptance and approval to gain leverage, a la the "competing kingdoms" model discussed earlier, and this strategy will find its way into their romance. People may hold something from the past over their spouse, or they may find fault with some attribute of character, or appearance, or something from a person's background—pretty much any way in which people can be unfavorably compared to others will serve this purpose. This unfavorable comparison to some ideal will be used to devalue one person in the other's bid for dominance.

Another issue of acceptance can occur: someone's deeply held belief that they are not acceptable. Someone, at some point, told him or her that they could not be loved due to a flaw perceived or real. The truth is, acceptance and love are not things purchased, not even with perfection. But it is easy to give this lie the benefit of the doubt and internalize this view, especially as a child. People with this belief are perpetually insecure. They view themselves as "not enough" in some key way, and they view their relationships as always in jeopardy as a result. No matter how such people are reassured, their insecurity remains. Why? Because their sense of security is based on something they can never achieve: perfection. Do you recognize the false but embraced "truth" here? And there are other ways acceptance may

> The truth about who we really are can set us free from these lies.

go missing, either in reality or perception. These all represent issues of identity as we discussed earlier, and they can only be dealt with effectively at that level. The truth about who we really are can set us free from these lies.

The genius of God is displayed in covenant as He destroys these dynamics, removes identity-leverage, and solves insecurity, if one only understands the nature of covenant. The reason we enter a covenant is that we chose to love a person and desire to join lives with them. We did not pay for this right with something we have done or might do. This represents a choice by each person to give and receive the fullness of another's life. The most fundamental reality of all is that one is accepted, fully and completely, once and until death do us part. There is nothing further to prove. The choice has already been made. What could be a more secure position? Unless one does not fully understand this position.

Covenant is the real and logical basis for *unconditional love*. Acceptance has already been offered, vowed, physically and spiritually transacted, and therefore fully accomplished. Striving after acceptance while in covenant is like rising early each morning and begging the sun to rise. More than unnecessary, this reflects a total misunderstanding of reality. One cannot develop the true potential of marriage while one is misdirecting effort begging the sun to rise by soliciting ongoing reassurance. Any posturing to the effect that the other person is unacceptable is what? On a par with asserting that one is still single even though they are married. In Philippians 3:16 we are instructed, "Only let us live up to what we have already attained." In other words, we should make every effort to be worthy of the acceptance already extended to us. Insecurity can be appropriately replaced with confidence, poise, and graciousness. Fear can be replaced by understanding and concern for others. Shame for one's supposed disqualifying faults can be replaced by gratitude for being made in the image of God, and loved by Him, and now by one's covenant partner. As we experience and offer complete acceptance of each other over time, there is a rock-solid security in each other and in the relationship that allows other things to begin to grow, within ourselves and within the relationship.

RECIPROCITY

In God's design, covenant is mutual and reciprocal. Relationships grow deeper and faster when two people are trying to out-try, out-understand, and out-bless each other. Relationships are always a balance between giving and taking, but in some relationships one person is all give while the other is all take. A lack of reciprocity violates the very nature of covenant. This is not the relationship God intends. This pattern calls for growth on the part of both parties.

At the same time, the vows we made to love the other person are not contingent on the behavior or responses of the other party. For a time, or in a given situation, one may not be able to return blessings or meet the other's needs. This is where vows about "better or worse, sickness and health" come into play. Temporary or permanent circumstances may present opportunities for growth of one virtue or another in either party. The interesting thing about God's plan is that our vows include every virtue necessary to maintain and grow the relationship on the part of either party in any and every circumstance. There is no "not in my job description" here, because, though God has laid out a few roles for male and female in Scripture, and through society has overlaid this with more role-specific duties that people either sign onto or vigorously oppose, consider all of this in light of covenant—that each is in the other. Thus, either party can pick up slack or fully assume any responsibility at any point. This approach allows the couple to function—and to develop potential and abilities—across the widest range of life.

If a person's approach to their partner and the relationship is "whatever it takes, whatever is needed, whatever I am, or can become" when facing a small task or a major challenge, if each has the work ethic and willpower to do whatever he or she is doing as well as each can, a tremendous teamwork will develop. If they vow to leave nothing undone, not only will all the necessary things get done, a teamwork will grow that allows the couple to take on new opportunities, trust that their partner will come through, and trust that they will come through when needed.

HONORING

The word *honor* has many facets. We have talked about it as the crowning virtue from which true love flows. It means to esteem someone most highly. It means to give gifts that speak of someone's consummate worth or to publicly proclaim their value as a person. Honor also means to be faithful to something, to follow through and accomplish something committed or purposed. And there are other shades of meaning. We are to do everything we can to honor our beloved in all these ways.

A marriage is holy ground before the Lord. Our mate is a sacred trust before God, one we are given the privilege and joy of knowing and loving. We are to protect, defend, uphold, build up, proclaim, expend every resource for, develop every potential in, and exercise all care to be devoted to this one whose ultimate value resides in being made in the image of God. We must be very careful as we interact with our mate and as we discuss and depict our mate to others; we must be careful to offer him or her our very best; and we must prayerfully, with great gentleness and consideration, encourage and inspire him or her to be their best. Our eyes must be focused on transformation in the face of imperfections, replacing those imperfect areas with God's character according to God's plan. God has a plan and a purpose for each spouse, and also for each family. The ultimate expression of our honor, and of honoring each other and our marriage, is to fulfill God's plan and purpose for each individual and for the family as a whole.

In regard to honoring, there is particular attention focused on the man in the leadership role delegated to him by God. The man is instructed to love his wife (Ephesians 5:25), and the woman is instructed to respect her husband (Ephesians 5:33). Not everything about either will be honorable, worthy of respect, or easy to love. And while problems must be addressed, and honesty is part of a covenant relationship, still God desires that as much as possible the two lift each other up. This is in stark contrast to the world, which teaches us to tear each other down because of these same imperfections. We must understand these two voices, these diametrically opposed instructions on marriage, if we are to prevent the enemy of God from stealing our birthright in covenant by following that enemy's lead.

Honoring each other consistently, in public and in private, creates another aspect of rock-solid security for the couple. Not only will the other person continue to be by one's side, he or she will be there as a best friend, a trusted ally, a loyal partner, and a passionate lover. If one finds that this approach from the other can be relied upon during the greatest challenges, or when one is most vulnerable, something wells up from deep within the heart, a more profound experience of love and being loved. There are two ways our vulnerabilities can be handled in a marriage: God's way or the world's. And we know what the world's way looks like.

HONESTY AND TRUST

We spoke in the first volume in this series of the trust issues in our society, how people reasonably distrust each other because trust must be earned and often it is not. In order for the emotions of love to grow over time, we must trust and respect the other party to the point that we are willing to trust in them and entrust our lives to their care. To continue to build a love for a lifetime, we must conduct ourselves with a level of integrity that is found in very few places in our culture, and we often must learn how to do this. The first thing to understand is the central role that trust plays in every other aspect of a growing relationship, and then to commit to being trustworthy as one of our highest priorities. At the very least the two should make particular efforts to speak truly and accurately so their words can be trusted. This might be one of the most reasonable litmus tests for whether someone is a worthy candidate for marriage. If one cannot trust the words of another, is it reasonable to think of entrusting one's life to that person?

Early in a marriage trust issues invariably arise as two people are getting to know each other at close range. Most of these issues will be simple misunderstandings. If there are issues of substance, as noted earlier, our proper role in covenant is to be the ally of our partner in developing their integrity—and not to play the policeman, judge, or executioner. Over time we must continue to provide a vast array of reasons for the other person to trust us at deeper and deeper levels if the relationship is to reach its potential. If not, we instead provide reasons we should *not* be trusted, and hearts inevitably cool. Trust must be earned, but also offered, and the overall lack of integrity in our culture can certainly create trust issues. Trusting is part evidence, part choice. We must be as careful to trust the trustworthy as we are to distrust those not worthy of our trust.

> Trust must be earned, but also offered, and the overall lack of integrity in our culture can certainly create trust issues. Trusting is part evidence, part choice.

Respect and trust are two of the largest foundation stones of a growing love relationship. If this foundation is damaged, emotional communion—*trusting in* each other—will be wounded. The key for both parties is to use the close proximity of marriage to pursue truth, honesty, and integrity in all things. We must always be mindful of maintaining the trust of our covenant partner. Trust is far easier to maintain than to rebuild.

If each does build this foundation, if situations are described accurately, if people do what they say they will do, if people accurately convey their viewpoints and motives, if their words and actions are not only strictly accurate, but powers of attention are used to offer grace to each other and to portray each other in the most favorable and constructive way possible—that is, if it is proven over time that one can trust not only the factual accuracy of another, but their intentions (their love)—then the two can begin to trust each other at progressively deeper levels. At the time of marriage, the two had gained each other's trust, but the things to be trustworthy about were actually few in contrast to the wide range of revelations and issues within covenant. Once trust across this realm is based on experience rather than hope, another level of confidence and trust is experienced. The other's faithfulness, and one's own, becomes a settled question within the relationship; this in turn allows even more things to grow within each person and between the two.

TRANSPARENCY

We all have our secrets, don't we? Many people are raised thinking they have a right to privacy that is absolute, that people can be in their lives only by invitation, and only where invited. Their rooms and cellphones are places where no one has the right to intrude or observe. Often as adults we do not publicly display our true intentions, our real motives, our past mistakes. We often do not make it known that we are conflicted, uncertain, confused, or clueless. And we often hold our most tender and vulnerable issues very close to us, carefully concealing tender or wounded areas. Why? All of this makes perfect sense in our world. The competing kingdoms that surround us will predictably exploit our weaknesses and vulnerabilities. They will gladly gain advantage over us if they know our real intentions, our true motives, or what we really want and need. We have been trained to be anything but transparent by our world, but in covenant these rules change completely.

What does God want to see in regard to transparency? His perfect love, and only His perfect love, allows us to be transparent with Him. We need to understand why this is so. All of us have been taught by our world that acceptance and love are conditional; and we have each somehow concluded that if another could see into the depths of our soul they would see things that would prevent us from being loved. Only when we realize that nothing God sees within us will quench His overwhelming love for us will we dare show Him, or ourselves, the darker sides of ourselves. In fact, does He not already see these things? This is the message of grace. He loves us not because of or in spite of, but *in light* of everything we are—because of who He is. It is also vital to realize that, although He loves us as we are, He does not intend to leave us as we are. Things that need to change do need to change. But we will carefully shield these things from our view if our understanding of His love is flawed. Instead we will put up a flawless image for the world to see, to gain its approval, and we will do as Adam and Eve did before God after they rebelled, covering over our vulnerability before Him and hoping He will not notice.

> This is the message of grace. He loves us not because of or in spite of, but *in light* of everything we are—because of who He is.

To grow out of or to be transformed into something different, we need to participate in the process God has ordained for this purpose. This requires total honesty on our part about our starting point. And it requires that we go through a series of steps in partnership with God to accomplish needed growth and transformation. If God intends that marriage play a central role in our growth and transformation, what will this require of us? We must first be honest about ourselves. We must be transparent, first to God and ourselves. But if we are to be aided by our mate, must we not also be transparent to them? If our marriage is according to the world's model of competing kingdoms, what happens if we reveal our vulnerabilities? But in covenant, with our acceptance a settled question just as God's love for us is a settled question, we can risk revelation of our deepest issues.

This is a process to be sure. Hearing about the unexpected struggles of another may impact the fabric of a relationship. In certain scenarios this might be best done with the guidance and support of a counselor. But for most of the things we conceal, our points of insecurity, our questions and doubts, our mistakes and miscues, the burden we feel by concealing them is far greater than the burden we will impose by revealing them to one who loves us. In covenant all things are shared, including burdens; they are no longer only ours. Now the resources we have to confront issues are no longer only our own, they include the resources of the other party. Thus, the reason we might conceal things, to creating that winning, perfect image for the world or our spouse, now fades in light of God's plan for our growth. This plan requires that we acknowledge our starting point with brutal honesty (on our part, not that of our partner), learn God's goal for us in this area, and begin the process of growth and transformation to get from point A to point B. One of the most important elements of this process is accountability, and this accountability depends on honesty and openness.

We are all surprisingly imperfect, and at the outset we are also part of a world that throws rocks at others for their imperfections. God deeply desires that we move toward several things: becoming real in our own view of ourselves, in our relationship with Him, and with our covenant partner; and that each partner deals constructively with the issues that their covenant partner brings to the mix. In fact, God's goal is that our hearts in covenant reflect the unconditional love He has toward us. There is a learning curve here in all directions, including for our covenant partner, but God's plan will take us up this learning curve quickly if we carefully listen to Him.

There are benefits of pursuing transparency beyond trouble-shooting major issues. Most of the time our motions toward personal concealment are simply habit. We are not really trying to hide anything of significance, we just are not in the habit of disclosing ourselves. We have never been in a relationship where it was important, or perhaps safe, to be transparent. Until now. What God wants is that we know each other and love each other as we actually are. If we can create a zone of personal safety within a marriage so that we can know and really be known, a vast number of benefits flow from this reality.

Here are two. First, we experience being accepted in a new way. We have been formally accepted by the other person as we enter covenant, but this a bit different from experiencing their embrace in full view of our imperfections. Transparency is the most powerful way the other person can demonstrate acceptance of us just as we are, and vice versa. Second, transparency in marriage is not only a fountain of *other*-discovery, but also of self-discovery. If we have been used to not looking closely at many things about ourselves, there are many things we have learned to not see. If we have mostly been playing to the expectations of the people around us, working at image creation, we have not taken the time to explore ourselves to find the many good things—hidden treasures of potential, capacity, talent, desire, and drive that God has placed within us—while we were blinding ourselves to our shortcomings. In our culture, we become simply an image, an avatar, playing for the approval of a hostile crowd.

In covenant, by contrast, we are to aid our partners in building to maturity the life that God has placed within us. Imagine the relief one will feel when he or she can come out of hiding, when that person no longer has to be concerned about what someone else knows or discovers. The energy formerly devoted to crafting our image—and keeping secrets—can be directed toward building lives and character.

> In our culture, we become simply an image, an avatar, playing for the approval of a hostile crowd.

Struggles and potentials are, in one sense, flip sides of the same coin. The more we overcome our weaknesses and vulnerabilities the more we will be able to develop our potential and build our lives. To the extent that our weaknesses and vulnerabilities continue to rule our lives, our potential goes undeveloped and our lives suffer. In covenant this impacts not only ourselves but our partner and family as well. We are loved where we are, but God does not want us to remain there. It is for this purpose, among others, that He developed this plan of relationship. It helps immensely if we shift our view of weaknesses and shortcomings, our partner's and our own, from "threat to our way of life" to "opportunity to build life." As we mentioned earlier, conflict is a doorway to growth. So is self-revelation.

What does this mean in practice? We should strive to be not just technically accurate, but open and honest in all of our communications with our mate. We should try to be fully forthcoming. How do we see a situation, how do we feel about it, how do we see it relating to ourselves? We want to be transparent, totally open for inspection. Again, in covenant there are no zones of privacy, no protected personal spaces. One of the deepest drives within us is simply to be observed by another person ("Mommy, Daddy, watch this!"). What we will find, if we stop playing hide and seek and make ourselves visible and available to our mate, is a new level of meaning and satisfaction even in the most simple things.

In my marriage, simply knowing that Holley knows something is occurring in my life gives meaning to the situation because it is something we now share. This is in contrast to things that may be interesting or fun but are not shared. Somehow these are much less meaningful. This drive to know and be known is most satisfied when two are sharing freely the things in life and the things within themselves. There is truly nothing like having someone you love watch you, and share in your life, and share her life with you as you do the same for her, then explore the deeper meaning of all of these things. Even the little details of daily living can have deep spiritual significance, deep emotional meaning. Walks, ice-cream cones, deer walking through the yard, something said by a child or grandchild, a picture that brings back memories. These shared things are the fuel that keeps the fires of love burning.

Do you remember how Jesus most often taught? In short stories about life situations called parables. He used the most simple of encounters, the most mundane things of life to teach lessons of remarkable depth. If we pursue a course of transparency, guess what else happens? Life itself becomes more transparent, more rich and meaningful. And we see God at work in many ways that had been beyond our view. Why would all this flow from an effort to be transparent? Because we are now jointly committed to sifting through the haze and finding the truth. Transparency, you see, is the opposite of deception—and its mortal enemy. People seek entertainment and virtual reality because actual reality is unsatisfying. Transparency is the foundation for building a reality that is worth inhabiting and sharing.

What is the end point of transparency for each of us? To have nothing to hide, no secrets, nothing in our depths of which we are ashamed. Obviously, this is a process, first of discovering what is within—and our marriages aid this immensely—then dealing with what should not be according to God's plan. As we pursue this course over time, we live without fear of discovery. We have a clean conscience. There is vast power in this, in living a coherent life in harmony with God's Word, in being a person in harmony with God's heart. We speak truth. We live truth. We become—substantially—God's truth. Never perfect, to be sure, but at peace in His loving hands.

SAFETY

God intends our marriages to be places of refuge from the world, places where we can relax, restore, refresh, rebuild, recover, and replenish. The world can be a rough neighborhood from which we need refuge. But is that what home always looks like, a refuge? Sadly, home can be the roughest neighborhood of all. This occurs because the oneness of covenant is not lived out, because competing kingdoms are at war. Home can even be a place where devastating abuse scars and misdirects lives. If we are not living out God's plan, the vacuum is filled with something *not* of God, and this can vary from cold to brutal to criminal.

In covenant, we are to actively create a place of safety for each other. This is the place from which we take on the issues of life and the problems of the world. In marriage, as we are working out things between ourselves and within ourselves, anger is not uncommon, nor is it wrong. Anger is the emotion of problem-solving and protection. This is a part of how God wired us. At the same time, good things can be misused. Our obligation to create a safe haven extends to our anger. When a situation is emotionally charged, this is a call to search out issues, problems, expectations, and solutions. We can feel and express anger, as well as other expressions of urgency and imperative in ways that do not threaten our covenant partner. These emotions exist to urge us to find solutions, and they should be harnessed for their intended purpose. The perversion of the world is to harness one's anger to facilitate an attack, to get one's way, to dominate. Kingdoms not just competing, but at war. Such moves need to be identified by every married person as directly opposing the plan of God for marriage. Ephesians 6:12 says, "Our struggle is not against flesh and blood, but against the rulers, against the authorities, against the powers of this dark world and against the spiritual forces of evil in the heavenly realms." Nowhere is this more true than within a marriage. Our wife or husband is not our enemy or our opponent, but our best and deepest friend, and our marriage is sacred ground. "Be angry, and yet do not sin; do not let the sun go down on your anger" (Ephesians 4:26, New American Standard Bible).

Various things can impact the atmosphere of safety in marriage. Character issues of one can threaten both parties. Anything from carelessness to dishonesty to addictions can create a profound lack of safety for a mate. This should offer added motivation to deal decisively with these shortcomings, to grow up, to properly fulfill one's role in building the relationship.

Another common thing that directly attacks the atmosphere of safety is one spouse sharing disparaging things about the other in public, with friends, or on social media. Any move to share dishonoring information to leverage the other party, to gain sympathy, or for any other reason is a move to publicly dishonor them. While this is common currency in our world, the person who displays marital problems, even if they view themselves as the "innocent party" initially, now becomes a major part of the problem. The way to create safety in the midst of the imperfection of both parties is to jointly approach all such problems in a confidential manner. If the problem is serious enough—abusive, addictive, or criminal behaviors—professional help should be sought immediately. Overall, though, the only things worth sharing in public are successes.

If we do create the safe haven God intends marriage and family to be, we will be much better equipped to meet the challenges of life. We will experience the joys and fulfillment that God offers in relaxation and pleasant diversions, and we will create a place that is not only a refuge, but a sanctuary, holy to God. God will bless ground that is devoted to Him. God knows that we need rest from our struggles. This is why the Sabbath was given to humanity: not only to worship God, but also to allow essential rest. Our homes are intended to fulfill this same role, to be a place of peace and rest, as well as a special place of worship for the One who gave us our families.

SECURITY

Security certainly involves physical, mental, emotional, and other aspects of safety, but it adds the element of the future. In going forward, are things most important to us truly secure? The most fundamental aspect of marital security is full confidence that the other person will be there tomorrow, and every tomorrow, till "death do us part," and that they will remain our ally and friend instead of becoming our enemy. Another major aspect of marital security is knowing what we can trust in regarding the other. Where do they stand and what can we expect from our partner? What capabilities do they actually have, and what is not within their ability?

Beyond this, there are many aspects of security. We save for future needs and wants, we have insurance for untimely death or disability, we invest for retirement needs, and we develop skills that produce the income to support our family. Another element of financial security is matching needs, desires, and income. It is crucial as adults to differentiate needs from wants and to learn to manage resources so that our needs are met; and our wants, if necessary, are deferred, or wisely met when we have a surplus. This is even more important for the finances of a family than for an individual. And finances are a realm where marital teamwork is called for at every level, from setting lifestyle goals and priorities to plans to develop needed income, to expense tracking, to trouble-shooting and crisis management. If the one who typically handles financial matters is incapacitated, temporarily or permanently, the other must be well versed in this realm to step in as needed.

Our culture has shifted to funding lifestyle with debt. "Available credit" is not to be confused with "financial surplus." There is no financial reality that places our future more at risk than significant debt, and no more foolish reason for debt than wanting a more affluent lifestyle than we have developed the skills and character to provide. "Someone else" is not tasked with bankrolling us as adults. This is one of the most fundamental roles of adulthood—earning and managing money—and there is no shortcut to financial security (inasmuch as such security is possible). Jesus spoke more about money and its use than any other topic, because one's financial decisions illustrate so graphically one's values and priorities. We are called on before God to be good stewards of what has been entrusted to us. He owns it all; we are simply entrusted with goods and resources by Him, ultimately for His purposes; or, perhaps, we divert these resources toward other goals, a decision which predictably produces adversity in the future. Here is much fertile ground for character assessment and growth. This is also a realm where transparency is vital. There is no role for a significant expenditure that is concealed from a mate. One must carefully examine any urge to conceal a financial transaction; this should be a red flag to self.

Other elements of security also merit attention. Health is important, so exercise, diet, and appropriate health care are part of building the best future. Building family relationships, being part of a church that reflects the heart and mind of God, living in a place suited to family needs, and many other similar things form our lives. Praying and working toward things that build our best future are a wise use of time. This brings up an element people often do not think about, or to which they do not devote appropriate attention: planning. Particularly in the last few decades, the focus of so many has narrowed to the current moment. Wisdom is seeing the end from the beginning and choosing the course with the best result. The only way we can learn to see the end point is by looking for it. This takes time and thought, and often on the front end it will require consulting more mature and experienced people. Failing to plan is planning to fail.

But there is a deeper question in terms of security, isn't there? Some problems of life are self-inflicted consequences, but some are not. Life is hard, adversity can come out of nowhere, and reversals often cannot be predicted—but are predictably a part of life. Despite all of our efforts, planning, praying, building, and personal development, we will encounter hardship and great loss during our lives, sometimes loss of things that mean the most to us. Is our life over if things we cherish are taken away? If we are to truly secure our future, we must understand what is most important about our future.

My wife and I have noticed through all of the pleasures, challenges, and storms of life that, no matter where we are geographically, our true home is in each other, in our love for each other, and in our love for God. This is our true earthly security, for together we can face things that are much more challenging to face alone. And even the challenges and adversities have added meaning and purpose as we face them together. These things build us, and from *us* flow many of our earthly blessings, even in the midst of these adversities. If everything else in our lives was stripped away, we would simply rebuild together. And if one of us is taken away to our eternal home, the other, in covenant with Jesus, will fulfill his or her purpose here on earth as we await a joyous reunion. Jesus also mentions directing our efforts wisely toward building for eternity versus building temporary things at the expense of eternal things. This is another realm where values can be wisely examined.

> My wife and I have noticed through all of the pleasures, challenges, and storms of life that, no matter where we are geographically, our true home is in each other, in our love for each other, and in our love for God.

In covenant with God our future is truly secure. This relationship secures the most important things about ourselves, giving us a life

227

that extends beyond this earthly life to eternity. At the same time, we must hold with an open hand all our relationships and possessions on this earth, for at some point these will disappear no matter how tightly we grasp them. Compare the unassailable security of a great marriage that has grown out of a deep and growing relationship with God with security that is (falsely) founded on feelings, position, status, money, appearance, fame, or any of the myriad measuring sticks by which people compare themselves with others. Compare it, even, with a marriage with no security based in the afterlife.

One spouse will very likely leave the other behind for a time, perhaps a long time. Even if our marriage is the most wonderful love affair on earth, on this earth it will end. But until it ends, it will be our home and our fortress. God has created this love to be fortress and home and has made our hearts so we can continue to build and grow our love in any circumstance. If, that is, we learn how to love according to God's plan. Our fortress is in each other, with each in the arms of God. This is God's plan.

PERMANENCE

"Until death do us part." This phrase seems to presume on the future in many ways. Life changes, circumstances change, we change. How can we possibly know that we can make good on this vow? Note also that the fulfillment of this vow is not completely within our power. Another person's decision-making is involved. At the same time, God wants us to understand at the outset that loving, and continuing to love, are based on our choice, not our emotional reactions or our in-the-moment view of our best interests. Our love is certainly not some random thing that falls upon us like morning fog, only to disappear as mysteriously and uncontrollably as it appeared. Thus, we vow our lifelong fidelity to each other and trust in God to teach us and shape us so we can love as we have vowed to love.

There is something profound that happens within us when our future rests within the love *and the commitment* of a person to whom we are entrusting our very lives. There is a sense as a single person that we have been waiting for our lives to really begin at some point. As we learn about the reality of covenant this perception makes perfect sense. There is something within us that knows that our future and our future happiness are bound up in this new beginning.

As a single person, we are free to float from one thing to the next, tethered to things only by temporary desires and tenuous promises. But there is a longing to have our lives affixed to something permanent, to build something with meaning and purpose beyond ourselves, something that will endure after we are gone. It is God's plan to provide all of this through the covenant of marriage. What do our hearts most desire? The assurance of another's undying love, someone's vow to pursue happily-ever-after by our side. A great love story would never end with happily-for-awhile.

If two people have made perfectly clear their profound love for each other, this love may survive lengthy periods of separation due to war, sea voyages, grave illness, or other pressing responsibilities. People will wait virtually forever for one they love, one whom they know is doing everything in their power to return to them. This mutual understanding taps into the depths of commitment possible within the human soul. But such endurance is predicated on one thing: knowing someone has chosen us and our love with every fiber of their being. This heart is the true foundation of covenant. Such devotion has been celebrated in poetry and song throughout human history.

On the other hand, people will not wait long for "maybe," "sort of," or "let's see." Our hearts are not stirred to their depths by "We'll try it for a while and see how it goes." There is something about the finality of marriage that clarifies people's intentions: do they really intend to give themselves to another wholeheartedly, or . . . do they want to draw whatever they want from the life of another without offering their own in return? If this commitment is sincerely made, notice the effect it has on the hearts of those

> Our hearts are not stirred to their depths by "We'll try it for a while and see how it goes."

who make it. Expressing our belief in one another, then living this out, creates a momentum of deepening commitment, one that results in the two entrusting themselves to each other at deeper and deeper levels. This is the ultimate expression and impact of an affirmed belief. Love is never static, it never stays the same. It is not a one-time decision. ("I told her I love her once, and if I change my mind I'll let her know.") Instead, it is a growing and compounding series of decisions of deeper and more focused commitment. Or feelings fade, attention to the relationship wavers as other priorities crowd in, and the central role in life that this relationship ideally should have will begin to be pushed aside and replaced by other priorities. This represents a different affirmed belief about marriage and one's marriage partner. This, too, is a progressive thing. Note the imperative of making a deep and strong commitment, then maintaining our focus on this commitment for a lifetime and acting in accord with this commitment. That is, our three powers, strengthened over time by persistent use, will continue building our marriage. This is the ultimate and best use of personal choice.

One fascinating aspect of "believe-in-each-other" love is that the two people feel as if they have known each other . . . always. Once such powerful mutual commitment and trust becomes a reality, once people have opened themselves to another in this way, their love takes on a timeless quality, or seems to reside outside of time. And this is an accurate perception, for such love and commitment do not belong to the physical, chemical, and electrical world we inhabit, but are gifts from God in the spiritual realm. Covenant is a spiritual reality, not a chemical one. Thus love is a uniquely powerful thing, able to transcend distance, barriers, and challenges, including time itself. In fact, if we are believers in Christ, our eternity will be most strongly characterized by love, as our present should be. God intends marriage to prepare us for that eternity by teaching us lessons of love that no other human experience can provide.

In covenant we enter a relationship with another individual, but are also connected in new family relationships. Perhaps we did not consciously intend to offer the other person's extended family a permanent place in our lives, but we did. Thus, the permanence that is God's plan between the two extends in all directions, joining these families henceforth and creating a new matrix of ongoing relationships. In a world where relationships are as disposable as drink cups, where people are so geographically and relationally mobile that far fewer long-term heart bonds are formed with extended family, the idea that our extended families matter is as foreign to most as the idea that "till death do us part" is a serious and binding commitment. Do you see the contrast between God's plan and the loneliness factory that is our world? In covenant God has given us opportunity to build permanent relationships on every side.

> Do you see the contrast between God's plan and the loneliness factory that is our world?

Our hearts are wired to belong to something bigger than ourselves. God puts in place a structure of nuclear family and extended family intended to gratify this need. Through our extended families we have multiplied resources, natural allies, and wider possibilities for deep relationships that are part of this new, permanent fixture in our lives. At the same time, just as a marriage may not reflect the fullness of God's desire, often extended families offer more challenges than opportunities. But the more people understand and commit themselves to God's plan, the more the benefits of God's plan will fill lives and hearts. The point here is that God's plan via the covenant of marriage extends far beyond the couple and their children, both across the community and through time. We can be assured that by attempting to fulfill God's plan for our families we will be blessed even if the results of our efforts are less than perfect relationships.

INTIMACY

What is intimacy? Our minds may quickly run toward the physical, but there is much more meaning to this word. We discussed transparency and the joy we get by simply being observed, seen for who we are and appreciated. Intimacy speaks to the responses, the interactions, and the inner experiences that take place in this atmosphere of transparency. It refers to the acceptance, the sharing, and the embrace. Someone whose mind, heart, and life are wide open to you, even inhabited *by* you. And vice versa. True intimacy is two people giving and receiving the purest essence of loving things from the core of their being.

God said, "It is not good for man to be alone" (Genesis 2:18). While the masculine pronoun was used here—since Adam was the only person in existence at the time—I doubt this reality is gender-specific, but instead is human-specific. One of the deepest needs God designed within us is to join together at these deepest levels to express, to receive, to share. Intimacy is the experience of having these needs abundantly met. Physical love is a periodic celebration, and a strong depiction, of something that God intends to be an ongoing state of being between husband and wife on an emotional and spiritual level. God's intent is that our marriages develop into places of lifelong, unbroken intimacy.

This is the consummate expression of His gift to us—covenant; the highest expression of His love toward us, second only to offering us the eternal intimacy of a relationship with Himself. Though intimacy is about sharing the depths of delight, it is also about sharing other things. In fact, it is about sharing *everything*. It is about no secrets— again, complete transparency—and about sharing the mundane and the mountaintops, the laughter and the tears, the hopes and the fears. It is about walking in the rain and sharing deepest pain. This is the principle of covenant sharing lived out day to day.

Why is God so comprehensive, thorough, and exacting about His instructions on how we are to treat each other in marriage? Because everything He tells us to do and be toward each other builds this atmosphere of intimacy. Everything we come up with, or that we have been deceived into accepting about how we are to treat each other that is at odds with God's instructions, simply puts intimacy at risk. These things create a sense of separation and alienation.

What we experience in a truly intimate relationship is the reality of union and communion that is created on a spiritual level as we enter covenant. This change is real and fully completed on one hand, but not fully perceived. Nor is this change fully reflected in the relationship. We are to then go about the process of building this relationship. Intimacy in its most full sense is a reflection of the full development of the reality of the relationship, this spiritual union and communion, in the fabric of daily life.

Think of the times you have experienced the most profound joy with another person. In almost all of these situations we are experiencing, in the moment, something we could best term *oneness* with this person. We are in complete harmony, totally in sync mentally, emotionally, and spiritually. God refers to love as "the perfect bond of unity" in Colossians 3:14. Paul (in Philippians 2:2) said his joy would be complete if those he was shepherding were "of the same mind, maintaining the same love, united in spirit, intent on one purpose."

> One of the most profound joys of marriage is merely being in each other's presence, of experiencing the other person as they experience life.

This sense of communion may be found in sharing an activity or simply sharing a quiet moment. One of the most profound joys of marriage is merely being in each other's presence, of experiencing the other person as they experience life. It has been said that if we find *this* joy in another we have the foundation of a great marriage. If, instead, we need to be amused, amazed, and entertained in the presence of the other person, otherwise we are bored, then something is missing in the relationship that no activity can replace.

Of course, intimacy also refers to sharing romantic and sexual activities. The misread here is to separate out the physical from everything else. Why? Because God built our lives to flourish when sexual intimacy occurs in the context of the unity of heart, mind, and spirit that can only be created within a wholehearted, lifetime commitment that accompanies an actual joining of souls: the Covenant of Marriage.

The openness, vulnerability, full exposure, and loving care of sexual activity—all of these merely reflect these same attributes across the spectrum of a relationship built as God directs. The sexual encounter draws from all of these other realms of relationship, celebrates the entirety of the relationship, and in turn builds something of importance into the relationship. The joining of bodies in sexual intercourse creates, through initiating covenant, the joining and merger of identities, and ushers in all the monumental changes that occur within and between two who enter covenant. Going forward, as we engage in this same activity frequently (as God instructs, 1 Corinthians 7:5), this returns us to the consummate experience of oneness, reinforcing in our experience the joining that has already occurred.

What do we note in our relationship if we are building intimacy into our marriage? If we are cultivating a pattern of honesty and transparency, if we have good reason to believe that we know the other person as well as they know themselves, and if an atmosphere of trust, respect, and loving response has been created, another important element is added to the relationship: peace and rest. It is hard to keep up a con, to maintain an image, to work the game. If we devote our lives to earning acceptance, we commit ourselves to a neverending and ultimately losing struggle, for true intimacy is not at the end of this road. We can never be *enough* to be accepted, because acceptance does not come from being enough in the first place. What if we realize that we do not need to engage in this struggle at all? What if being *ourselves* is enough? We do not really need to work at being ourselves, do we?

> We can never be *enough* to be accepted, because acceptance does not come from being enough in the first place.

If we are accepted and embraced as ourselves—the reality of covenant—we can truly rest in the presence of the other person. We can find that place of refuge, safety, and security—that fortress within which we can recharge, restore, renew, and grow in the company of our best friend. The paradox is that we need to grow and transform into people who can build and experience such a relationship for the long run. Though accepted as we are, we cannot remain as we are and experience this fullness. There is something here that requires us not only to grow, but to grow together. The starting point for this is choosing to create the best relationship of which we are capable at each step, doing everything we can to create an atmosphere of unbroken intimacy. And as we are accepted, we must accept. The other person also is *enough*.

God says we love because He first loves us. As we embrace and inhabit the reality of His love, it is His intent, His heart, His command that we learn to love other people as He loves us. Intimacy grows in a marriage as we increasingly reflect the perfect heart of God toward each other, at least as much as our current stage of maturity allows. The growth of intimacy will parallel our own growth as we learn new lessons from God about how to truly love. This growth is the spring from which flows the most wonderful of experiences, the source of happily-ever-after, a lifelong love affair. The only love that is strong and enduring enough to last forever is God's. He is gracious enough in His plan to teach us how to love as He does, one small step at a time.

WHOLEHEARTED

Wholehearted means that a person is completely directed toward one end, with no reservation, no confusion, no doubt. He or she is not conflicted or uncertain. This kind of life is the result of refining our reasons, of doing the hard work of clarifying what we really want and actually need. It is the product of shifting our reasoning from affirmations of deception to affirmations of truth for the important questions of life. If this refinement is in sync with God's plan and His truth, then our desires will match up well with the cause-and-effect universe that we inhabit, our desires will form around good things, and in pursuing our desires we will enjoy many more good consequences than bad ones. If our marriage matches up well with the true nature of marriage, with the structure and dynamics of our heart, and with the plan of God for our lives, we will reap wonderful consequences. A sense of meaning and purpose will infuse even the most mundane aspects of our marriage. If this is the case, our wholehearted efforts will be matched with heartwarming gratification and satisfaction. And, as our hearts and minds enjoy these benefits of carefully following God's plan, our commitment will intensify, our focus will be more fueled by passion, our efforts energized as the haze of confusion and deception that is our world is seen more clearly for what is actually is, and the allure of the things of the world fades. As if a morning fog is burned away by the rising sun, and God is more clearly seen for who He is. As our love for Him grows, this fuels more and more passionate expressions of that love. This growing passion and love also flows into the other focus of our lives—our marriage. This is what I have been experiencing for decades in my own life.

PASSIONS

How would we term a state where our deepest being is being expressed? A state where our mind, heart, spirit, and body are all feeding into this expression in perfect harmony? A state in which every ounce of the personal energies of two people are directed toward a single mutual point? The term I use is *passion*. We generally use this word to describe something that ignites powerful feelings, or our expression of those feelings. In our culture this word most often refers to sexual activity. But there is a much more broad context in which this word can be applied. I would use this term to describe a deeper and more powerful way of living. A life where the power of unqualified beliefs, wholehearted commitments, authentic expressions of identity, and mature character combine to build the life we are capable of building. Passion is the emotional energy that drives us to build this life. Passion drives us to settle for nothing less than the best we can do to build this life.

Passion is also what we feel as we develop our potential within, or abilities and capabilities, building things in the world that express something of who we are.

The opposites of passion are malaise, the paralysis of confusion, or a lifeless, depressed state. Or dissipation, where our energies are misdirected and spent on seemingly important things—entertainment, image-building, getting to the top of a ladder that is leaning against the wrong wall—while important things are ignored. God's goal is that our lives be characterized by passion, both as an individual and as a couple.

We have a finite amount of energy for living. We get to choose how we will spend this energy. Some things cause this energy to disappear into the universe, giving nothing in return. Other things give back to us, build us, grow us, reenergize us. That is, these things fuel our passion. For life in general, we may learn to focus our energies effectively and efficiently, accomplishing as much as possible, making the most of opportunities, building important things. Or we can flail around, spending our energy developing things of no real benefit. We can really think about how we are going to spend our precious time and life-force. We can dissipate our life-force by spending it in virtual reality, or building relationships that are not actual relationships (most of social media), or pursuing physical sensations devoid of meaning (illicit drug use, et al.). All these pleasantries we can fill our lives with also expend our energies. These are like the ropes we mentioned previously. To the extent that these things represent false value systems and misdirected priorities, these also hold us in place; these things keep us from growing, maturing, and moving forward in life. Becoming an adult in our culture now seems a negative thing. Is it really better to not be doing or becoming anything of significance?

As we learn to see more deeply within ourselves, as we mature, and as we learn how to learn—and as we learn how to identify and to rid ourselves of the world-inspired impediments to our lives—we will find dimensions of ourselves that have not yet manifested, things that will matter to us and others. We may learn that we have an undeveloped musical talent, or leadership capacity, or interest in ancient history or . . . nearly any other significant pursuit of which men and women are capable.

The difference between being a catch basin that collects all the world's ideas about living versus ridding ourselves of wrong and counterproductive ideas is the difference between floating through life in weakness, frustration, and loneliness, leaving nothing worthwhile in our wake, versus living a life that is passionate, powerful, and productive, making a difference and building a meaningful life. This difference comes down to passion versus confusion. This is direct evidence of the war between God and His enemies, of the war between what is true and what is not, between right and wrong, good and evil. Satan comes to kill, steal, and destroy. Do we not see this occurring slowly—or in the moment—in lives all around us? But the thing is not to just avoid the pitfalls of falsehood. The point is to build the passionate lives that are there and waiting to be built, the passionate marriage that is there waiting to be developed. This is life played by an entirely different set of rules, the rules of the Kingdom of God.

> This difference comes down to passion versus confusion. This is direct evidence of the war between God and His enemies.

If we realize that we are here to maximize what God has deposited within us, not just for our own sake, but to enhance the lives of those around us, we will approach self-discovery and self-development much differently. Imagine a seam of gold found in the rock beneath your backyard. You could certainly benefit from picking up an occasional nugget that pokes up out of the dirt. But what if you realize there is far more gold beneath the surface waiting to be uncovered? Enough gold to entirely revolutionize your life, to impact it at every level in every way? Would you devote the time and effort to mine what you already possess? It is in your backyard, after all.

In the same way, we can simply note the parts of ourselves that pop into view, or an occasional truth we encounter, and make occasional, small improvements; or we can make the effort to really get to know ourselves and to develop our full potential, along with developing the potential of our marriage. God developed the Covenant of Marriage for exactly this purpose. In covenant we owe our covenant partners not only anything we possess but also any potential we have that will enhance their lives. Thus, this quest for self-knowledge and self-development actually represents us living out our covenant of matrimony.

If we devote ourselves to a life of learning, growing, and developing, things seem to build, one upon the other. One capability that is developed leads to the growth of another. One opportunity that is developed becomes a stepping-stone for to build yet another important thing. There is huge joy simply in becoming good at doing one thing after another, of learning a new skill or developing new understanding. All of this, in turn, offers yet more opportunity for personal growth. Holley and I began investing in real estate early in our marriage—in truth, when we had no money to invest. There are ways one can acquire properties with little or no upfront money. As we learned about this realm and began to buy some properties, we had to learn many new things, develop new capacities, and further refine ourselves to take care of new responsibilities in the face of already full lives. Many opportunities we have developed in more recent years draw directly from growth that had to occur for us to be successful in these earlier real estate investments. God often brings new opportunities our way only after we have mined previous opportunities, growing and developing so we can make the most of the new ones.

Each new capacity enables us to be of more benefit to other people, and to build an even better life. I am in my sixties, and I'm still reaching out to learn new things, master new skills. Like learning how to write. Still a work in progress, right? There is a growing overall power of life that flows from this perpetual building process. Holley and I take on many projects together in areas of mutual interest. And in areas we do not share, we encourage, support, and appreciate the other. All of this is just as much an expression of intimacy as the physical act of intercourse. And all of this adds mental, emotional, and spiritual energy to that physical act.

As Holley and I began building our relationship, we each had a few interests strong enough to be termed passions—our relationship with God, for instance. As we grew together, joined in covenant, and faithfully lived out God's plan as best we could every day, we acquired many more areas of passion in our lives. Our lives are now literally full of these things. We shared a vision for a Victorian-era home but were sobered by the massive financial implications of owning a real one—no insulation, antique foundation, wiring and plumbing issues, and more—the definition of a money pit. So, we architected our own house plan, then acquired the antique elements to build a new house that is an 1885 Victorian look-alike, consisting of a thousand or so pieces of old houses bolted together. We have built several businesses together, we ballroom dance, we have hiked dozens of trails on our travels, Holley's culinary talents have emerged as a passion, and we've developed many art forms to some level of proficiency. In recent years there are several areas of study I have pursued extensively, many of which form portions of this book series.

I also write, research, and teach on medical topics. Holley and I built a medical practice in which I have innovated several highly effective strategies for dealing with joint and regional pain. Our clinical results have brought patients to our office from, thus far, forty-nine states and sixteen foreign countries. We are currently teaming up with two of the best researchers in this realm to do controlled studies to document the results of our techniques, which are superior to stem cell and other regenerative medicine treatments currently available. Holley has studied in other realms that complement this practice, including receiving a Master's degree in wholistic nutrition. Holley is also an excellent teacher on spiritual topics. I point all of this out simply to explain why I have little patience for people who say they have "no time" in their own lives for truly important things, like regularly studying God's Word.

All of the above things and more were developed while seven children were being raised. All are now going on to build their own families. Our ninth grandchild is due about the time this book is to be printed. Another realm of personal development, to be sure. The point being, we have developed a vast array of high-level skills across the decades that are the source of many good things in our lives and the lives of others. But at the time our life together began these things were there, for the most part, in potential only. We simply did what God instructed to develop these things within the context of our marriage.

I hope you can see now the reason for the steplike sequence in which the description of marriage, and of our marriage, has been presented. One must start at the beginning and build the foundation stones of the relationship, then build wisely atop this foundation in order to construct something as complex as a family—and have this be one of the most fun things you have ever done. As all of these things were developed Holley and I had to iron out our understanding and our approach; we had to figure out what was true in the midst of all of this on a daily basis. And we talked about these very things daily. We figured out how to build together and grow together, and just did what was in front of us on a daily basis. It was really a bit shocking to spend the time looking back at our earlier lives, to see all that has grown and developed during our journey. We never had that much of a long-term plan; we paid attention to what was before us on a daily basis. God obviously did have a very detailed long-term plan, out of our sight. And He graciously led us to build a life that we are passionate about.

Holley and I are passionate about our lives, about what God has taught us, grown us into, and built all around us. So passionate that we want to share the path that produces this life with others. Thank you for walking beside us for a while as we share that path.

> *For one standing next to a fire, if they do not*
> *appreciate the fire, it is as if they had no fire.*
> ANCIENT CHINESE PROVERB

CONTENTMENT

We have many choices in life. One of the most important choices we can make is to be contented. What? Isn't contentment about enjoying pleasant circumstances and constructive relationships? Doesn't contentment describe our experience when things, at least for the moment, are going well? Actually it is none of the above; this is one of the secrets of life. The apostle Paul summed up this secret nicely: "I am not saying this because I am in need, for I have learned to be content whatever the circumstances. I know what it is to be in need, and I know what it is to have plenty. I have learned the secret of being content in any and every situation, whether well fed or hungry, whether living in plenty or in want. I can do all this through Him who gives me strength" (Philippians 4:11-13).

How would we describe contentment? It is the experience of being pleased, of being satisfied, or having enough, or of the situation being enough. Why is finding contentment in life so important? Think for a moment about times you have been discontented. What is discontentment? We are not pleased, we are not satisfied, the situation is not good enough, we do not have enough—or the other person is not enough. Another way to put this is that our expectations have not been met. Our entire society—from advertising to media to motivation at work to expectations for our relationships—seems geared to produce discontentment. How? By seeking to convince us how important it is that we have this or that *thing*. We are presented with the idea that something vital is missing in our lives, something we could have if only . . . By the way, does this approach sound vaguely familiar? Remember Genesis 3? We are presented with such an idea and we, too, often embrace it. Our expectations are formed by these things we have come to think are important for our lives. We are challenged to go get those things we are now convinced will lead to contentment. The right job, right house, right car, right spouse . . . Remember, the Hallmark Channel teaches us that it's all about finding the *right person*. And, at the altar, we are convinced each of us has found this right person.

What is it, then, that drives all of these *right people* apart in the long run? "It wasn't what I thought it would be." "It just isn't working for me." "He/she was not who I thought they were." "They changed." "We grew apart." Then there is the deepest of these brutal truths: "He/she is no longer making me happy." There is a principle at play here we must understand if each of us is to find true satisfaction.

Discontentment is a choice, and this choice is the result of a training process. Contentment also is a choice, and we can also train ourselves to experience this state of mind and heart.

Let us think for a moment about the nature of discontentment and the nature of contentment. If we are discontented we are not willing to settle for what we now have. We want more, better, higher quality, more prestigious, more successful, more . . . *whatever* because we will not be satisfied otherwise. Our world teaches us that it is important to be discriminating, to not settle for less than the best. We deserve the best, after all. Somehow we have come to believe that the most important people are not the ones with the most virtuous character, but the ones with the highest expectations. High expectations equal most important person. The world teaches us that we will arrive at contentment when our expectations are finally met. Thus, we must devote our lives to getting other people to come through for us to meet our lofty expectations. Discontentment in this form suggests that our position in the big scheme of things should be higher than it is. If we were satisfied with our lives, after all, we would be content, not discontent. Who wants to discount their own value by being contented? By settling for less?

> The world teaches us that we will arrive at contentment when our expectations are finally met. Thus, we must devote our lives to getting other people to come through for us to meet our lofty expectations.

People who are trying to prove their importance via being discriminating train themselves to look for things to be discontented about, to complain about, to highlight as faults and flaws. Note also that, for this person, this form of discrimination applies only to life and other people. Discontented people typically do not spend much time pondering their own faults and flaws because their complaints are intended as an implied comparison between the deficiencies of others, and of life itself, in comparison with their own obvious excellence. Of course, not everyone is this far down the discontentment scale. And there are some things about which we should be discontented—our own character deficiencies and immaturity, for example. It is a good thing to desire that our lives be better, and even to desire that other people be better. One question is: Do we want *better* in an absolute sense, as in being better at our job or marriage, or do we want *better* in the sense of being better than other people? The first path is God's desire for us, the second reflects Satan's urge to falsely elevate himself. The next question becomes: Do we want to *actually find contentment in life?*

The bottom line is that we want to be content with our lives and our marriage. We want things, at the very least, to be OK. We want to *not need to fix* something major in order to be good with the way things are. Here is a key question: Do we want the situation to fundamentally meet our expectations—whatever those happen to be—or do we want our expectations to be fundamentally in sync with reality? This is a bit of a trick question, but a very real and important question. Then the next and most important question becomes: What actually produces contentment?

One thing worth noticing about people who will accept nothing less than the best: depending on their finances, their lives may be filled with expensive, high quality, beautiful, luxurious things. And something may feel good as they experience these things—pride in their (from their vantage point) superiority over others. Having been around some of these people, I cannot recall one whose lives were not also filled with complaint. Why? Because, if their priority is superiority, if their tool is comparison and their value scale is money and *things*, someone else will

> For one's internal experience is more powerfully created by what is in one's heart than what is in one's house, by the virtue one shows rather than the image one displays.

always have more. If they have decided to settle for nothing less than the best they will be eternally frustrated, perpetually discontented. This is a game no one can win for more than a while; a game each will ultimately lose badly. For one's internal experience is more powerfully created by what is in one's heart than what is in one's house, by the virtue one shows rather than the image one displays, by the value one creates in the lives of others rather than the value of one's portfolio. Every advantage these people value is temporary, transient, fleeting.

True contentment means that we realize our vital interests are secure. Nothing can fatally damage our lives, nothing can take away the things that are truly, vitally important. This is not to say that we will not suffer loss, feel pain, grieve, and wish things were otherwise. But if we realize that our most vital interests are secure, can we now be OK with the situation, whatever it is? In fact, the negatives in life with which we may easily be discontented may also be seen as *part of God's development process*. And since this process is something we are necessarily in the middle of, and something intended for our ultimate good, we do not want to escape this process. This is why we can bless even our adversity and give thanks even for the challenges in our lives (Philippians 4:6, 7).

For this state of mind to be real in our lives, we must learn what our most vital interests actually are. Our world misinforms us about this at every turn. Second, we must realize the source of supply for our vital needs. This is not, by the way, our covenant partner, though they are a big part of meeting our real needs. Our ultimate source of supply for everything truly important is God and our relationship with Him. He tells us what our vital needs are, and how He has met and will meet those needs, now and for all eternity. Are we listening to what He is saying?

Paul understood this. His view quoted in the Philippians passages above notes that God was his source of strength and, by implication, the source of all essential things. Once one understands this secret of life—that God has us in His hands, that He has provided everything in our lives to gratify us and please us, to teach us, and on occasion to correct our thinking—we can relax into the process God has us in and simply be grateful for the pleasures we experience. This state of mind—being OK with what God offers, and thus with what life brings, regardless of how we would assess the individual pieces—is the true foundation of contentment.

Satan's initial offer to humanity was that we would "be as God." Which means that we would gain the power to have things our way. Do you remember what else Satan did in this exchange? He offered Eve the first reasons she had ever considered to be discontented. God was not giving her enough. He was holding back, and she was suffering as a result. Does that pitch sound familiar?

The problem with the package deal Satan offered Eve to solve her newly created problem—her discontent—is that this plan does not work. It does not yield the hoped-for contentment: not then, not now, not ever. This is true in the long run even if, at the outset, this plan leads to some initial sense of reward while we are getting our way. Sin satisfies for a season. But why does it not yield deep satisfaction and gratification in the long run, even if we end up getting everything we think we want? Because this plan directs us to look for contentment, or happiness, in the wrong places.

It is not that we should have low expectations or desire less for ourselves and the other person than is possible. Look at God's expectations for us. They are impossibly high—at least from our initial vantage point. The questions are not whether we want the best or not, or whether we are willing to put out immeasurable effort to build the best marriage. The questions are about how we are going to go about getting there, and about our experience of self, relationship, and life overall in the process. The question is about how we are going to manage and direct our legitimate desires.

Do our expressions of discontent with our spouse usually energize him or her to meet our expectations? Or are they more likely to turn around and display their own discontentment with us? A nice counterbalancing question to ask ourselves is how we want our own shortcomings and mistakes to be handled. What is God's approach in this situation? He has far more lofty and exacting standards than we do, and He sincerely expects us to meet those expectations. *Over time.*

Through a process of growth and change, one laced with mistakes, false starts, misconceptions, and occasional epic fails. He wants us to try as hard as we can in the moment, but God is the ultimate realist. He expects, He loves, and He forgives. He also teaches, encourages, affirms, and challenges. His expectation for us is not perfection, but progress. He is OK with this in a way that our personal understanding of God often does not take into account. If we are to bring our expectations into line with reality, this is reality. If we fixate ourselves on the expectation of perfection for ourselves or for our spouses, will we ever be satisfied?

What would our expectations reasonably be? That another person can make me happy *in spite of* my commitment to creating my own unhappiness via my misplaced expectations? Let's be real for a moment.

Our experience of life is dramatically altered by the screwups, mistakes, and moral failings of our spouse, as much as by our own. In a marriage we will take hits; we will be hurt. What then? Did you notice in the passage from Philippians that Paul completely untethered any connection between his circumstances—many of which were distressing and painful—and his level of contentment? Paul goes into more detail about his personal challenges in 2 Corinthians 11:24-29. When you are having a bad day, you might refer to this list. Paul was content in any and every circumstance. Why? How? Because of His relationship with God.

> Paul goes into more detail about his personal challenges in 2 Corinthians 11:24-29. When you are having a bad day, you might refer to this list.

When we learn to see adversity in this way we can most benefit from God's plan, for we cease resisting it. One of the most powerful moves we can make make in life is *not* to ask, "Why me?" Instead, ask, "God, what are you trying to teach me?"

At the beginning of this section, I said that contentment is a choice. What is that choice, exactly? We can choose to affix our hope for happiness and contentment upon our spouse—more specifically upon our spouse meeting our expectations in matters great and small—or we can fix our hope on some other human institution, from our job to the political system. We can choose to define our own conditions for happiness and choose to settle for nothing less. Sort of like locking up our own happiness and holding it for ransom, demanding that the world meet our terms or we will never let our happiness out of prison. We can spend our lives trying to motivate or manipulate others to meet these expectations.

Or we can realize that we are living in the middle of a mess that we also had some part in creating. We can be OK with ourselves the way we are, and we can be OK with others the way they are. We can desire something better for all of the above, but at the same time not allow discontentment to destroy our own happiness or hinder the very process that can improve things.

We do all of this by employing our power of attention, focusing on the deeper truth of God's love and provision, and toward His love and care versus more minor issues, problems, and considerations—including our expectations. And we keep any current issue in perspective. Today's issue is just one of many we will confront over a lifetime in our partners and ourselves. It is helpful to direct our attention toward things we have to be thankful for in our relationship, our partner, and even in any given situation. The act of looking for beneficial aspects of challenging situations, things about which we may be thankful, has tremendous power to shift our emotional perception. God tells us in Philippians 4:6, 7 how to short-circuit anxiety, which is a by-product of discontentment. The secret ingredient of contentment is thankfulness as we turn to God and ask Him to supply our real needs.

FORGIVENESS

God has instructed us on every aspect of marriage. And all of us, with a little attention and effort, can carry out these instructions and get this all right, building the perfect marriage in less time than we thought it would take, right? If anyone believes this they have not actually tried it. Mistakes will predictably be made on any and every front. How close will we come to perfection in marriage *ever*, but especially early in marriage? The key is to get closer to these ideals over time, but can we fully master these things even across a lifetime?

Each of us comes into marriage with our own set of ideas and expectations about how this is all supposed to work, don't we? We come into marriage with hearts that may be wounded and aspirations that are off base. Our ideas and feelings may be in sync with God's system of truth and reality in some ways, but probably to some degree they are not. This means we may be hurt and offended when the other person actually transgresses God's agenda for our marriage. Or we may be offended and hurt when the other person does something that offends our ideas or deviates from the way our own family did things, or from the way our culture tells us we are supposed to do things. For instance, we may be hurt and angry if our spouse lies to us about something. Or we may become angry or hurt when the other party disagrees with our uncompromising approach to getting our own way.

But regardless of the many scenarios which might lead to hurt feelings and offended sensibilities in marriage, one thing is certain. We will experience pain, frustration, and loss in a relationship where every vulnerability we have is in easy reach. What then? Another thing also is certain. We will disappoint God through our own contribution to these scenarios, either by the way we initiate them or by the way we react and respond to them.

Fortunately, God has a plan: forgiveness. Before we look at God's plan in that area, we need to look at the typical "plan A" for dealing with hurt, pain, and loss in our society. This will help us understand how different God's plan is, and help us better understand its brilliance.

When we get hurt or offended, how have we been trained to defend our interests? What do we want, or think we need, from the other person at this point? What lengths will we go to in order to protect our interests? There are many possible answers to these questions, answers ranging from people who vigorously defend themselves when slighted in any way to people who refrain from defending themselves from serious, ongoing abuse. For the vast majority of people, when hurt or harmed they will take action to deal with the other person. We generally want two obvious things from the other person, and one thing that might not be so obvious. The obvious: we want the other person to understand how they hurt us, and we want them to take responsibility and fix the situation. These make sense, and to a degree both may be appropriate. The third thing, the thing we really want, however, is to gain power over people who might hurt us, leverage that will be useful in protecting ourselves in the future. How do we know this last item is in play for most people? Simply listen to the way people dredge up past misdeeds to use in current negotiations.

What are the deficiencies of this model? First, it does not take into account the perceptions and understandings of the other person. No notice is taken of what they were attempting to do. Second, this exchange is completely based on the value system of the person who takes offense. It does not necessarily take into account a value system that is far more important than either party's: God's. Some scenarios are really straightforward. Your spouse forgets something important, or carelessly breaks something of value, or says something inappropriate. They are clearly in the wrong. But is this the nature of most offenses? Most of the time, as people begin to discuss a problem that just occurred, what happens? Both parties claim to be in the right. One is hurt, and the other has a perfectly logical explanation for this unavoidable if unfortunate situation. What happens next? Usually the injured party voices a pointed accusation toward the one who will "not take responsibility" that at least implies something about motive and character. Both escalate the defense of their perceived interests and go on the offensive. Hurts multiply as accusations multiply, as people's motives and hearts are impugned, and the initial issue turns into a multifront battleground, a fight about the fight, as well as about the initial issue.

At this point, the person who took offense feels justified and believes that wounds delivered were richly deserved. They believe that such wounds will teach the other person to not act this way again. How successful is this approach in building unity of heart and mind in a marriage? Does this approach really settle matters? How successful is this approach in getting us what we really want—motivating the other person to love more deeply?

What is God's approach? Is it to refrain from being angry? No. Is it to patiently endure all things and to simply pray for the other person? Very rarely would this be the right approach. God's approach involves three things: properly diagnosing the problem, speaking truth in love, and forgiveness.

When we are hurt or offended, it is extremely beneficial to ask ourselves one question before engaging with the other person: *Why do I have this response?* Is this about a moral issue, a covenant violation, a violation of integrity, or about dishonoring me? Or is it about my expectations, my desire to be in control, or some value that really does not reflect God's priorities for me or the other person? Do I need to learn something in this situation before I try to teach someone a lesson?

> God's approach involves three things: properly diagnosing the problem, speaking truth in love, and forgiveness.

There are two ways we can react to someone's emotion-eliciting behavior. One way is to be *reactive*, the other is to be *reflective*. Anger is not the issue here. It is a separate issue. The question is how to present this situation in the way most likely to lead to a constructive outcome. First, the behavior should simply be recounted accurately—like holding a mirror to the person so they can clearly see their reflection, spoken as a fact, not an accusation. The posture is of an ally trying to help their friend see something, rather than an adversary attacking or a policeman pulling someone over. Thus, this is termed *being reflective*. The goal is first to let the person see themselves clearly and draw their own conclusions. This may be all that is necessary, but this step will not happen if the person is attacked or accused initially—this will almost always result in the person responding with a defense or counterattack. If one is *reactive* instead of reflective, if the main message is the anger, this is almost always voiced in the form of an accusation with an implied threat that the person had better do something about the problem. Accusations usually speak of motive and assign guilt. It is far more powerful to affirm the person's heart and motives instead, to acknowledge their love and concern about your well-being. Then highlight the mismatch between the word or action and what you know is in the depth of his or her heart. Isn't this how they really feel about you, and why you married them?

How you feel about this behavior comes next, once the two agree on what was done, and once you have taken the time yourself to become clear about the nature of the offense and the reason for your emotional response. The second skill to master is owning one's emotional response, for as we have mentioned, many of our emotional responses are actually the result of choices we have made. They are not fixed aspects of our identity, or of the situation; a feeling of offense is not synonymous with someone being guilty of an actual offense. Two people can have completely different emotional responses to the same situation, and the same person can have different responses depending on his or her frame of mind at the time. Are we exhausted, stressed, hanging by a thread, or having a great day? Does this impact our emotional response? The way to voice this is, "When you do *this*, I feel ____." We are relating—truthfully—the way the other person's behavior impacts us, but not making our response totally their responsibility. At this point the other person might apologize, or they might ask us why in the world we feel this way. Either might be a useful next step in the conversation.

If, after reflection, we think this is an issue of moral significance, it is beneficial to speak the truth clearly about what was done and why it is a problem in addition to how we feel about it. Then we listen. It is surprising how often there is an element of misunderstanding and miscommunication involved. We may not really know the whole story. Thus, the third key skill to master is termed *reflective listening*. This means we hear the other person out and reflect back to them what they are really saying. If they do not agree with our reflection of their point, we keep discussing until they agree that we understand what they are saying. They do the same for us. At this point we have subtracted the problem of misunderstanding. And we have subtracted perhaps 80 percent of the conflicts we will encounter in marriage. And for the 20 percent of the time in which a real issue exists, we have clarified all of the details.

If a true shortcoming exists, it is up to the responsible party to take full responsibility. This starts with an apology. But this means something different from the way apologies are often spoken in our culture. Often words of apology are spoken by someone who does not recognize or regret the damage they have inflicted, nor are they concerned that they did wrong and offended God; they simply regret that they have been caught in the act and are suffering the consequences. Such words are designed to take the pressure off the offending party, to entice the other person to again offer the warm embrace of relationship while the offending party intends to change nothing. Have you experienced this? God speaks instead of true repentance. This is a 180-degree change of direction based on understanding what is wrong with one's current course and embracing a new guiding idea. This means that one sees the damage caused by acting out an idea and regrets this damage. But also that one sees that a new guiding idea is required. Therefore, one affirms and embraces this new idea. We have already outlined this precise process along with disaffirming the old guiding idea. At this point, what the person did becomes the last thing he or she would do going forward. Transformation has occurred. A genuine apology simply acknowledges that this process has occurred. This also suggests that a couple should not content themselves with a pattern of ending such issues with a simple and superficial "I'm sorry" that is devoid of real understanding; that does not reflect real growth. If we do this, we miss a wonderful opportunity to know each other, and ourselves, more deeply.

As two people sort through marital issues in this manner, looking for truth, holding fast to what is right, and expecting the best of each other, helping each other to see new perspectives, does this build the relationship? Does this build hearts toward one another? I will tell you from significant experience that it does.

There are two more elements to God's equation. The first is humility. This is simply approaching other people and situations from the perspective that we all have much to learn. No one is fully and completely right. Everyone has a point and a perspective worth hearing and considering, especially someone we love, trust, and respect. At the same time, our human perspectives are all limited, our understandings are all incomplete. Only God has it right, all right, completely right. If we approach issues and conflicts speaking the truth—God's truth—and seeking the correct way in the situation to implement this truth, we are now allies with our spouse and with God on a journey toward God. This is stark contrast to an attitude of self-righteousness.

Holley and I, after years of experience, do not approach the other with any vestige of a critical spirit when the other messes up. First, this helps nothing. Second, the other person will commit the next screwup soon enough, and we have learned not to give out what we do not want to hear back. Third, we have such a successful way of growing in the midst of these scenarios that we do not mind them. There is very little emotional response now to each other's mistakes. Why? Because there is virtually never any long-term harm in these; instead they are just our next steps of growth. We are climbing a high rock wall, roped together. So, one's footing slips and kicks off a few rocks. The other gets hit by a rock. It stings a bit. So? We are trying to get to the top of the wall, and it takes both sets of eyes and each other's full support to find the best path up the wall. We coach each other on technique so neither falls off the wall—roped together as we are. This minimizes but does not eliminate missteps. Sometimes a technique is harder to master; it takes a few lessons to learn. So? We are trying to get up the wall. And we are.

> We are climbing a high rock wall, roped together. So, one's footing slips and kicks off a few rocks. The other gets hit by a rock. It stings a bit. So?

Now that we have put the issue out there, discussed it, and agreed on what really happened, the final element of God's plan is *forgiveness*. What is this? It is simply ceasing to hold the other party responsible for fixing or altering the situation. Why would we not want to forgive? It may be that the other person does not repent; they do not recognize what they have done to us or to themselves. We may still be in the position of making the point that something seriously wrong was done. It feels like forgiveness lets them off the hook, like we are admitting that the situation really did not matter that much, that the guilt of the other party is unimportant. Our own sense of righteousness dissents from making these statements. We want justice. But forgiveness is not making less of a situation than is real, nor is it a move away from justice. Forgiveness is really turning the matter of ultimate justice over to God and refraining from trying to enforce justice on our own. God has built consequences into the system, and God has promised to act directly, possibly in the short term and certainly in the end, to right every wrong and to deal with every offense with perfect justice. By holding on to offenses and trying to insert ourselves into the justice end of the equation, we are simply getting in the way.

Why would we want to subtract ourselves from this justice equation? First, God is much better at this than we are (read Hebrews 10:30, 31). He will recompense wrongs in ways that are far more powerful and effective than we could possibly engineer. More importantly, though, we do this because God told us to. In fact, He tells us that if we do not forgive each other, He will not forgive us (Matthew 6:15, Mark 11:26). Why is God so strong about this? There are several reasons, all of which are worth keeping in mind as we approach dealing with offenses from anyone, but especially from our covenant partner. What, exactly, is forgiveness? It is simply ceasing to hold the other person responsible for *repairing* the situation. It is therefore to make peace with the impact of this situation on one's life, trusting God to redeem this in our lives just as He deals with the offense in the life of the other.

If we are in covenant with God we have each been forgiven by God far more serious offenses than the one we are dealing with in the other person. The second reason we want to step aside from the judge's chair is that this reminds us of our proper place and role in the big scheme of things. This person has also committed far more offenses before God than before us. And God is working in their lives, desiring that they come to Him. Anything we do by way of revenge or retribution may hinder this process, and we would much prefer that God got hold of their lives than that we get hold of their lives—or their necks. Whatever issue is between us, this person has much more of an issue with God. If they are not listening to God, how much less likely is it that they will listen to us on this issue? If you must make the choice between letting God make the point to them and you continuing to make the point to them, who would you rather have address the issue? To forgive is not to forget or to negate the situation; it is for the less powerful being in this situation to step aside so the more powerful Being can use His superior power and wisdom in a process that may take some time. And though we suffered loss in this situation, is God not capable of blessing us for our obedience in ways that redeem this situation if we obey Him? Our willingness to forgive comes down to two ultimate questions: 1) Who is really in charge? 2) Does God love me enough to provide for my deeper needs in ways that provide gains that more than offset the losses? People did a lot of really bad things to Jesus while He was on earth. He left us a pattern to follow as we deal with many of these same issues.

What happens when we do not forgive? We replay the offense in our minds over and over, and every time we do so we experience the unpleasantness of the initial wound. Here is the problem: the first abuse of our hearts occurred with the offense, but at this moment—as we choose to replay this event in our mind and heart—the person is not even around, yet our hearts are filled with pain and anger. So, who is really inflicting this unpleasantness on us? Are we now not simply joining the other person in abusing ourselves? Unforgiveness binds the heart and mind to the situation in an ongoing way, picking off the scab and keeping the wound open. Our minds will ever be searching for just the right way to redress the wrong. Unforgiveness is a gift that keeps on giving—to ourselves. The relationship cannot be right, now or ever, unless our terms are satisfied. We resent the person, their im-

Do you know someone who is bitter? How did they become so? By a simple process: unforgiveness plus time.

pact on our lives, and the loss they have inflicted upon us. This fixation on these situations in our heart grows over time into bitterness. As we continue to live in past painful situations, these situations exert more and more influence on our overall character and experience of life. The bitter flavor of these situations begins to infuse our entire being. Do you know someone who is bitter? How did they become so? By a simple process: unforgiveness plus time. If two people are accumulating even small bits of unforgiveness over time in marriage, what happens to hearts? God wants us to turn outcomes and punishments over to Him and move on with our lives, restoring and continuing to build relationships that will inevitably sustain wounds due to our imperfections.

How do we forgive when we do not feel like doing so, do not want to do so, and our lives hold daily reminders of what someone has done to us? We must use the three powers we discussed earlier in this book. We have discussed reasons why it is a good idea to forgive. The first step is to consider what God has instructed, plus some of the practical reasons to support a decision to forgive in the situation. The second essential thing is to decide to forgive, to use our power of affirmation to choose this course. Next, we must use our power of attention to redirect our minds and hearts away from creative ways to have our revenge, and let God handle this matter in the other person's life and in my life. When I am in this process, I turn my imagination from creative ways to redress toward praying for the person. This is a spiritual battle, and hostile spiritual forces have the capacity to blind eyes and close up ears to truth. Pray that eyes and hearts are opened to truth, pray for the person to be blessed with a new heart or a more godly heart (Luke 6:27-35). The bottom line: we will not feel like forgiving until we have affirmed forgiveness and reinforced this affirmation more than once. We must choose the path of forgiveness, walk this path, and see its benefits before this becomes our heart's desire.

At this point, something needs to also be said about the person who engages in serious abuse on an ongoing basis. These people do not acknowledge the nature of their behavior and are aggressive about silencing those who would reveal their behavior. They profess love and invite another person to display love toward them by repetitively forgiving their abuse and continuing to submit to it. Despite promises to "change," true repentance does not occur. What God wants to see in a relationship is forgiveness that is coupled with seeking and acknowledging truth, and mutual forgiveness accompanied by growth in love by both parties. Forgiveness should not be confused with a conspiracy of silence to conceal destructive or criminal behavior. Abusers often seek out people who are sincerely trying to love as God commands, who have the best of intentions. It is true that God tells us not just to forgive seven times but seventy times seven (Matthew 18:22). And we are to forgive abusers and unrepentant people just as we forgive those who truly repent.

But we are also called upon to speak the truth in love, which in this case acknowledges the ongoing intention of a person to abuse. True love is founded firmly upon truth. A relationship where truth is concealed and behavior mischaracterized is not a loving relationship; it is manipulative. When damage is severe enough to be labeled abuse, there is ongoing danger, from which a prudent person will protect himself or herself. Those who continue to enable abuse or addiction harm not only themselves but the one they are trying to help through this approach. Codependency is not synonymous with love. Professional help should be sought and these destructive patterns confronted vigorously.

GENERATIVE

Covenants are generative. That is, they create things that would not exist in the absence of the covenant joining. This reflects the creative character of the Author of covenant. The most obvious thing created by a marriage covenant is children. New lives are begun via the same act that began new life in each covenant participant. These new lives are created as we physically celebrate a Covenant of Marriage. But there are other, less obvious things to understand and appreciate if we want to understand the big picture of God's plan.

As we have discussed in detail, the Covenant of Marriage creates a new identity and a new nature for both parties. Consider all the things God had in mind through this alteration and merger of identity. As two people are altered and joined, they are put in a position to become the most loving, mature, and wise that they could possibly become. I can only speak at this point from personal experience, but in our marriage Holley and I have been exposed to myriad activities, hobbies, interests, areas of learning, and opportunities through our relationship that we would likely never have been exposed to on our own, many of which were mentioned in an earlier section. Learning new things and mastering new skills has become the pattern of our lives in our marriage. This pattern is vastly different from our previous pattern of living. Prior to marrying Holley I became well-educated, got a medical degree, trained as a urologist, and was active in many areas. But through our marriage there is an entirely new avenue of personal development. Flowing from our own growth, Holley and I are always looking for ways in which we can use abilities and resources to bless others. God has shown us how to learn how to learn, and the primary way He did this was through our learning how to do a good job of being married. But this translates into being able to more quickly master other complex tasks, having the confidence to attempt this, and having the aid and encouragement of our partner to do so.

Another thing created uniquely through covenant is a particular type of reward. While many things matter in life, feel good, are gratifying, or are satisfying in some way, there is one realm of life from which arises the deepest, most profound, and most satisfying reward: marriage and family. There is no experience that compares to true intimacy, that compares to the experience of covenant faithfully lived out. There is nothing like looking into the eyes of your child for the first time; or like giving your child to someone else's child, both now grown to adulthood, in marriage; or looking into the eyes of your grandchild for the first time. There is something profound about seeing life continue through us into new generations, about being able to impart valuable things from the past, about watching the future unfold in lives that mean something to us. Even little things and small joys mean much more when shared with our best friend and lover. Much deeper is the sense of reward as we work together through prolonged struggles, overcome huge obstacles, and see God at work delivering and blessing in the midst of overwhelming challenges. Perhaps the greatest joy of all is simply looking back over decades of faithful, loving relationship and seeing how we have been fashioned into the people we have become by the journey we have shared. Then, seeing children moving forward in their own journey, growing in their own relationship with God, and becoming something of increasing beauty as they walk in faithful submission to our loving Father. There is nothing of worldly status, or achievement, or accomplishment, or wealth, or power that can offer these rewards. These are from God, poured into our hearts as we faithfully live out His plan for our lives.

> There is something profound about seeing life continue through us into new generations, about being able to impart valuable things from the past, about watching the future unfold in lives that mean something to us.

A marriage is the most complex, interesting, challenging, and rewarding thing that humans have the opportunity to be part of other than a relationship with God. In many ways the experience is more tangible and powerful, more here-and-now, compared to the things that await us in eternity. Marriage is something shared with another person that we can touch, see, and hear on a moment-by-moment basis. But behind all this is the reality that marriage, when filled with the rewards God intended, is a big piece of preparing us to live and love in eternity, and its rewards are but a taste of what awaits us in fullness. As God's Spirit is in each of us, and as our joining is His gift to us, we also serve as tangible expressions of His love to each other and to a watching world. As much as marriage means to an individual and a couple, it is about far more than the nuclear family.

God's plan is to impact the world through covenant, one by one. Surrounding a marriage are multiplied opportunities for relationships: each now shares in the other's family of origin—parents, brothers, sisters, et al.; there are relationships with children, the children's friends and their families; then there are adult couple friends, and other relationships that would not have occurred without marriage and family. This web of relationships and connections knits society together and adds additional meaning and purpose to all of these lives, especially as people are matured via covenant.

In contrast, imagine a group of single people weaving in and out of each other's lives. There are simply far fewer reasons to build and sustain deep relationships in the single world. There, it is merely about others being value-added to one's own life. Now imagine an entire society without marriage and family, and consider the difference in the depth and maturity of the people, the difference in their developed capacities to love and relate, and the contrast in the priorities which would dominate a society without marriage and family versus a society based on this fundamental social unit.

Now imagine a society filled with people in faithful covenant relationships with each other who have followed God's plan, and thus become mature, wise, loving, and capable to the extent of their inborn abilities. (Note that many people see countless others around them who have achieved far less than their potential and assign the responsibility for this lack of personal development to "society." What are they saying about "society"? If society had done something differently, these people would somehow turn out to be far better and more capable persons than they have turned out to be? God's plan is not for "society" to produce this outcome, but for faithfulness to His plan for living to produce this desired outcome in the lives of a growing network of wise and mature people. There is, in fact, no other pathway by which this personal development can happen.)

Envision these supportive and intact families raising children who are mentored and disciplined to reach their potential in character and ability. Further, envision the meshwork of constructive relationships among these people, the social structures built by these people, and the civic and national governments that would be crafted by such people. This ideal has not yet been fully achieved on earth, though we have at points been much closer to it than we are today, especially in our own nation. But we have come nowhere near having the fullness of this plan in operation in our world. Why? I would suggest the reason we have seen so little of this plan in operation is because people have so rarely implemented it in fullness in their individual lives. At least few enough so that this is not the prevailing culture in our churches, much less in our neighborhoods, schools, and cities.

At the same time, God's plan has produced enough stability, enough maturity, enough general virtue to hold our society together, at least until this point. His plan has also supplied most of the genuine virtue seen across cultures and time. The durability of God's plan in a world that largely rejects Him is, in an odd sense, evidence of the love He has even for those who reject and despise Him, for He betters their lives as well in the ways only He can. This simple verse makes that clear.

> *He causes his sun to rise on the evil and the good,*
> *and sends rain on the righteous and the unrighteous.*
> MATTHEW 5:45

Virtually every society on earth, throughout all of history, has recognized the family unit as the basic building block of society. Only in communist societies and a few other totalitarian societies, like the Nazis, have governments tried to replace the family as the fundamental social structure. They have tried to accomplish this by asserting that the state is primarily responsible for training and educating children, then they proceed to indoctrinate children into the ideals espoused by these governments. Nowhere has this led to a more ideal society, though this is always the stated goal of social revolutionaries. Instead, as these governments attempt to replace the order of God, while universally opposing faith in God as a threat to themselves, these governing ideas and groups can easily be seen as an initiative of . . . whom? Who has been trying from the beginning to sell humans on the "virtues" and "beauties" of a world without God? And how has this consistently turned out, from the beginning of history until this evening's six o'clock news?

The most important things generated by covenant are lessons on love. We have talked about building love in marriage and family, and the personal impact God intends covenant relationships to have. One thing we must learn about love is that love does not ensure wonderful relationships. One may love, yet a relationship may be completely broken. God notes this as He tells us, "If possible, as much as it depends on you, be at peace with all men" (Romans 12:18). As William Wilberforce, the great British legislator and public servant who did more than any other to end slavery in the British Empire, famously said, "Duty is ours, results are God's." Love from one heart does not ensure any particular outcome in a relationship. Consider Jesus, the definition of perfect love, and note the responses of everyone He encountered during His earthly life. Or since. True love involves freedom to choose one's response; this is the freedom God offers each of us in relationship, and this freedom exists in the response of others toward us.

Lessons learned about love through marriage, then family, equip us to engage with the rest of the world with an entirely new level of wisdom and maturity. We are capable of loving in ways we never would have if not for the school of covenant. Thus, we are capable of impacting others in new ways, ways that much better reflect God's heart. We can be used by Him in new ways. Our new capacities, and the new opportunities we are presented with as a result, are another reflection of the generative nature of covenant.

The thing I want to leave you with in this discussion is a growing awareness that covenant is an answer powerful enough, generative enough, good enough, to fully address the evils of our day at the global level of societies and nations, all the way down to the challenges of our own marriage on a daily basis—if this plan is fully and faithfully applied. If we truly want to devote ourselves to building a better world in general, and especially a better world for our children and grand-children, the most powerful step we can take is to place ourselves in the hands of God and live out His plan for our lives, becoming in the process the people He intended us to become, living out the new life He has graciously given us in ways that accurately reflect His charac-ter and nature.

One of the centerpieces of God's plan for the world is developed and mature marriages and godly families so that all who view such people can see that God is good and that He blesses those who seek Him. The most powerful rebuttals to Satan's lies are hearts and lives fashioned after the Creator, truly transformed lives. As covenant is a remarkably powerful force for good, so violations and perversions of covenant are remarkably powerful to give birth to pain and loss. Thus, as we build our marriages, it is not just about us. We are, in a larger sense, a part of God's initiative to present a working and attractive alternative to a lost and dying world.

SUMMARY

These are but a sampling of the elements of a relationship built by faithfulness to the principles of covenant. As there are an array of things we are supposed to do, and be, there are an array of outcomes in hearts and in functions of the relationship. I hope you get the sense for how one thing builds upon another in each realm we discussed, and how each realm adds to the others. Honesty, trust, transparency, and growth are all intimately connected. In fact, every element that God adds to this relationship—every single thing God says to do or be in this relationship, everything that covenant teaches about relation-ship, and every implication of living out its reality—interlocks like a beautiful puzzle. The relationship is beautiful to look at, but it is more than appearance, it is also function, and consequences, and heart im-pact, as well as many other things. Any piece missing from this puzzle matters. The appearance loses something, but so does function, and so does the outcome of the relationship. For best results God's plan must be embraced in its entirety. That is why commitment and faithfulness are such a prominent part of God's plan. This is why Jesus would accept no synthesis, no melding of His plan with other ideas or agendas. Covenant is the very heart of Jesus' plan for each of us.

To have our best marriages we must believe, and believe in Jesus and His plan to the extent that we are willing to carry it out. We must submit ourselves to this plan in every detail. Great effort has been expended in the first two volumes of this series to explain why this level of commitment is vital if best results—the best marriages and the best us—are to be built. With this in mind, let's next look at two of the parts of God's plan that draw the most fire from the enemies of God, where the enemies of God have focused the greatest attention in our culture. See if you can determine why these two areas would be chosen for attack.

QUESTIONS FOR THOUGHT

1. Some days in our marriage we may feel very connected, and other days not so strongly, or at all. Everything we are called to do, or be, toward each other flows from the reality of our connection and the reality of our transformation of identity. How do we deal with a situation in which we are to act like something is real that we do not feel in the moment?

2. How does true love grow between two people?

3. What would it mean in a relationship for two people to fully accept each other based on covenant joining instead of holding out conditional acceptance: "If only you will . . . " What would you feel about yourself? What would you feel about the other person? Would this change the way you approach problems and issues in the relationship? How?

4. Accepting each other on this basis is simply a decision to acknowledge reality. But the rest of the relationship must be built. The most foundational decision is to honor each other first of all, above all. Why is honoring so important? How would failing to honor impact the relationship?

5. Why is honesty the next most important foundation for the relationship? Though obvious to some degree, let's think about how honesty impacts trust, transparency, safety, security, the sense of permanence, and intimacy. Would it help us if we realize that an ironclad commitment to tell the truth to each other, to be fully forthcoming, to have no protected personal space where the other is not welcome, or even aware, are powerful investments in building every other element of the relationship? Trust and respect are the bedrock upon which everything else good is built. How can you go about building these foundations in your relationship? What little compromises have you made in integrity in your relationship? What are you risking by doing this? What is the path to building what is most important in your relationship?

6. How does confidence in your partner's lifetime commitment to you impact your heart? What environment does this create between you? Is this another aspect of simply acknowledging the reality of covenant joining? How does your confidence in your spouse change your approach to issues and problems in the relationship? On the one hand, the person—and the problem—now will not simply disappear from your life. And this problem or issue is now not only theirs but yours. How does this change your thinking and your approach to dealing with this issue? Does this offer additional motivation for a couple to learn how to grow, change, and transform?

7. What is true intimacy? If we want to build intimacy in marriage, what specific things might we focus on building? What experience does intimacy create for us? True love means being deeply and completely known. We cannot be intimate with a misconception, can we? On the other hand, the experience of being known, accepted, and warmly embraced for all that we are creates the in-the-moment experience of being loved that most deeply nourishes and blesses our hearts. Is this an experience worth any effort to create, for ourselves and for our beloved?

8. What is it to be halfhearted, to live a passionless life? And what is to be wholehearted, passionate about the many things in our lives? What is the difference? How does one move toward being wholehearted? How does one build passions? How does marriage fit into this plan?

9. If I said the true goal of a marriage is not to be happy, but to be content, would you agree or disagree? If I said happiness is mostly dependent on circumstances while contentment is dependent on use of our three powers, would you agree or disagree? If I said it is better to have our desired state of mind not completely dependent on circumstances, would you agree or disagree? How might we do this?

10. What role does forgiveness play in the growth of a marriage?

CHAPTER TEN

The Parts of God's Plan Most Disdained By the World But Most Necessary for Success: Submission

Blessed are the meek, for they will inherit the earth.
MATTHEW 5:5

Most people automatically associate the word meekness with weakness. To be meek, it is thought, is at best to be nonassertive, at worst to be run over. Meekness, though, is not about weakness but about power. Think of a heavyweight champion boxer listening patiently to someone mouth off on a sidewalk. Is there anything that needs to be proved here? Power under control. Think of Christ on the cross being taunted by the crowd. They mocked His Godhood and His power. He easily could have incinerated everyone in sight to silence this foolishness, but He did not. Is there anything that needs to be proved here? Power under control. He had more important business at hand. Meekness is possible when we realize we do not need to waste our power to prove a point; who we are is secure and cannot be assailed even by those who are trying.

One of our urges in life is to be powerful—for our own protection, so we may have an impact, so we can build the best life, so we can be respected by others. And much in our world is geared to creating the impression of power. Let us think for a moment, though, about the nature of true power. This is God, described as *omnipotent*, or all-powerful. In what has become a repetitive theme in our discussion, in this realm we are also presented with the choice between pursuing power a la the world, or the power of God. If we really want power in our lives, the most sure route to this is to allow the power of Christ to be fully effective in and through us. This is best accomplished via spiritual growth and maturity, and in cultivating a life fully surrendered to God. The issue of submission in the Scriptures is a direct contradiction to the path to power pursued by the world. Let us keep all of this in mind as we continue our discussion.

With everything we have discussed thus far as our foundation, if we are to build our marriages after God's pattern and create the inner quality of life God desires for us, we need to carefully consider God's instructions for the administrative structure of marriage and family. It is vital to do this because, as God reveals His plan in Scripture, the world around us aggressively asserts that God's injunctions are the most damaging and degrading things we could be asked to follow. Here is the point of greatest distinction between the "competing kingdoms" model of marriage and God's plan: The world's plan asserts that marriage consists of two kingdoms, separate but equal, living in a negotiated peace but also competing for the real prize. To the victor go the spoils. It is vital that God's plan for the administrative structure of marriage be sharply contrasted with this and understood as God intends. Our world has completely distorted the path to happiness in marriage, and for life in general, and the results are already in for the experiment of grafting progressive ideals into marriage: a fivefold increase in the divorce rate within the Christian community since 1960, and so many struggling marriages among twenty-and thirty-year-olds that many in this age range avoid marriage altogether. Let us therefore focus on God's path to marital happiness, and for the sake of contrast take a closer look at the world's path—the path to conflict, pain, and relationship damage.

Why is *submission* such a terrible word in the world's way of thinking? Because it describes giving up our true path to the good life, which comes via getting our own way, right? If we submit to someone else, we are placing ourselves *voluntarily* in a position of losing, of acknowledging that we are less powerful, less influential, and thus of less value than those to whom we are submitting. The very word, submission, is a lightning rod even in Christian circles—unless we understand two things. First, why God requires it in marriage; second, that true submission is nothing like the world mischaracterizes it to be. God deeply loves us. Therefore, everything God instructs us to do is for our good, ultimately meant to build love in two hearts for each other. If God's plan is actually what it is mischaracterized to be, love for a lifetime would not result from that plan. But this does result from God's plan. In fact, it results in fullness only from God's plan. If we really understand the vast difference between God's wisdom, power, and understanding and our own, and understand that He loves us more than we love ourselves, is it reasonable to trust Him and His Word, to trust in Him and entrust ourselves to Him? We have spent several chapters explaining why this is not merely a reasonable position, it is the only working plan. Believing in God and loving Him inherently involve submitting to Him. Is this toxic, or is it necessary?

And before we submit to God, we must do something else outrageous in the eyes of the world, and this is mentioned in the interest of full disclosure. We must *surrender*. This, again, evokes images of laying down our defenses before a hostile force, possibly allowing ourselves to enter a state of slavery, or worse. But let us look more clearly at the two sides as one ceases to resist. The hostile force driven by bad intentions is actually us. The one to whom we surrender, before whom we lay down the implements of rebellion, is God. He wants to invite us into a family relationship, and He wants us to cease leading our own lives to destruction. He wants us to stop striving against the one true, perfect lover of our souls—and this is not our spouse, regardless of how wonderful they are. We are perfectly loved by the One who created every aspect of us, of marriage, and of the world we live in. Is there any good reason we would not prefer His guidance to any other? What we must surrender is the idea that there is any more reasonable guide for living than the Living God.

Surrender and submission provoke profound anger in those sold out to the world's ideas. Why? Because these concepts are the most direct contradiction to the world's fundamental guiding principle: getting our way is the only path to happiness.

* * * * *

Anyone who loves me will obey my teaching. My Father will love them, and we will come to them and make our home with them. Anyone who does not love me will not obey my teaching. These words are not my own; they belong to the Father who sent me.
JOHN 14:23, 24

The problem arises when we extend the idea of submission from a perfect, all-powerful, all-knowing, all-loving Deity—which is difficult enough—to a very imperfect human being to whom we are married. Or has this idea of submission been "rightly" discarded in our modern world? I want to take some time to work through this particular issue because it is surprisingly important in building the quality of marriage we desire. We want to look at what submission means in the sense it is used relating to marriage, and to what it does not mean. We want to look at the alternatives to submission in marriage, both from the standpoints of outcomes and priorities. Why, in other words, would it seem so vital to us not to submit in the way God instructs us? Next we want to consider how we actually build a great marriage and an outstanding quality of life in contrast to the way our society instructs us to conduct our marriage and pursue our best lives. Then we want to look at how—and why—we might be misinformed by our world about the real path to the best marriage.

First, let us look at a key passage on submission in the Scriptures, in Ephesians, and see what questions this passage raises for each of us. Then we will see if we can answer these questions. In this passage the first verse refers to mutual submission, the second to submission on the part of the wife, and the third to submission as the husband's role.

Submit to one another out of reverence for Christ.
EPHESIANS 5:21

*Wives, submit yourselves to your own husbands as you do
to the Lord. For the husband is the head of the wife as Christ
is the head of the church, His body, of which He is the Savior.
Now, as the church submits to Christ, so also wives should
submit to their husbands in everything.*
EPHESIANS 5:22-24

*Husbands, love your wives, just as Christ loved the church
and gave Himself up for her to make her holy, cleansing her by
the washing with water through the Word, and to present her to
Himself as a radiant church, without stain or wrinkle or any
other blemish, but holy and blameless. In this same way,
husbands ought to love their wives as their own bodies.
He who loves his wife loves himself. After all, no one ever hated
their own body, but they feed and care for their own body, just
as Christ does the church—for we are members of His body.*
EPHESIANS 5:25-30

The questions I see in these verses follow; feel free to develop your own.

1. What is submission?

2. How can a woman reasonably display the same level of submission toward an imperfect human, even a very good human, and much more toward a very flawed human, that she would reasonably display toward God precisely because of His perfection?

3. Does this not place women in a second-rate position, a decidedly unequal and demeaning position, in regard to men?

4. How can a husband "give himself up" for his wife in a way that has an impact on her that remotely resembles the impact Christ has on the individuals who comprise the church?

5. Since the initial injunction in verse 21 is to mutually submit, how is a husband to submit to a person who is simultaneously supposed to be submitting to him?

6. How does the concept—and practice—of loving each other relate to all of this?

There may be other questions these verses raise, and I would encourage you to seek your own answers as we work through the following points.

What is submission? Let us contrast two pictures. First, a wife who is afraid to speak for herself, or even think for herself, who scurries around behind her husband cleaning up his mess and catering to his every whim. And a husband who acts like it is his God-given right to have his own way, period. Second picture: a Chief Operating Officer of a company with an office next to the Chief Executive Officer. The COO has vast areas of responsibility and competence and largely exercises his or her discretion on a daily basis. These two officers have great respect for each other and cooperate closely. Company policy is crafted by input from both people, and they rarely disagree over policy or procedure. On the rare occasions where this occurs, after perhaps spirited discussion, the CEO has to make the final decision. And, by the way, both officers have a huge ownership position in the company, so the greatest benefits flow to each when the right decision is made for the company as a whole. Thus, do you think these officers care more about being the one who is right or about *getting it right?*

Which of these two pictures do you think God had in mind when taking about submission? While in practice the CEO rarely overrules the judgement of the COO, he or she is granted the prerogative to have final say over every aspect of the company according to the company bylaws. Thus, in one sense, the COO is "fully submitted" to the CEO. In reality, the reason there are multiple people with multiple roles in the company is that everyone's best efforts are required to achieve the company's potential. The CEO and COO are almost always so busy fulfilling their own responsibilities, and they cooperate so closely, that an outsider might never notice that this administrative hierarchy even exists. They would merely see close collaboration and cooperation. (By the way, is this the kind of company you would like to work for?)

*You know that those who are regarded as rulers of the Gentiles lord
it over them, and their high officials exercise authority over them.
Not so with you. Instead, whoever wants to become great among
you must be your servant, and whoever wants to be first must be
slave of all. For even the Son of Man did not come to be served, but
to serve, and to give His life as a ransom for many.*

MARK 10:42-45

One of the sharpest contrasts between the Kingdom of God and
the world system is in the nature of authority and in how authority is
exercised. In the world system authority and power define the value
of the leader, and the worth of each individual is determined by their
place in the hierarchy beneath the leader. The one at the top has the
power, controls the resources, reaps the benefits, and is viewed as the
most important. All the rest are trained to admire, even worship, those
with power, influence, fame, and money, for their positions give these
people what it takes to have their own way over others. This means,
according to the world, that they are inherently more important than
others. But this runs cross grain with something inside us, doesn't it?
People admire but also resent those who have vast power, wealth, and
influence. People also view the "important people" as being unfairly
privileged, benefitting from some cosmic inequity that overlooked the
most important persons of all: themselves. We realize at the most fundamental level that these people are actually *not* more important than
ourselves or anyone else.

These viewpoints together highlight three curious realities. First,
we are all made in the image of God; thus, all are equally important
in one very real sense. But in another sense we are all unequal. We
have unequal capabilities, we are unequally wise, we work unequally
hard, and we have unequal life circumstances. Visible and measurable
rewards are unequally distributed across the face of the earth. The
third reality is that Satan, a created being, unquestionably *not* God,
believes his path to upending the Creator is to gather power and influence over others, and through the power conveyed by this influence

overthrow the Creator and rule in His place. We have assurance from the Almighty that this pretender's plan is doomed to fail.

Yet this plan continues to be pursued avidly by Satan, obviously no fan of the concept of hierarchy under the rule of God. And Satan's counterplan is being avidly pursued by those following his lead, who curiously seem to not mind being under Satan's authority as they join him in rebelling against the rightful authority of God. People following Satan often operate under the ultimate delusion: as they turn from following God, they think they are assuming the role of captain of their fate and master of their soul. But this is not at all the case. The ultimate question is not *whether* one is under authority. Even Satan, ultimately, is still under God's authority at this moment and for all eternity, a reality that will become clear at a certain point in the future. The only question is *who* we choose as our authority. The only one under no one's authority is God. Yet Jesus—God—fully submitted to the Father. What does God say about the proper role and use of authority?

God says that the true leader is servant of all. What does Satan say about leadership? Satan demonstrates that his leadership is about domination and deception. He is trying to increase his actual value in the system through leading as massive a rebellion as possible, one he apparently believes can still succeed. Can you see in the efforts of people attempting to climb to the top of the depth chart this same desire to enhance one's ultimate worth, one's position in the universe, to put oneself in a position to be the most gratified, served, and adored? Is all of this enemy-inspired thinking a deception from one end to the other? Yes. This is leadership under which one would chafe, for it is all about proving to you that you are of less value than the one at the top.

This brings two things into question: First, people's erroneous view that their true worth is related to their place in the hierarchy. Their true worth is found in being made in the image of God. And what about the rewards that really matter, that really satisfy, that are true rewards? Where do these come from? I would suggest that they come from the one who made our hearts, who fashioned our lives, who knows how to bless us more than we know how to bless ourselves. I suggest that any rewards that last—especially for eternity, but even ones that endure through our lives on earth—are found by following God's plan for our lives. Any benefit, as we have noted, which is promised that entails departing from God's plan is an illusion. Our rebellious efforts will certainly have consequences that we do not expect, and we will not enjoy the rewards we do expect. The lives of the rich, famous, and powerful are full of such long-term outcomes.

How can people practice mutual submission, and how can a woman submit to a man's direction, especially when she knows she is right? Let me reiterate something earlier said about covenant. Our true self-interests change as we enter covenant. This reality should not be underestimated. First, our self-interest now incorporates the interests of the one who has become one with us. Second, our former self-interest pertains to a being who literally no longer exists. Our current self-interest, properly understood, includes three things simultaneously: first, a correct understanding of our real needs; second, a correct understanding of the needs of our covenant partner; and third, the needs of our relationship—our family. The correct path of decision will reflect the synthesis of these three.

In covenant there is no "mine and yours," only "ours."
In the same way, there is no "Because I said so . . . "

In practice, as Holley and I are considering any issue or decision, we lay out everything we are thinking on the matter. Then we look at the reasoning behind what we are thinking. Why do we want this or that, or why do we think one option is the best idea? We talk through things to get to the values and motives that are most important for each of us. As we discuss, not uncommonly we find ourselves exchanging positions, each taking the other's initial position. Very often, viewpoints converge as we are discussing the deeper issues involved. Even when they do not, this may be an extremely valuable time to reflect further on what we really need, or on what is most important, so viewpoint differences are not a bad thing. They make us look even more closely at our own heart, at each other's heart, and at the big picture. Once we come to accord on the highest priorities in this situation for both of us, the next question is how to address the issue. Again, there is much discussion. Throughout, this is not about being right, it is about getting it right.

Often we arrive at a view of the situation and a "right" solution that is far from where either of us started. Working through real-life issues in this way is a huge part of God's plan for our growth, individually and as a couple. And if we reach an impasse? This has happened maybe a couple of times a decade, but when it does, Holley takes the position that God has made me primarily responsible for the outcome since I am charged with making the call. We both realize that our abilities to predict the outcomes of even the most simple decisions are limited, so it makes no sense to push our viewpoint beyond its real value. And we both realize, even if it appears a mistake was made, that God may well use this situation for our ultimate benefit. This is much more likely if we are making a point of following His pattern for decision-making and involving Him in the process through prayer and seeking His will. It should be obvious, but let me emphasize that each step of this process is bathed in prayer. We are both seeking the ultimate source of guidance, and we both realize that this guidance may come through either of us.

Does anything about this scenario make Holley feel inferior, one-down, devalued, or overlooked? You are welcome to ask her yourself, but you already know the answer.

In the Kingdom of God there is an entirely different foundation for the worth of the individual. Each of us is equally valuable to a loving Creator. Why? Because we are made in His image for His purposes. We are loved by Him because we are in His image. Further, when we enter covenant with God we are given new life, His life, as we are indwelled by His Spirit. There is no particular thing we are, or must accomplish, nor is there any error or crime that we commit that alters our basic value as a human being made in God's image, or that alters our worth if we are in covenant with God as a re-created child of the Father, adopted into His family forever. Why? Because our worth derives solely from our value in the eyes of the Father, and from our relationship to Him. Rewards may vary; worth is a settled question.

Our world teaches us to strive for the top spot, to gain all the power and glory we can. God teaches us something very different. In fact, Jesus spent three years of continual conversation with his disciples shifting their views from those of the world to God's views on authority and its exercise; He focused on this since they would soon be exercising authority in the Kingdom of God, leading in His Name. Multiple conversations are recorded where the disciples were arguing about who was the greatest or who would sit at the right and left hand of Jesus when He was on His throne in the coming kingdom. And there are multiple places recorded where Jesus corrected His disciples' viewpoints. Rather than seeking one's own power and glory, Jesus pointed His followers in a radically different direction if they wanted to be great in the Kingdom of Heaven.

> *The greatest among you will be your servant.*
> MATTHEW 23:11

One cannot overstate how this conflicted with the view of self-importance of nearly everyone around Jesus. Servants were of little or no value in anyone's eyes. They had no power, no possessions, no influence. By definition they were people who were told what to do. How is this a good thing, especially if getting our way is the thing? And, by the way, this view is not confined to our culture. It has characterized every culture throughout history because it has been sold by the same being to humans who have continued to fall for the same deception throughout history. Jesus elaborated on this idea in another passage.

> *You know that the rulers of the Gentiles lord it over them, and their high officials exercise authority over them. Not so with you. Instead, whoever wants to become great among you must be your*

servant, and whoever wants to be first must be your slave—just as
the Son of Man did not come to be served, but to serve, and to give
His life as a ransom for many.
MATTHEW 20:25-28

Some time later, Jesus illustrated this point by clothing Himself with a towel and washing the disciples' feet, which would have been the job of the lowest-ranking servant in the home. Peter initially resisted this display of indignity, but Jesus continued to press His point (John 13:1-17).

While this does not make any sense in the world's way of thinking, it does make sense in God's economy. How? God's greatest commands involve love. One indispensable element of genuine love is understanding and meeting the needs of other people. If one is exalted over other people, that person by definition views their own needs and prerogatives as more important than the needs and prerogatives of anyone else. Leaders in the model of the world do not get to know those under their authority in a way that allows them to genuinely meet their deepest needs. Nor do they care to do so or see any reason why they should. To give orders, or to get one's way, one must only know what one wants to happen and have the necessary leverage over others. The needs of other people are instead made into campaign slogans or tools of manipulation.

In contrast, to follow God's directive to love other people, we must know them, respect them, and act in their best interests. Meeting someone else's needs makes the statement that this person is worthy—worth the effort, important enough to be noticed and cared about. Can you see how this affirmation of the worth of others begins to contradict the idea that we are the center of the universe? To act in another person's best interests, you must learn what is needed by them and what is important to them. Who is the person most in touch with the needs of another person? The one who is serving those needs. The verb is "serving," but the noun is "servant." One who is serving the needs of others is by definition a servant.

Jesus goes one step further and equates greatness with being slaves. This is one step down the hierarchy even from a servant, to the lowest rung of all. This is the kind of person who would be chained to an oar in the hold of a ship. What is the point of this? Simply that our interactions with others in the Kingdom of God should be purely about enhancing the lives of everyone we meet in every way we can. There is to be no part of our efforts that is intended to elevate ourselves above others. Jesus wants us to delete the world-inspired concept of status-based and power-based worth from our thinking in order to focus on something altogether different: loving other people. This is not to say that our own needs are unimportant and should be ignored. Our needs are just as important as the needs of others, and that is the point. They are equally important, no more and no less.

It should be noted that Jesus descended from His place of honor and glory in Heaven to position Himself as our servant. In that position He was ill-used, scorned, betrayed, and brutalized, then unjustly murdered, all for our sake. If He asks us, in return, to endure one small indignity or another, is this really too much to ask? But His instructions are not about simply deflating our egos; they point us toward a lifestyle that is formed around serving people and building real relationships rather than falsely exalting ourselves at the expense of other people, a move that poisons genuine relationship.

The deeper reality Jesus is revealing in this statement is that the rewards in life that matter most come from following and pleasing Him, and from being blessed by Him, not from a self-perception of importance or from the vote of the crowd. The rewards that matter most of all begin now, but will last for eternity, and these may bear little resemblance to the reaction of the crowd in the moment. Note how the crowd responded to Jesus for details. In the face of these instructions from God, the strength of our attachment to worldly ideas of self-importance is truly amazing, as it was for the disciples. Do you think Jesus wants to shift our views just as He wanted to shift theirs? Beyond our attachments to worldly status, power, position, and wealth, Jesus wants us to see that the underlying thesis of the world's plan is fatally flawed—*getting our own way* is not the path to the best life. That comes through *following His way*. Why is this such an important distinction? Do you think God, in His wisdom, might have set up the perfect tool to teach this distinction in the issues of life, small and large, right in the middle of our marriages?

Imagine two figures, one a pyramid, the other a chain. The world's view is that the leader is at the top of the pyramid. The buck stops at the top, more bucks than for anyone else, in fact. Ultimate power is vested in the ultimate leader, and greatest rewards come to the one at the top. Who is the highest paid person in any company? In contrast, in God's view we are all links in a chain. Children obey parents, husbands are head of the administrative structure of the home, and spiritual authority is given to certain offices in a church. We are also to obey laws and pay taxes. Each link is under the authority of the one above. Husbands are not at the top of the pyramid, nor are those in spiritual authority in a church. Each is in their proper place in a chain of authority that extends from those under our care, to us, to those in authority over us, then to Jesus, who is in turn under the authority of the Father. Note the times when Jesus would have preferred something different from what the Father had ordained, as in the Garden of Gethsemane. He asked the Father to "remove this cup from me" (Luke 22:42), yet He ended His appeal by saying, "not my will but yours be done." Jesus leads the way in all things, even in submission within this chain of authority.

One thing we often do not consider is that God has the right, in the same sense that the CEO of a company which employs us has the right, to review and redirect anything we do. The difference is that the CEO's oversight only extends to company business. God's right of review extends to every word, thought, and deed. God has in fact said He will take note of every word, thought, and deed and will recompense us for every one of these in light of His Word and His will for us (Matthew 16:26, 27). We have not seen this set of consequences fully in action (yet), so we do not often have this reality in mind as we go about our daily lives. But the extent to which we have submitted ourselves to God will at one point in time become extremely important for all eternity. One of the realities of living is that God is trying to train us to live in the Kingdom of God in a way that will gain blessing and reward for us in the end, and He does this because He loves us. He offers us the opportunity to follow Him. True love, after all, is a choice each must make. God informs us of the consequences of obeying or not obeying, but He does not compel obedience. He continues to offer us the choice to submit ourselves to Him. As we experience the benefits of following God's plan in marriage, and in other realms of life, we gain more motivation to follow Him with more enthusiasm and more exacting obedience. Our passion is kindled for God's ways.

> Yet from the redemptive heart of God flowed a plan through which these disasters produced huge blessings even though the pain and loss were real.

Holley and I have noted at several points in our lives situations we thought were genuinely worst-case scenarios; we faced personally devastating things. But looking back, each of these proved to be the seedbed from which grew some of the greatest blessings in our lives. Not only did we not get what we wanted in these situations, we got the last thing we wanted. Yet from the redemptive heart of God flowed a plan through which these disasters produced huge blessings even though the pain and loss were real. We had to deal with these impacts, and in the short run that seemed to be all there was of these situations: pain and loss.

The lesson learned looking back is, when adversity arrives, to first make sure we are on solid ground as far as behavior and heart. Then, as mentioned before, rather than asking "Why me?" to ask, "Lord, what are you trying to teach me through this situation?" Then we can safely trust God with the outcome of our lives, even though, based on everything in our field of view, it looks like our lives have just sustained a devastating loss. But what inside us changes if we realize this is not the end of the story? What if we realize God is still at work even in these things?

Why mention all this as we are discussing submission? Because we are often tempted to not follow God because we fear one outcome or another. We have the mistaken impression that our lives will be better in the end if we avoid an outcome that frightens us, even if that means taking charge ourselves and clearly going outside God's will in some way. By the way, does this pattern seem familiar? At times, Satan entices us to brush past God and follow him; at other times he terrifies us into running from God and straight into his waiting arms. If instead we trust God and walk with Him no matter where He leads, we will discover several things. First, we will see that God's priorities for us are deeper and more important than our own; second, we will see that God has the power and wisdom to navigate us through life in ways that will ensure the safety of everything that truly matters; and third, we will see that we can trust God's love, His desire for our best, in every way, at every point, more than we can trust ourselves.

God may pry something we deem very important from our grasp, which may even be very important and its loss quite painful, to teach us and prepare us for something of more importance He will place in our hands later. If we hold on too tightly, resist too much, become dissatisfied or bitter, what direction have we chosen? The other thing we will see is that our estimation of our ability to predict the future, or to predict the full significance of a particular outcome, is extremely overrated. We are more often wrong than right about what is going to happen, or its importance, in sharp contrast with God. Once these things are proven to us by experience, submission to God becomes something we wholeheartedly desire. Of course, the only way these things are proven is by trusting God and watching what happens over time in painful or threatening situations.

There is one other aspect of submission that is a direct result of the joining and merger of identity in covenant. We are used to the notion that if one wins, the other loses; if one gets their way, the other does not; if one is strengthened, this happens at the expense of the other. We believe these things because we have seen these principles in operation our entire lives. For every winner there is necessarily a loser, right? Covenant completely erases this dynamic. How?

In covenant, joined in identity and nature as he and she are, one's victory also belongs to the other; one's blessing and advancement belongs to both; one's loss and pain belongs to both. The strength of one benefits both; the honor of each is shared. So how much sense does it make for one partner to undercut the other? And how much sense does it make to covet the authority vested in the other from whatever source—positional on an organizational chart or earned by training or competence? In covenant, our highest honor is to honor the other. Therefore, how would we reasonably respond if others honor our beloved? In covenant there is no rational basis for competition of any type. There is no basis for envy, nor for a feeling of superiority. This points back to the imperative of understanding covenant, for this is the only reason it would make sense to have this viewpoint toward another person. How does this play into the issue of submission and mutual submission, of submission first to Christ, then to truth, then to each other, instead of submission only to our individual and perpetually distorted sense of our own best interest?

> In covenant there is no rational basis for competition of any type. There is no basis for envy, nor for a feeling of superiority.

BUILDING A LIFE OF SUBMISSION IN MARRIAGE

A life of submission to God is not an easy life. It is one filled with blessings but also with challenges. It is, though, the best possible life. How do we develop such a life? This is simple: one decision at a time. But we will not even begin seriously attempting to live these things until we have sufficient reasons to do so, nor until we have effectively rebutted the world's reasons for not doing do. I have attempted to provide such reasons in brief. You may need to spend much more time considering these issues before arriving at your own conclusions, and I encourage you to do so given the importance of the question.

Assuming that you do want to pursue this life in your marriage, here are some practical ideas and steps.

It is crucial, if a mature covenant pattern is to be developed in a marriage, that both partners move toward the same goal: mutual submission and mutual love. If one partner is "not there yet," the other partner modeling godly behavior can help keep a lid on some of the conflict, but, obviously, "mutual" means mutual. Two people are ideally in a learning process, encouraging each other, supporting each other, helping each other, caring about each other—that is, in the process of learning to love each other as God directs.

I mentioned the pattern Holley and I follow. The first step is to remember the bigger picture. First, we are not to see *our* ideas as *the only appropriate* endpoint and the other person's views as the obstacle to all things good and right. We are to consider the other person's interests as equal to our own, since they are—in covenant, both equal and our own. If two people are taking each other's interests into account, seeking to know and understand each other, then daily decisions rarely require extensive discussion.

When a significant difference of opinion exists, and further discussion is warranted, this should be directed toward finding the best answer, not toward one simply getting his or her way as the other gives in. If done properly the discussion will not look like a conflict, but instead more like a planning session where all factors, reasons, and contingencies are laid on the table and examined. Real needs and desires are further examined, factors are weighed, and all is prayerfully considered. God's will for this situation is sought through prayer in a spirit of collaboration. This process will almost always produce an agreed-upon answer. This process will also do more than almost anything else to clarify our real needs and deepest priorities. This is one of the best possible ways to get to know each other.

When, after thorough discussion, a difference still exists about the best course, a decision must now be made between the best options. Notice that the injunction to submit is not initially gender-specific, but a mutual one. Both parties in a marriage at this point are to step back and prayerfully consider whether it would be better to defer to the passionately voiced alternative presented by the other party. Taking this step back often leads to reconsideration and then crafting a mutually acceptable compromise. If there is still an impasse, God gives the call, and responsibility, to the husband.

This is a picture of decision-making in a mature relationship between spiritually mature people. But this is not where anyone starts, or where any couple starts. People in relationships leading toward marriage and people in marriage have varying levels of maturity, varying levels of understanding of the nature of marriage, and varying levels of understanding themselves. Many may still be living out the "competing kingdoms" model of marriage far more than the covenant model. How does such immaturity and lack of understanding change God's command to husbands and wives? The answer: It does not.

Early on the issue of submission likely will come down to a few focal points: a situation where a decision is under consideration or has already been made, in which one party thinks they are right and the other party is wrong . . . dead wrong . . . even seriously wrong. And something is at stake that really matters—reputation, family finances, the children's future, or some other weighty matter. Or there may be a decision where one person is not considered, perhaps not consulted, and this impacts both. Or there is a scenario where one party's desires seem, in their mind, to be the trump card in the discussion. Therefore, there is no real discussion.

How do we handle such situations? First, is a genuine moral issue at stake? If a proposed course of action violates one of God's other commands—is it dishonest or illegal, for example?—then submission is inappropriate. At this point we should submit to the higher moral authority: God. The concept of submission is also never to offer one party leverage to abuse the other. It should already be clear that abuse is a fundamental and grievous violation of our covenant vows.

But if this situation is about competing perceptions of best interest, or about personal desires or priorities, as is most often the case, we are now presented with a familiar scenario: do we brush past God's clear instructions and pursue our own perception of our best interests, or do we follow His commands? One more reality must be grasped: even beyond a sense of self-interest, our ability to predict the overall outcome of a decision is less than perfect. (If humans were really good at predicting outcomes based on looking at current factors, there would be many more people making lots of money in the stock market.) We are often less effective than we realize at predicting the overall consequences of any decision. The one who actually ordains outcomes is God. There is a moral cause-and-effect universe with which we interact, and outcomes can be much better predicted if we understand this cause-and-effect realm. However, God is still able to surprise us with unexpected blessings that flow from apparently bad choices. Or, following an apparently best choice, we may be faced with unexpected challenges. If we are to follow the wisest course, we should seek the most prudent decisions in every case while at the same time being careful to follow God regarding things like chain of authority. In any situation, we do well to leave God room to teach lessons to everyone involved and make sure we are tuned to His lesson for our own life.

Even if one party is more about getting their way, is fully centered on perceived self-interest, and even acting like a jerk, the best move is for the other person to follow God's pattern. In practice, this would look like listening to the other person's concerns and ideas and trying to craft a plan that takes both parties' interests into account. The moves of listening, trying to understand, and being responsive to the other's view will generally defuse a conflict scenario into a discussion. It is not a godly move to simply give in to an intransigent debater in these situations. Instead, press more deeply into what is driving the person to insist on their way. And, in the end, since almost no decision is going to result in irreparable harm, leading the way toward the right kind of conversation, offering submission in the matter, then trusting God for the outcome is appropriate. Simply being listened to and cared about will have influence on the one who needs to learn God's pattern. It is also appropriate to point out that submission on this issue is *because of God's pattern and for His sake*, not simply bowing before human pressure or manipulation, and that such submission reflects our mutual responsibility before Him. At the same time, let God work in hearts, and refrain from pulling up past decisions for present debating points.

Instead, pray for the person and be an example of godly behavior. In this scenario, the wife or husband may be the more spiritually mature person; this pattern is applicable in either direction under the "mutual submission" injunction.

What about the husband, particularly the reference to him "giving himself up" for her, "washing" his wife with the Word, playing a role in her purification (all from Ephesians 5)? The rest of this passage, which compares the role of Christ and the church to husband and wife, centers on the husband loving the wife in tangible ways and recognizing her as his own body. These statements have in view the role marriage is intended to play in growth and transformation. How, in sum, can the husband conduct himself in marriage in a way that has the most beneficial effect on his wife? This is quite simple: by devoting himself wholeheartedly to loving her as he devotes himself to becoming the man God created him to be.

His love will not be perfect or mistake-free. His decisions will not be flawless, nor will his heart and motives always be pure. But if the man takes the position of loving and serving, as well as leading, protecting, providing, and fulfilling all the other roles of a covenant partner, then his wife will in all likelihood be free to grow to her potential before the Lord as a person, wife, and mother if they have children. This is not to say that the wife cannot provide, lead, and be responsible for her own growth before God, and play key roles in her husband's growth and transformation. It is a practical reality that either party, surrounded by the elements of a good marriage, will thrive in ways that are simply impossible for a single person or a person in a challenging marriage.

While we are discussing the positive impact both parties can have on the other, we must also note another possibility. There are people who are not trying to wholeheartedly follow God and His ways, or to follow them at all. These will vary from typically worldly-selfish people to toxic and manipulative people, all the way to emotional or physical abusers—but these same people may, at the same time, be covering themselves in a veneer of Christianity. In most scenarios with such people, being treated according to God's patterns will warm hearts and build relationships. This in turn will encourage the other party to seek a deeper relationship with God for themselves. But there is no guarantee that godly behavior will positively impact another person. At times loving behaviors even invite the other person to escalate manipulative and destructive behaviors. Being open and vulnerable to some people only offers them more leverage, more opportunity to use and wound the other. Scriptural injunctions to love unconditionally are tempered by those recognizing that such love may not be sincerely received or returned (Romans 12:18).

Jesus interacted with many people who did not turn from their ways to follow Him. Some, seeing His life and power, responded by trying to compromise, silence, and ultimately destroy Him. This is why selecting a covenant partner who not only professes a relationship with Christ but whose life is clearly impacted by that relationship is so important. But not every Christian is married to a Christian, and even some people who profess to be followers of Christ can be dangerous. Thus, the injunction to love is tempered by the injunctions to be wise (Matthew 10:16) and to not put ourselves in harm's way (Matthew 7:6). The Scriptures also warn about entering covenant with an unbeliever, which is termed being "unequally yoked." Beware of the urge to save someone by entering covenant with them, to rescue someone drowning in sin by inviting his or her life into your own. Despite the love we might feel for someone in this situation, we must be careful not to go outside God's specific instructions (see 2 Corinthians 6:14). Submitting to someone who has no chance of offering godly leadership in marriage is clearly not what God has in mind. With this in mind, while discussing what submission is, we also need to consider what submission is not.

Submission is in no way an invitation to abuse, to offer inappropriate treatment, or to devalue another individual. If an administrative authority leads in a way contrary to God's Word, it is appropriate to deal with this situation in the Lord's name. Various ways this might be done are beyond the scope of this chapter. This should involve counsel from other mature Christians and perhaps even involve church authority.

There is an approach to difficult people that is termed *codependence* that is sometimes confused with love and submission but is neither. This is giving in—submitting, in one sense—to being a part of or enabling the destructive or self-destructive behaviors of another person. Another term for the person who looks the other way is an "enabler." People who are abusive or addicted often attempt to recruit helpers—spouses, family members, parents, children—to cover for them, to clean up their messes, to provide what is needed so they can continue their addictions, to help them cover up behaviors that are damaging or even criminal. What would a covenant heart be toward such a person?

Real love is based on truth and the best interests of all involved. There is a concept called "tough love" used by Christian counselors, an approach in which behaviors and lies are confronted and consequences are allowed to impact one who is refusing to turn from destructive behaviors. In any situation where seriously dysfunctional behaviors are involved—such as narcissistic or borderline personality disorders, and in situations where there are addictive and abusive behaviors—professional help is imperative. God's injunction to turn the other cheek (Matthew 5:29) refers to refraining from engaging in back-and-forth insults. This is not an injunction to submit to ongoing physical or emotional abuse.

There is also a role for pastoral or professional counseling if significant violations of covenant principle are present. If we want to build the best marriage, we want to continually be aiming for God's pattern for such a marriage. Obviously the first step would be a couple's study of God's plan for marriage, such as reading this book together. For some, though, the importance of building a marriage according to God's plan will not be of interest unless something is impressed upon them: the damage that is being caused by their own actions. This requires involvement by a third party, a pastor or counselor. At this point, the person may be more open to alternate approaches.

It is fascinating—and distressing—to see how Satan's perversions of understanding submission have twisted God's commands into something of a flash point even in the Christian community, and a source of outright derision for those not in covenant with God. Submission is never about diminishing the worth of another. If anything, the pattern in Scripture is of the more powerful one submitting to serve the needs of the weaker for the sake of love. Submission is not a one-sided thing but a mutual and reciprocal thing, and part of the spiritual and character growth processes for both parties. God's plan only works if husbands love their wives as Christ loves the church. This is God's plan to put the husband in the most powerful position to love and serve his wife and family. This plan only works if the husband recognizes and operates under submission to the One who is the link in the chain above him and is not only carrying out His plan himself, but instead leading everyone under his charge in this direction. And the wife's role, respecting her husband, offers her access, full involvement, and all necessary influence to move the marriage toward God's plan. The wife must simply decide which is more important and more worthy of her efforts, God's plan or her own.

> Submission is never about diminishing the worth of another. If anything, the pattern in Scripture is of the more powerful one submitting to serve the needs of the weaker for the sake of love.

Why are we going to such lengths to discuss this topic? Because there are two places where Satan has most successfully attacked marriage and family over my sixty-year lifespan. The first is God's authority structure within marriage and within the family between spouses and between parents and children.

We will cover his second point of attack—sexuality—in the next chapter.

ACTION POINTS

1. Move from conflict toward collaboration.

When listening to the issues that most couples tie up over, my most common reaction is, "And you're getting wrapped around the axle about *that*?" Often the most trivial and petty things are the most contested things. It will make no difference in the big scheme of things whether it goes this way or that. It is all about winning and losing. If we start by subtracting this dynamic from a relationship, we have taken the first step toward a constructive partnership. Many people have been so surrounded by contention and strife in close relationships that they cannot envision a relationship as God intends. Every step away from pointless conflict and toward considerate collaboration is a move toward God's plan and a more satisfying relationship.

2. Shift focus from getting our way to serving and loving others.

We are so trained to focus first and foremost on our own desires and agenda that this requires effort. It is not that our needs and desires are unimportant. We have behind us God, His resources, and His power to meet our needs. Therefore, confident that our needs will be met in the end, we have the luxury of being able to devote attention to building a better life for other people who perhaps do not have such resources to draw from. Jesus said it clearly: "It is more blessed to give than to receive" (Acts 20:35).

3. Learn to use anger appropriately.

Anger is not our enemy; it is a capacity built within to protect and defend, to energize us to overcome threats and solve big problems. But we must learn to harness our anger for our own good and the good of others. While appropriate anger is felt when our life or our vital interests are threatened, we often misinterpret not getting our way as a threat to our most vital interests. Thus, we often display anger when our prerogatives are challenged. This anger is inappropriate. To deal with such a pattern of anger, we must understand that many things about ourselves and relationships are more important than getting our way, as we have been discussing throughout this section. We must clarify and refocus our priorities.

Our spouses are not enemies to be defeated by our anger, nor are they obstacles that can be manipulated by anger. It is certainly not wrong to speak with honest anger. "The heart of the wise instructs his mouth, and adds persuasion to his lips" (Proverbs 16:23, NASB). But it is wrong to attack another's character, to dishonor him or her, or to wound for the sake of getting one's way. It is right to be angry about a breach of integrity, a violation of God's Word, or a covenant vow. But one does better by dealing with such things with humility since we will predictably find ourselves on the other end of such conversations. It is always a good guide to treat other people as we would like to be treated in the same situation. Employ anger as the energy that pushes you to solve problems, to confront issues, to overcome obstacles, both within yourself and in a relationship. God created anger for very good reasons and as a useful tool when properly employed.

QUESTIONS FOR THOUGHT

1. How do you feel about submission to God? How do you feel about submitting to another human? How does being in a covenant relationship change how you feel about submitting to another person? Or does it?

2. How important is it to you to make every possible effort to make what you think is best actually take place?

3. How confident are you in any situation that you know what is best in the long run for yourself and others?

4. Have you ever personally experienced a situation where a "worst-case scenario" outcome was later turned by God into something good and important in your life? How often do we look only at outcomes we think we understand in the moment and forget the bigger picture, and our even bigger God? How does this impact our view of submission in marriage?

5. Jesus spent three years, 24/7, with a group of men conveying three messages: 1) His true identity; 2) that they therefore could totally believe in Him and believe every detail He conveyed to them; 3) the nature of the relationship among them—servanthood instead of leadership and hierarchy as it was known in their world. (Note also that these men were about to enter into a new covenant relationship with God, and with each other, as we will see in the next volume in this series.) How would you describe the lessons Jesus was trying to teach about leadership? How does this impact our view of submission in marriage?

6. When we have the urge to not submit to something that is actually in the best interest of our partner, what is pulling on the other end of the rope? When we have the urge to not submit to a request by our partner that we are not sure is actually in their best interest, what is pulling on the other end of this rope? Should we handle these two situations differently? In what way?

7. Does submission mean downplaying our own wants and needs versus those of the other person? If not, what does it mean?

8. If I said the path of submission is not the path of "giving in," but the path of growth, would you agree or disagree? Why?

9. What is the difference between submission and codependence? How does this difference relate to truth, integrity, and love?

10. How is one's approach different when a couple is practicing mutual submission versus only one taking this approach? Even when two people are committed to following God's plan, might one expect early on that the relationship would shift back and forth between these two? How, then, might one prepare for this in the relationship?

CHAPTER ELEVEN

The Parts of God's Plan Most Disdained By the World But Most Necessary for Success: Sexuality

Sexual intercourse is about new life: giving one's life, receiving the life of another, and creating a new life, a joined life, within the participants. In addition, it is God's plan to create new human beings within the structure of a loving family.

May your fountain be blessed and may you rejoice in the wife of your youth. A loving doe, a graceful deer—may her breasts satisfy you always, may you ever be intoxicated with her love.
PROVERBS 5:18, 19

What God has joined together, let man not separate.
MARK 10:9

It is God's will that you should be sanctified; that you should avoid sexual immorality; that each of you should learn to control your own body in a way that is holy and honorable, not in passionate lust like the pagans who do not know God; and that in this matter no one should wrong or take advantage of a brother or a sister. The Lord will punish all those who commit such sins, as we told you and warned you before. For God did not call us to be impure, but to live a holy life. Therefore, anyone who rejects this instruction

*does not reject a human being but God, the very God
who gives you His Holy Spirit.*
1 THESSALONIANS 4:3-9

*Flee fornication. Every sin that a man does is outside the body; but
he that commits fornication sins against his own body.*
1 CORINTHIANS 6:18

*The acts of the flesh are obvious: sexual immorality, impurity and
debauchery; idolatry and witchcraft; hatred, discord, jealousy, fits
of rage, selfish ambition, dissensions, factions and envy, drunkenness, orgies, and the like. I warn you, as I did before, that those who
live like this will not inherit the Kingdom of God.*
GALATIANS 5:19-21

*They exchanged the truth of God for a lie, and worshipped and
served created things rather than the Creator—who is forever
praised, Amen. Because of this, God gave them over to shameful
lusts. Even their women exchanged natural sexual relations for
unnatural ones. In the same way the men also abandoned natural
relationships with women and were inflamed with lust for one another. Men committed shameful acts with other men, and received
in themselves the due penalty for their error.*
ROMANS 1:25-27

GOD, THE ULTIMATE ROMANTIC

If you read the Song of Solomon—which I recommend doing—
you will see God's depiction of romance and physical desire, a beautiful picture of love. God built our hearts to love, to pursue a romantic relationship, to win the heart of our beloved, to join together in a
happily-ever-after love affair that includes satisfying heart, mind, and

sexual drives and urges which were built into us by God. Everything that inflames our hearts into an inferno of passion for another person taps into mechanisms God created in our mind and heart for just this purpose, mechanisms designed to draw two people together into the closest and deepest relationship possible. Building a relationship upon which a marriage can be founded, then building the marriage, requires vast energy and effort. And vast energy resides within most of us waiting for this opportunity, longing for this hope, aware at some level that this is the centerpiece of our future. Because God made us so.

Sexual expression is a vital piece of God's plan for love—in its proper context. God's plan is that sexual desire fuel the growth of a romantic relationship that is going to lead to creation of a covenant. So that this will happen in the most powerful and productive way, God designed the powers of our mind, heart, and body to be guided by certain principles and realities. He has a plan to harness, in a constructive way, the raging fire we term "falling in love." What is powerful for good can, unfortunately, also turn into a destructive thing—fire can warm a house or burn it down. We do not want to be deceived about someone's romantic intentions toward us, nor do we want to be deceived into engaging in sexual activity that does harm to our relationship instead of building it properly. God has given us powers—the three powers we have been discussing—necessary to direct our passions in a constructive direction in full obedience to Him. The most important thing to understand about sexuality is that obedience to God equates with our most wonderful sexual experience.

As we are walking through life with our needs, desires, and dreams, encountering opportunities along the way, it is helpful to remember that God's plan is designed to lead us to the best and most satisfying lives possible. He wants to protect us from hidden dangers. He is the ultimate romantic, and He wants us to enjoy this part of ourselves, this dimension of relationship, to the full. He wants us to feel the full power and delight of romantic love and its physical expression. He wants us to thoroughly enjoy something that is at the very heart of His plan of covenant: sexual activity.

GOD'S FINGERPRINTS ON LOVE

One reason I am so certain there is a God is that His plan for romance and sexuality lines up so precisely with how we are created. His plan might not line up particularly well with misinformation about sexuality that has been embraced by our culture in recent years. But even here, His Word explains perfectly why this misinformation exists and where these distorted messages about sexuality come from and why. ("For our struggle is not against flesh and blood, but . . . against the spiritual forces of evil in the heavenly realms," Ephesians 6:12.) I know these are broad assertions and quite countercultural. As countercultural as a really good marriage. God is not on the board of directors of Planned Parenthood. We are going to take the time to work through these assertions, for the beliefs we affirm in this realm are among the most important decisions we will make.

"Be memorable."
KY PERSONAL LUBRICANT TELEVISION COMMERCIAL

"Avoid immorality; be faithful to the wife of your youth."
GOD

Don't we all want to wake up next to someone who loves us deeply and wholeheartedly? Next to someone who is committed to us for a lifetime, who has committed to walk through any and every circumstance of life by our side? Next to someone who knows how to treat us, how to protect our hearts, how to help us be the best we can be, and how to help us find the greatest rewards our life can offer? Next to someone who will stand by us in a conflict, whom we can trust with our most sensitive things, who will sacrifice anything and everything for our sake? Let me point out that each of the above **So why do we settle for less than this? Because our world tells us this kind of relationship simply does not exist.**

elements is an important foundation stone for the most amazing and rewarding physical relationship possible. So why do we settle for less than this? Because our world tells us this kind of relationship simply does not exist. And if we try to build a relationship guided by the world's priorities and strategies, it will not exist. But these kinds of relationships can definitely be built. God has a beautifully designed plan to produce these things.

Far beyond offering us the best in-the-moment experience, God's plan offers us the path to maturity, preparing us for the rigors of marriage and family life. His plan builds the mind-set, attitudes, values, priorities, and self-discipline, which in turn produce the character, strength, and perseverance to be an excellent covenant partner, the kind of person to whom one's life could reasonably be given. One of the centerpiece strategies for character development in God's plan is choosing and following through with sexual restraint in the face of growing physical and emotional attraction.

The focal point of romance, love, marriage, and family in God's plan is sexual intercourse. Everyone inherently knows that this act is unlike any other in its power and importance. But most seem not to understand this power or how it is used to greatest benefit. Fortunately, God does know the answer to these questions, and He has gone to great lengths to share this information with us. There are a very large number of comments and directions in the Scriptures about sexual conduct. What role does sexual intercourse play in God's plan?

INTERCOURSE INITIATES COVENANT

We have discussed how covenant is entered, via sharing identity-containing fluids with another person. Sexual intercourse corresponds perfectly, in creating the Covenant of Marriage, with the sharing of blood that creates a Blood Covenant. Semen—an identity-containing body fluid—and a female's intimate body fluids, often mixed with blood when a virgin has intercourse—are shared. There are two pictures in sexual intercourse that depict the spiritual reality of covenant, as a covenant is initiated: the entry of the husband's body into the body of the wife, literally inhabiting her body; and depositing something that contains his identity within her. This exchange of fluids not only creates the covenant but may also create an entirely new life in the process, or during any later sexual encounter. Sexual intercourse creates new life in covenant, and new life in the form of a child.

IS A WEDDING REQUIRED TO CREATE A COVENANT?

Is a wedding required in addition to intercourse to create a covenant? In fact, a covenant can be created with no intent at all on the part of the participants. Two people merely need to engage in sexual intercourse. The occasion when people would be least apt to assume that intercourse "meant something" in terms of relationship would be when intercourse is engaged in with a prostitute. This is about money and lust, not love. However, God informs us of a spiritual reality (that is not apparent to the participants in prostitution) in 1 Corinthians 6:16, which says, "Do you not know that he who unites himself with a prostitute is one with her in body? For it is said, 'The two will become one flesh.'" This is the same terminology God used while giving the covenant of marriage to Adam and Eve. There is no question from this verse that a full-fledged covenant relationship is formed by having intercourse with another person regardless of the context or the intentions of the persons involved. This act and this act alone—engaged in by two people for any reason—creates a marriage covenant relationship between two people. Does this begin to explain God's clear and consistent instructions prohibiting this activity outside of marriage? And why, in most cultures throughout history, have sexual activity and marriage have been linked as they have?

Flee sexual immorality. All other sins a person commits are
outside the body, but whoever sins sexually sins against
their own body. Do you not know that your bodies are temples
of the Holy Spirit, who is in you, whom you have received from
God? You are not your own; you were bought with a price.
Therefore, honor God with your bodies.
1 CORINTHIANS 6:18-20

INTERCOURSE CELEBRATES COVENANT

The act of intercourse is a beautiful physical picture of the reality of covenant. One person literally inhabits the other, just as the two now inhabit each other in nature and identity. That an orgasm, accompanying the covenant-creating exchange, is a consummately pleasurable and overwhelming experience is further testimony to the significance of this event. And in the ecstatic experience of orgasm, if one is perceptive enough one can experience the boundaries between the two people blurring. I noticed early in our marriage that I could perceive this via some sort of visual imagination, as two slightly different colored fluids flowing together, swirling and merging. As a man and woman are lying in an exhausted embrace afterward, it can be difficult to discern where self ends and other begins. Again, this reflects the reality of covenant, for this boundary in a spiritual sense ceases to exist as covenant is entered.

A consistent element in all covenant ceremonies is a way of remembering. In blood covenants there is a mark on the body or something always worn to remind people of their covenant. In the New Covenant we are told to engage in a ceremony often termed "Communion" or "The Lord's Supper," and to do so on a regular basis. In this we drink wine, or a type thereof, and eat bread to commemorate and illustrate, in a tangible way, our covenant with Christ. We literally take a representation of Christ into our bodies in a manner that reflects Jesus' words (John 6:53) and His specific instructions (Luke 22:19). In God's plan for marriage, sexual intercourse recalls and celebrates this covenant with one of the most intense and delightful experiences of which humans are capable, revisiting with our beloved the event that initiated our new life together. God tells us to engage in this act regularly (1 Corinthians 7:3-5), just as He instructs us to take communion on a regular basis. Of course, the other "mark of remembrance" is a wedding ring. The ring is put on once, in essence to remain forever. As it is part of the initial ceremony, wedding rings are more analogous to the one-time-public-pronouncement of baptism than to the Lord's Supper.

Sexual intercourse, with all its foreplay and afterplay, all the romance and affection, all of the sweet and wonderful ways two people can be toward each other emotionally and physically, is a wonderful celebration of covenant, of the couple's relationship. The more of life Holley and I traverse together, the more history and relationship we have built, the sweeter, deeper, and more meaningful our physical intimacy has become. It is often implied that sexuality is the domain of the young, that youth is somehow an advantage in this realm. This is simply not true, in our experience at least. Each act of intimacy draws from the entirety of our relationship and experience and builds upon previous encounters. This celebration literally becomes sweeter, deeper, and more meaningful with each passing year.

Being faithful to our spouse, not merely in a technical, sexual sense by not having intercourse with someone outside of marriage, but in the full sense of faithfulness to God's plan—to our covenant and its vows, to God's instructions about how to treat each other, to our responsibility to grow into people who can increasingly live out our vows to each other and God's instructions to us—also is *the path* to a wonderful physical experience, as well as a wonderful emotional, mental, and spiritual experience in sexual intercourse. The key thing to understand about God's plan is that there are no parts that exist in isolation, no parts that work well apart from the others. God's plan is a seamless whole, a plan that encompasses the entirety of our being and entirety of our lives. One can certainly continue to have sexual intercourse and have a struggling and painful marriage. But one's sexual experience in this scenario will be nothing like the experience of those who are walking closely with God, being blessed by Him as they substantially live out His plan. This experience descends to total meaninglessness for those who engage in this act for recreation and idle amusement.

Intercourse within marriage has many purposes and functions beyond remembrance and fun. The underlying principle is that our intimacy should not be used as leverage or a political tool, but instead be a sacred place that is visited frequently. God's command lines up with many realities about us—our need for physical touch and affection, our need for romantic attention, our sexual urges and desires, and it even recognizes that a man and woman may desire or need different things at different times. In instructing us "not to deny one another" (1 Corinthians 7:3-5) God is instructing us to be sensitive and accommodating to the needs and desires of our partner. Why can we not be simply governed by how we feel or what we want sexually? If we are not "in the mood," why does this answer not end the conversation? The answer is that our identity, our nature, and our bodies belong to each other. Our feelings are very important, but so are our partner's. The same is true with our desires and drives. This is not to say that one's desires should control the situation in either direction, but it is to say that the desires and needs of both should receive more consideration than occurs if one thinks his or her mood should rule over all other considerations.

In covenant we are to offer to the other any resource we have, any potential we possess. Our best response is to make every effort to be everything we can be for each other while at the same time respecting each other's real limitations as humans. The only injunction of God regarding timing is: often. Even if one is not in the mood or at their best, a willing approach to a partner is a wonderful reflection of the way every aspect of the relationship is ideally conducted if it is to reach its potential. And disinterest often changes to interest if one approaches their reluctant but willing partner with a kind and considerate heart.

We are to passionately explore this sacred ground. Some who have heard injunctions and negative messages about sexuality—perhaps well intended, but misguided, in an attempt to scare people into avoiding premarital sexual activity. Some may carry this negativity into marriage and assume that this is something "good" people do not really do (much), and if they do, they are not to enjoy it. This could not be further from the heart or intent of the Author of physical intimacy. This is an activity built for intense enjoyment, and to pointedly refrain from enjoying it, or to fail to contribute wholeheartedly to the enjoyment of our covenant partner, is an approach completely out of sync with God's intent. There is no limitation God places on the nature of our sexual expression within marriage beyond its exclusivity between the participants. God built our bodies with many areas that feed into sexual arousal. There are no limitations on our exploration of these areas beyond the desires and tastes of the participants.

> Never miss an opportunity, men, to tell your wife how beautiful she is—inside and out. Nor should women miss the opportunity to affirm the masculinity and attractiveness of their husband.

We want to be at our most attractive for each other. We want to take good care of ourselves. We want to please each other visually as well as in every other way. But life happens, birthdays happen, medical issues happen. Our culture vastly overrates the relationship between physical appearance and sexual attraction, and we should be on guard against this distortion. People's countenances, their heart, the ways they live, their character—these are far more important measures of an individual human being. Beyond this, we have committed ourselves to accept and affirm the other person because their identity and nature reside in us, and ours in them. This reality should inform the affinity we feel, and the affirmation and acceptance we display toward our covenant partner. We took them in sickness and health, for better or worse. And, before God, we still take them. Our attraction to them, the way we value them physically, is an important element of lifelong relationship-building. Never miss an opportunity, men, to tell your wife how beautiful she is—inside and out. Nor should women miss the opportunity to affirm the masculinity and attractiveness of their husband.

How does God's plan create such a wonderful intimate experience? Acts of physical intimacy are intensely private. They create their own world inhabited by just these two. This depicts the exclusivity of marriage. Sexual intercourse is a wellspring of relationship. It teaches us many things about each other and ourselves. We learn about sharing, giving, and finding joy together. We explore bodies, desires, and sensitivities. All the elements of God's plan are reflected, including trust, vulnerability, transparency, intimacy, gentleness, kindness, and every other way we have vowed to treat each other if we are to create the most delightful experience for our covenant partner and ourselves. The other elements we have vowed—total acceptance, the permanence of the relationship, wholehearted love, protection, provision, and more—create the foundational emotional environment in which hearts can truly be vulnerable and open toward each other, fully trusting in each other. These realities of the relationship profoundly influence how we experience the physical act.

The goal of God's plan for this act is that our minds, hearts, wills, bodies, and spirits be in perfect harmony. All the elements inherent in covenant are required for the fullness of physical intimacy to be experienced. To the extent that any of these elements are not in good order, we will be personally conflicted, and it will simply be impossible for us to be fully open, transparent, and trusting with the other person. Our bodies will still "work" in a physiological sense, but much will be missing, even in a marriage when we are living out, at least to some degree, the reality of this relationship.

And what might be missing if we are not in a marriage? That is, when we create a covenant through sexual relations outside of marriage, we enjoy some of the pleasantries associated with marriage, but in no other way assume the responsibilities, duties, and obligations of covenant. Nor in any way acknowledge the reality of this relationship. In no sense in this scenario can true openness and vulnerability—the core of intimacy—be experienced. Instead, "consensual" nonmarital intercourse inevitably involves dishonesty and manipulation. It is an exercise in selfishness in which two people are trying to get something, but something other than a marriage. Thus, they violate every spiritual and moral reality surrounding sexual intercourse and marriage, damaging themselves at the deepest level in the process as noted in the Scriptures at the beginning of this section. Nowhere is the activity of the enemies of God more evident than in our society's movement toward embracing destructive sexual activity.

IMPLICATIONS OF SEXUAL INTERCOURSE

PREMARITAL INTERCOURSE IF THE COUPLE INTENDS TO WED

If we understand everything to this point, it goes without saying that our culture's recent attempts to change God's plan of marriage are far from God's intent. But is there any real harm if two people enter a covenant before they are publicly joined in a wedding ceremony? We noted earlier that the quality of marriages correlates closely with how the marriage relationship is understood and conducted; the closer these are to what marriage is designed by God to be, the better the marriage will be. Conversely, the more that marriages depart from the principles and practices of covenant, the more problems occur in the relationship and the less satisfying the relationship will be. Thus, what does *not* help a marriage is for the two people to be confused about the nature and foundation of their relationship. It is crucial that our approaches to each other—as we are building the most important relationship we will have on earth—builds the correct foundation if the marriage is to reach its potential.

By engaging in prewedding sexual intercourse a covenant is created. Though this relationship cannot be perceived in its fullness by the participants, still this reality is in full force. If we conduct ourselves completely out of accord with this reality—maintaining separation in most other realms of life, and refraining from giving in to each other's lives in the ways called for by covenant—we set up an internal conflict in both people. The first thing we establish in our new relationship is our unfaithfulness in most aspects of our covenant. The expectations we hold for our marriage and the marital relationship we build, based on the plan we are following, will likely be a poor reflection of covenant. Thus, we weaken the bond that holds us together and interfere with the blessings this relationship is designed to confer. Let us take a closer look at the many implications of this initial unfaithfulness to our covenant and our covenant partner.

We have already considered at length the amount of commitment and devotion it takes to build a relationship that is in accord with the spiritual reality of a marriage covenant, a lengthy phrase that simply means "build the best marriage." Early in a relationship patterns are being formed, and these patterns are much easier to build correctly in the first place than to tear down and rebuild—if we even realize that these patterns need revision.

But before we further dissect the problems caused by pre-wedding sexual activity, we must ask, "What good reason is there, or what irreplaceable benefit is found, in ignoring the clearly stated command of the Author of marriage?" The first thing to see in this conversation is that there is absolutely no benefit in the short term or long term of pre-wedding intercourse. Also, this raises the question of the importance of a wedding, if everyone who has intercourse is already actually married. A wedding, though now a nice and socially acceptable gesture, does not undo the confusion and damage already created. At this point, it reflects at best token, half-hearted obedience to God. The other reality to emphasize here is that engagements are often broken. If we do care about obeying God, and have in our minds negotiated a compromise that we hope will still be acceptable to God—by intending to marry—despite His clear instructions, what if the engagement is broken? Unfaithfulness to a relationship we were not even aware we created now multiplies. What we most need to see, though, are the benefits of obedience on this question.

How, and when, would two people who have been following the world's plan (have intercourse when you feel you are ready, or when the other person makes themselves available) arrive at the view that their relationship is a sacred and special joining of two people in a one-flesh bond? God wants perception and reality to coincide in the most powerful possible way because this is the only way marriages can be properly built; this is the only way the two will make the kind of decisions that build the relationship to its potential. Spirits, minds, hearts, and bodies must be in harmony with reality—which is covenant, in the larger context of God's overall moral law. Premarital intercourse, living together, and other almost-married activities simply continue to reinforce the couple's belief that sexual intercourse and marriage are not inextricably related, when in fact they are synonymous. If one believes sex can be termed a "casual" thing, how devoted will one be to the sexual exclusivity of marriage? We can simply look around to answer this question. Rates of adultery in marriage are much higher in recent decades than in my childhood in the 1960s, when the common cultural perception was that sex was to happen within marriage, period. Divorce rates increased manyfold in this same time period.

Sexual activity before a wedding is prohibited because it strikes at the heart of God's plan for marriage. This plan depends on not just creating a covenant relationship but doing so consciously, willingly embracing all that covenant entails. Intercourse before marriage creates a covenant, but lacking is acknowledgment of the nature of the relationship, the decision to embrace the totality of this relationship, and therefore any other element God has built into His plan to ensure the success of the marriage. Rather than making the effort to build into character and viewpoints, then into behavior, all the elements that lead to success in marriage, someone who has rejected the reality of covenant—though they may seek "marriage" as whatever form they ordain it to be—simply will not have the alignment of factors in heart and mind needed to build the best marriage relationship.

Life is hard, and we need more than our own resources, more even than the joint, pooled resources of a couple to get through life. At various points we all find that we need God's resources to make it through the challenges of living. In a wedding, we stand before an altar and ask God's blessing on our union; we invite His help and support for our marriage. How ironic that two people would stand before God seeking His blessing on their marriage if they have made a point of discounting and dismissing the most important thing God said about building their marriage, which is the timing of creating their covenant. If people make a point of ignoring God when it suits them, how enthusiastic will God be about digging them out of holes they will predictably fall into by continuing to ignore Him? Of course, God is gracious and merciful and will help those who call on Him. But He will not pour out His blessings on those who ignore Him in the same way He will pour out blessings on those who consistently display their love for Him through their obedience.

Marriages are not failing in unprecedented numbers because the plan of God is flawed. What G.K. Chesterton famously said about Christianity as a whole can also be said of God's plan for marriage: "Christianity has not been tried and found wanting. It has been thought difficult and not tried."

WHAT DO WE WANT TO AVOID UNTIL THE WEDDING NIGHT?

While the Scriptures do not speak with precision about what specific romantic activities do and do not initiate a covenant, the physical realities seem obvious: any activity where the body of one enters the body of another, and any activity where intimate body fluids are transferred, appear to qualify as covenant-initiating events. This appears to include oral sex. But rather than trying to determine the exact point of this line in order to get as close as possible to it without going over (using a condom does not create an exception to this rule; there will be a transfer to some degree even with this "protection," as attested by a pregnancy rate significantly greater then zero with their use), God's plan is that we choose to redirect our outside-of-marriage sexual energy toward relationship building.

BUILDING THE BEST ROMANTIC EXPERIENCE

Our goal is to build the best relationship we can build leading to the best marriage we can. God has created us so that there is a synchrony between mind, heart, body, and spirit when we are building a relationship in God's pattern, with proper things occurring at proper times. The getting-to-know-you process is all about timing. One person opens up a little, reveals something of themselves; the other then reflects understanding and also reveals something of themselves. One gives some gift of attention, or food, or flowers, or encouragement, or something they think will matter to the other person. The recipient responds so the giver can judge if this is something that should be repeated, or others gifts tried. Then the receiver reciprocates with something of fairly equal value. If someone is over-revealing for the current depth of the relationship, or is overwhelming in gifting—say, filling the room with bouquets—it does not feel like a blessing; it feels like the other person is not sensitive to one's heart. When someone is trying too hard, or not trying hard enough, it negatively impacts the normal rhythm of a growing friendship. Some relationships are lengthy dances of on-again, off-again, but eventually two people must demonstrate their commitment and caring in unequivocal and consistent ways for hearts to fully open to each other.

God created this sense of timing within us, along with a sense of modesty and reserve. One amazingly useful sense we can develop during the relationship-building process is learning to listen to this rhythm within ourselves and developing sensitivity to it within the other person. Two people in a growing relationship are often not at the same place in the process. Respectfully giving time and space, and learning to discern what the other person needs to take the next step, will build the kind of cooperation in the relationship that will be beneficial later as the couple begins to approach decision-making together.

The overall experience one wants to create for the other person is one of safety, security, trust, and transparency. These are the foundation stones upon which true intimacy is built. We want the other person to feel perfectly comfortable just being themselves. We do not want to force issues nor push forward in a way that either heart does not desire. If both parties demonstrate that they can create such a place together, this lays more of a foundation for everything else the couple wants to build. God's plan is that we not only have the delights of falling in love with each other as we are building the relationship but that we are also in a training process, learning how to relate, learning about ourselves as well as the other person, and developing our senses and discernment as well as cultivating consideration and respect for each other.

Remember, God's ultimate goal is that marriage radically transforms each of us. The small adjustments and accommodations we make during courtship are a tiny glimpse of what is (ideally) to come; and the blessings that flow from taking our best friend's interests into consideration begin to teach us that we can safely and beneficially shift our focus from our agenda to a shared agenda, from our interests to shared interests, and toward the ultimate development of mutual interests.

THERE IS MORE TO ROMANTIC ACTIVITY THAN INTERCOURSE

In the same way that getting to know someone in mental and emotional realms is a slow and steady progression, physical contact also has a comfortable and appropriate level that corresponds to the current depth of a relationship. Dr. James Dobson, in his book *Love for a Lifetime*, has a list of thirty or so different types of physical contact that correspond to growing closeness in relationship. These move from first touching another person to having intercourse with them. Holley and I studied this list during our first weeks of dating and committed to two things. First, we would avoid covenant-making physical activity until we were wed. Second, we would take these steps in order, gradually getting to know each other physically in tandem with getting to know each other in every way. There are too many benefits of this plan to list here, and I cannot recommend it enthusiastically enough. (This would literally be a book, and perhaps should be.)

Here are some of the benefits: first, we were completely comfortable with each other physically, from start to finish. There was no internal conflict or relationship conflict related to physical contact. We were on the same page, and before we turned to the next page we agreed to do so. This kept our physical, mental, and emotional life in complete harmony. The key is to not jump ahead, to not force forward in a way that creates discomfort or awkwardness. Taking the time to savor this journey, to thoroughly enjoy this process of revealing oneself and discovering the other, is one of the most delightful experiences of life and one of God's many relationship gifts to us. Before marriage, God obviously intends limits to pre-marital physical closeness. In every person's heart and mind God builds a boundary around covenant-creating sexual activity. One can blow through this boundary, and our society makes a point of training us to do so. But if we choose to acknowledge and respect this boundary, it feels like we are respecting the other person, and being respected—because we are. Consideration is mutually displayed, and displayed toward God. Though our society tries to pound into us the notion that something is lost by respecting this boundary, not only is nothing lost, everything worth having in a relationship is strengthened.

> In every person's heart and mind God builds a boundary around covenant-creating sexual activity. One can blow through this boundary, and our society makes a point of training us to do so.

The next benefit is trust. We learned that we could be in close proximity yet completely trust each other physically. Do you think this would build trust in other areas as well?

The next benefit was that the energy of our attraction was directed toward other ways of getting to know each other. We were crazy attracted to each other, but as we confined our considerable passions to certain limited physical expressions, the rest of our romantic energies went toward figuring out new ways to bless each other, to show how we felt and how much we cared. It was about eighteen months from our first date until our wedding. Living out our commitments to each other took considerable self-discipline and self-control—and tested and built that self-discipline and self-control. At every step, do you know what we had? As much fun as we ever had in our lives, but not just on occasion. We had an unbroken, eighteen-month run of fun.

Most couples have a much more up-and-down relationship, one that alternates between growing together and backing away. I'm convinced that the virtually continuous growth of our relationship had much to do with our plan to consciously and slowly build the relationship in every way, including physically.

We thought and talked about how to best get to know each other. One of our first areas of cooperation was figuring out how we could get to know as much as possible about the other in each stage of our growing relationship. One thing that did not grow slowly, by the way, was our hearts for each other. We were over-the-moon out of our minds for each other within a week of our first date. But even from this starting point, somehow our hearts for each other continued to increase, though by week four I did not think my heart could be any more on fire. But it was, week by week, for the next eighteen months until our wedding. Nor did this growth of heart stop after the wedding—or even slow down. Of course, Holley is a wonderful person, and we both brought good relationship skills to our union. But what happened between us seemed decidedly unusual. I attribute this to consciously building as many elements of covenant behavior as possible into our relationship at every step. These are, after all, the ways we want to be treated and the ways we want to treat our beloved. We made a point of trying our best to do nothing but this, even before we wed.

What do you think we proved to each other, and ourselves, during this time? We proved that we would not be ruled by momentary passions, but by our commitments. Do you think this was a valuable thing to learn about each other in light of considering a covenant relationship? How about the alternative? What if one or both people just cannot resist an extremely strong urge? What unfortunate possibility just became much more likely at some point in the future if our actions are guided by in-the-moment urges instead of our commitments? What if, on the other hand, our course is guided by convictions in every area that really matters?

HONORING GOD'S PLAN BUILDS NECESSARY CHARACTER

This leads to the next benefit of honoring God's timing for sexual activity: character building. Our sexual drive, combined with our culture's messages to satisfy that drive given any opportunity, plus the fact that our heart is now on fire for another person—the ultimate context in which we are supposed to display our love for each other physically—create the perfect temptation. Now, it is not about something that is wrong to do in an absolute sense. This is about something we both fully intend to do at some point. The only question is timing. We are going to learn a very important lesson, and there are actually two lessons from which we can choose: 1) the power of temptation; or 2) our power (in Christ) over temptation. Engaging in certain behaviors will change everything by initiating a covenant. This will change each of us at the deepest level and radically change the nature of the relationship. The real question, therefore: When should we cause these changes? Do you think God may have planned this exercise—delaying intercourse with someone we love—as a premium character-building experience? Why do we have, throughout history, an engagement period for marriage? Why not hear "yes" to our proposal and then get friends and family together the next week or the next day? Why the delay? Consider the elements of character that must be developed to keep a commitment to purity, not only for a few days, but for months, when the "issue" has been—almost—decided. Might the attributes needed to delay consummating the marriage until one actually has a wedding come in handy in other realms of life?

Another thing we need to learn is to think clearly. We need more than "God says so" in this pressure cooker. We need good, strong reasons to support one decision and refute the other. Can you see what we are talking about? We need to develop a conviction about this issue if we are to not bow to pressure from one direction or another. We spoke of this process earlier, and it involves more than just reasons, does it not? The process of developing a conviction also involves examining our own beliefs on this topic and subjecting our current beliefs to examination in light of absolute truth, God's Word. This is not "God says so, so that is the end of it." This is the process of searching out the truth and understanding why a God who loves us so much wants this for us so badly. We need His heart on this matter, and every matter. But first we need His mind—the real reasons. Therefore, we will look at a few more reasons not to preempt our wedding, and some reasons why waiting until after the wedding is such a good idea.

Is intercourse essential at any point outside of marriage? Can we safely delay it and not come to some kind of harm? Of course. People have been delaying intercourse until marriage for millennia. To refrain from engaging in this behavior, despite all urges, drives, encouragement, coercion, or peer pressure to the contrary is a decision anyone can make. If we develop the capacity to be guided by sound principle instead of bending to temptations, it is simple common sense that this will promote marital stability and success. This same pattern of self-discipline will open many other doors to success in other realms of life.

Those who govern themselves according to desires, personal prerogatives, and opportunity are simply not going to display the same consistently constructive behaviors—in obedience to vows and God—because they have not trained themselves to become capable of doing so. Thus, one's decision about premarital sexual behavior actually reflects a much more deep and broad decision—about the kind of person one intends to become, and about the level of respect one plans to display toward one's spouse-to-be, in addition to God.

THE IMPORTANCE OF A WEDDING

Everyone wants their marriage to be the best party ever. We want to be surrounded by friends and loved ones. We want them to have a great time and celebrate this most special of all occasions with us. People spend tremendous amounts of effort, time, and money to create the perfect wedding for themselves and their guests. Everyone wants the most powerful and meaningful experience, don't they? How would waiting until the wedding night play into making our wedding day such an experience?

You have to wonder why God has gone to this much trouble to institute and preserve weddings as the entry point for marriage for all these years. Why aren't covenants typically created within minutes of an accepted proposal in whatever private place two people can find in the moment? If God thinks weddings are this important, there must be a good reason. What does it look and feel like if we do things His way? What if we harness the full power of God's plan? Let's look at a wedding and see if we can get some sense for why God's plan, including the timing of sexual activity, is as it is.

THE FULL POWER OF GOD'S PLAN CELEBRATED—AND UNLEASHED

A wedding publicly acknowledges our intention before God to enter holy matrimony. Honor and respect are first and foremost to God in a wedding, the Author of all this. Then we touch on every part of God's plan. We come before Him at an altar, or in some way stand in His presence, addressing Him as well our beloved and those assembled. We speak vows. Especially if we understand the commitment we are making, and the weight of our words, our hearts are now fully aligned with God's plan to create a new person, part of a new family, to become one flesh with another new person. This event is the most beautiful, emotion-filled, celebrated event of our lives. Why? Because the celebration corresponds to the gravity and beauty of this imminent life change. Rings are exchanged—beautiful, pure, precious things. A representative of God speaks words acknowledging the union of the couple before Him, blessing that union and holding the new couple up before God, family, and friends.

Then there is a party, a huge celebration of family and friends, a huge outpouring of good will and best wishes. In this reception there are still ceremonial vestiges that illustrate covenant, such as the two feeding each other cake and wine. The couple then is ceremoniously whisked away in a nice, perhaps well-decorated vehicle to actually join together in the bond they have spent the day celebrating, vowing, and illustrating.

As they are thus transformed, joined, and made new, can you see how the power of the celebration was perfectly aligned with the reality of the transformation from single people to couple, from best friends to one flesh? How standing before God and acknowledging His role in designing this relationship, then leading these two together toward this relationship, then vowing to accept and faithfully live out this covenant, not only defines the reality of this relationship but impresses on the couple the magnitude of the transformation that will soon occur? This is an "all things have become new" moment. The wedding focuses attention on the all-in nature of this imminent joining. All of this makes sense emotionally, mentally, physically, and spiritually. The overall experience of a wedding impacts the couple at each of these levels if they have any awareness of what they are hearing, seeing, and doing. And the couple's first intercourse, following this celebration, is just as momentous a thing as all of this would suggest for just these reasons. This plan harnesses the full power of God for life change—not only the change itself, but the couple's perception of this change. Both, as we have seen, are vital. If the couple is to inhabit their new relationship as God intends, they must understand the relationship and choose to follow His plan for it. In a wedding we see a nice sampling of God's entire plan to inform, conform, and transform. This gets the newlyweds off to the best possible start.

> And the couple's first intercourse, following this celebration, is just as momentous a thing as all of this would suggest for just these reasons. This plan harnesses the full power of God for life change.

Why would someone not want to experience the fullness of God's plan in this way? I suspect the current arms race of more and more extravagant and expensive weddings is just over-compensating . . . for the fact that the ceremony has been stripped of much of its actual meaning. Rather than gathering before the Lord to honor Him and accept His gift of relationship, a wedding is more of a formality, a photo op, a we-had-the-biggest-party kind of thing. Rather than an "all things have become new" moment, what exactly is being celebrated?

What if two people enter a covenant when they believe they are "ready" for sex, but not ready to fulfill many, or any, of the principles, duties, and responsibilities of their covenant? What if they continue to affirm in their minds, hearts, and lives that they are separate individuals simply waiting to see if the other person adds enough value to their respective lives to continue to stick around? Even if these people eventually have a wedding, what are they building between themselves and within themselves? What have they decided marriage is? How have they trained themselves to be toward each other? What does faithfulness mean to these two? What is the potential of their relationship? Were these two really ready for sex?

The best marriages are built very carefully. I shared earlier that at every point Holley and I learned as much as we could about God's plan and followed it carefully. To me this explains the continuous power we experienced in the relationship as it grew, the power of blessing after blessing, the power inherent in God's plan and in lives guided by Him. This is not because our lives were easy and straightforward. Our personal circumstances were as challenging as anyone's. But as we confronted each challenge and dealt with each situation in the ways described, we grew, our relationship grew, and issues and problems were resolved, at times in ways that led to even more lessons. Our circumstances were decidedly not perfect, but we found ourselves building a remarkably rich and strong relationship and quality of life in the midst of all this. The bedrock reality of our relationship was our commitment to live before God in obedience and before each other with integrity. I believe the trajectory of our relationship ever since reflects God's plan substantially—though certainly not perfectly—implemented through all the challenges of life. The circumstances were not perfect at any point, not even close, but our relationship and quality of life in the midst of normal life has been an experience I would not trade for anything.

To me, the most compelling reason to follow God's plan for life and marriage is what happens when we do. We often do not believe our lives could be much different from our experience to date. Nor did I on the front end. I had no idea the course our lives together would take and likely would not have believed it if I had been told on the front end.

Now, to Him who is able to do immeasurably more than we ask or imagine, according to His power that is at work within us . . .
EPHESIANS 3:20

SEXUAL INTERCOURSE AND NEW LIFE

One of the most important reasons to carefully observe God's plan—intercourse at the time of personal and public proclamation that we are "all in," publicly forming a new family under the guidance and protection of God—is that this initial intercourse can produce more than just new life for the participants. It can also produce another new life, a child. As a physician, I can assure you that nothing that is done to keep pregnancy from resulting from intercourse is 100% effective. The only thing that will reliably keep pregnancy from occurring is abstinence. If the proper things are done in the proper order according to God's plan, children are born into a family with a mother and father. The mother and father are not only in a fully committed relationship, they are now involved in the training process God has ordained to make them the best parents they can become to the children their intercourse creates. If the parents are harnessing the opportunities covenant offers to learn to love, to consciously build their lives together as one flesh, to have character shaped and molded, to be transformed into the men and women God created them to be and become, these parents will learn invaluable lessons about love. People do not learn these lessons if they do not participate in God's training process. They will be better parents if they have learned these lessons. Parenting, in turn, teaches us lessons that help build and grow a marriage. This is also part of God's plan.

The importance of a two-parent household is hotly debated in the social science world, as is the importance of whether parents are married or not. The importance of the gender mixture of parents is questioned, as is essentially every other aspect of family life God has ordained. As if people with a few years of college education, access to a computer, and no meaningful personal life experience in the realm in question are in position to overturn and reinvent a social institution that has been present and vibrant for six thousand years. One must also carefully define "science" in this realm. What experiment could one design, after all, that matches the benefits of God's plan against the alternative? One can look at two, or three, or five measurable parameters, but how can one really determine the relative quality of life produced by these approaches? If a scientist could even define these approaches and distinguish them—which they cannot. Despite these real limits to scientifically studying the application of any or all moral issues, scientists offer calming and encouraging words about single parenthood, or abortion as remedy for the predictable consequences of mistimed and inappropriate intercourse. Or divorce as the obvious answer for marriages that never became anything remotely resembling what they might have been.

It should be clear to any thoughtful person with significant life experience that a child does better with two loving, married parents in a stable household than in any other scenario. And, given that a pre-born human being, if simply left alone for nine months in the womb will grow into a being who can live outside the womb, there is no point in this continuum where this being somehow converts from "non-person" to "person." They are persons on a continuum of growth from the moment of their conception, when they already contain as a single cell every potential they will ever have. To take this life in the womb is no different in any absolute sense than taking this life at any other point. This point has been graphically illustrated and confirmed by proponents of abortion as they lobby for the "right" to deny food and water to babies who escape late-term abortions and are born alive—only to be killed by neglect under medical and parental order if the abortionists get their way, as they have in several states at present.

Does it matter, then, in this scenario, whether the child is six hours old or six years old? In any other context, such behavior by parent or physician would be termed child abuse if unsuccessful in ending life, and murder if successful. Even if such behavior is "legalized" by the state, would the nature and character of such behavior be altered by the vote of a state legislature or the gavel of a judge? Or would the state now become an accomplice to the murder of the most defenseless of humans—as it has already become in some cases. Current arguments on this matter now strip away, once and for all, the artifice that these advocates only intend to kill "non-persons."

While God has a plan to redeem the life and circumstances of every person on earth, this does not relieve people of the responsibility for placing a child who might be conceived by irresponsible sexual activity (according to God's definition, not Planned Parenthood's) in harm's way. The supposed benefits of out-of-wedlock sexual expression are an illusion across the board, while timing according to God's plan not only creates a myriad of blessings and benefits, it also avoids myriad possible bad consequences, not only in the lives of the participants but also in the lives of children who are being created in large numbers by this irresponsibility. Life is promised when one chooses "not-God," but death in one form or another always ensues, including the literal death of many millions of unborn children. Satan's path leads to death; God's path leads to life. We must never lose sight of this reality.

THESE AND OTHER BENEFITS

Sexual intercourse and other expressions of sexuality are either a remarkably deep, rich, rewarding, fun, exciting, passionate, enthusiastic, thrilling, warm, soft, quiet, peaceful, communal, shared, poetic, beautiful, energetic, meaningful, rewarding, gratifying, satisfying, abundant, growing, learning, expressive, contemplative, worshipful thing under the guidance of our Creator—or something much less than these, depending on our choices. God has made this wonder available to us at any time. It is portable and can show up in surprising places at surprising times. It is free, though it costs us our lives as the price of admission—only to give more delightful and meaningful lives back. It produces fun, closeness, and children. It produces some of life's most memorable moments, none of which I am going to share with you. If we must wait a little, or a lot, and work hard, or even harder, to do this God's way instead of reaching for some "innovation" and alteration inspired by God's enemy, we can reasonably expect the blessing and favor of the Lord in our lives as we walk with Him and live out His will.

> It is free, though it costs us our lives as the price of admission— only to give more delightful and meaningful lives back.

To understand and defend against the things we have been taught by our culture, inspired as they are by this enemy, we need to have a more clear view of our culture's plan. And we always need to keep in mind what is behind this plan—and who.

QUESTIONS FOR THOUGHT

1. How is a marriage covenant created? What is the role of vows and a ceremony in the creation of this covenant? What goes missing if a wedding ceremony does not occur?

2. What impact might it have on a relationship for two people to be in covenant but to neither recognize the nature of their relationship nor live out any of the responsibilities of this relationship toward each other? Another way of asking this question: How do relationships predictably change when people start having intercourse outside of marriage (in their perception)? However one answers this question, one thing is clear: the relationship changes significantly.

3. How do you think current cultural ideas about what a sexual relationship "outside marriage" is supposed to be impact an individual's understanding of what this relationship actually is and how it is to be conducted? Do you think our expectations define

this relationship or the spiritual realities God has revealed? Of course, our expectations greatly impact how we actually conduct such a relationship, but do our expectations define the fundamental nature of the relationship or not?

4. Do you think a person's expectations, if out of line with reality, will impact their heart and mind going forward in certain ways? How? If we are persuaded to try to be something we actually are not, how would we expect this to turn out?

5. If we understand marriage, and ourselves, and build a relationship in keeping with these realities, how would we expect this to turn out? Is there anything about God's plan that does not steer us toward what is real, true, and constructive?

6. What character qualities are built by waiting until the wedding night to have intercourse? What other things are built into the relationship by waiting until the wedding night? What kinds of consequences are we setting in motion by choosing to wait—or choosing to not wait—until the wedding night? At what point will the fullness of these consequences become apparent?

7. Why have weddings been part of marriage throughout human history in every culture? If a wedding is conducted in accordance with Scripture and Christian traditions, referencing and illustrating all the spiritual realities of marriage, what specific impacts might this have on the bride and groom? How might the synchrony of the ceremony, the vows, and initiation of the covenant be of tangible benefit to the couple?

8. If you are married, or have close relationships with married couples, have you noticed anything you would identify that corresponds to the "one flesh" that God describes, the new life that defines entry into covenant? How do two who are newly married usually identify themselves? What is the significance of a name change? What other manifestations of this reality have you observed or personally encountered? Do you notice that, the more you think about this question, the more items you recall? How

would you compare the changes noted in a couple recently married with the changes you note in a person who has just become a Christian? Are the changes inherently possible in either relationship present at this point more in potential or in the moment? What does this mean about our reliance on our perceptions for understanding these relationships versus learning about them from God's revelation?

9. How many ways might the new life that occurs in marriage impact your life right now? Over time? Is it not interesting that the very act that brings new life in the couple also creates another completely new human life? And that the celebration of covenant God tells us to frequently engage in gives so much life to the relationship? This is among the most meaningful and delightful of human experiences—free and freely available, though at the same time at the cost of a lifetime commitment. How do you see this new life in areas of the relationship not directly related to sexual activity? Is there any aspect of living not impacted by this new life? How can you see God using this reality for His purposes over the course of your life?

10. Based on your exposure to His plan for marriage thus far, would you agree or disagree that covenant is the heart of God's plan for humanity?

CHAPTER TWELVE

God's Plan Under Attack

Because of the increase of wickedness,
the love of most will grow cold.
MATTHEW 24:12

The section on sexuality was saved for last because this is the portion of God's plan that has been most enthusiastically and successfully assaulted. This is not, by the way, a recent phenomenon. Problems related to sexual behavior are some of the most frequently mentioned topics in the New Testament. There are dozens of references to various inappropriate sexual activities, always in tandem with a clear and consistent message that sexual activity is to be confined to marriage. The response of the ancient world to this proclamation of the exclusive relationship between marriage and sexual activity was referenced in 1 Corinthians 6:13: "Food for the stomach, and the stomach for food." In other words, as the natural function of our stomachs is to receive food, so the natural function of our male and female parts is to be used for sexual activity, with no moralizing.

An updated version of this view was offered by the group Bloodhound Gang in their 1999 song, "The Bad Touch." "*You and me, Baby, ain't nothing but mammals; let's do it like they do on the Discovery Channel.*[4]" Thus, any moralizing in this realm is misplaced; this is simply a reasonable use of the resources at hand. God's answer, however, is found in 1 Corinthians 6:13,15: "The body, however, is not meant for sexual immorality but for the Lord, and the Lord for the body. . .

. Do you not know that your bodies are members of Christ Himself? Shall I then take the members of Christ and unite them with a prostitute? Never!"

If we understand that God has an enemy who wants to destroy God's image and works in the hearts and minds of humanity; if we understand that this enemy also wants to create as much damage in humanity as he can while at the same time seducing people to follow him, and thus to worship him, what would be the ideal target for this enemy to attack? If God's plan is maturity and character developed through strong families, what would derail maturity, distort character, and destroy families most effectively? How about destroying as completely as possible the concepts of faithfulness to covenant and sexual purity, upon which the family is founded. Further, if there was an absolutely delightful physical experience that God reserved for only a very specific context—marriage—how might it ingratiate this enemy to the mass of humanity if he offers this delightful experience to . . . everyone, anytime they want it, with no restrictions or rules and no additional responsibilities? Desire alone qualifies one for sexual intercourse. In fact, these two attacks on God's plan are one and the same. All of Satan's goals can be accomplished simply by doing the same thing with sex and our culture that he did with Eve and the fruit. Satan simply offers a plan for sexuality that seems, on casual observation, to be a better plan than God is offering. This is the story of the human race as we have turned from God to embrace deception again and again across millennia.

Satan's attacks on God's plan do not just show up in sources that are avowedly anti-God, like much of the media and scientific community. He has also inserted many one-off ideas into the teachings of many denominations. The pace of this as well as the degree of divergence from Scripture is rapidly increasing. In the Christian community we often start with views that are, on the surface, closer to the Scriptural model, like having intercourse only with someone we actually intend at some point to marry. A recent poll showed a majority of people aged 20 to 35 who regularly attend church do not believe premarital sex or living together is a moral problem or prohibited by God's moral law. Where did they get these ideas?

I wanted to lay out God's entire plan for the Covenant of Marriage in the detail this book allows, first so we can see something of the depth, breadth, beauty, and specificity of God's plan. To fully appreciate God's instructions and God's plan, we need to first understand what He has made possible for us to build. We must understand how much we have to lose by departing from His plan. God's plan is a complete package, a seamless whole, each aspect of which builds and sustains crucial elements. His plan is not improved by innovation, addition, or subtraction. In fact, as soon as we try to improve on God's plan, attempting to seek something that—from our vantage point—appears better than what God is offering us, we are no longer following His plan. We are affixing ourselves to a one-off plan, and we have noted that these ultimately come from God's enemies, even if we are unaware of this reality. By now we should be very familiar with this pattern as well as the agenda and being behind it.

CULTURAL TEACHING ABOUT UNMARRIED SEXUAL INTERCOURSE

One thing many people less than 40 years old today do not realize is that our culture used to widely embrace and promote the belief that sexual activity was to be confined to marriage. This view was voiced not only in churches, but in schools, the media, and the legal system. The invention, around 1960, of the birth control pill and other quasi-reliable contraceptives introduced for the first time the possibility of separating sex from childbearing, and this quickly led to the notion of separating sex from marriage, designating it a recreational activity between consenting adults. This was termed "the sexual revolution" because it upended what had been before—a cultural view in our nation of sexuality largely fashioned on God's Word. God designed the act itself to be so pleasurable that it became easy, once the risk of pregnancy was significantly reduced, to market what was previously thought to be "completely irresponsible and inappropriate sexual activity" as a good thing to a culture in the process of exchanging the imperative of personal responsibility for the imperative of personal attempts at gratification by alternate pathways.

Rather than cultivating personal qualities and habits that tend toward the success of marriage as the ticket to sexual gratification, our populace shifted toward simply gratifying sexual urges outright, not to mention toward other indulgences like mind-altering drugs. Would a gratification-seeking lifestyle develop character and habits that tend to increase, or lessen, the success of marriage? Was the sexual revolution of the '60s and beyond really a giant leap forward for humankind? While our culture devoted itself to avidly seeking gratification, did we actually find it?

When the previous standard was discarded, was there a new standard advanced that was clear, reasonable, and constructive? Are people now more safe, secure, and satisfied, sexually and otherwise, in our culture? Let's take a look at what has replaced a cultural standard that largely reflected God's. Once someone accepts the premise that God's rules are not applicable to his or her life, what do these unbounded lives look like? You do not need my answer; simply look around. When one takes the position that God's rules do not apply, there is no other clear, consistent code of conduct that applies beyond people doing whatever they feel like doing. To further emphasize the importance of God's plan, let's look at what this alternative plan translates into in terms of behavior and outcomes. What do people feel like doing when they can do whatever they feel like?

THE REAL COST OF SEXUAL INDULGENCE OUTSIDE MARRIAGE

Whatever the hoped-for benefits of sexual activity outside marriage, the reality is that vast amounts of human struggle, pain, and suffering flow from engaging in this activity outside of God's plan. Consequences extend to a whole subpopulation of single mothers who are supported by government funding (via taxing the rest of the populace) who, with their children, now form a permanent "underclass"; to a generation that has lost sight of marriage as an important life goal; to abortion. Worldwide figures from the Guttmacher Institute for the years 2010-2014 show an average of 56 million abortions per year[5], with a total of 1.72 billion children killed via abortion over the last 40 years[6]. While not everyone who has an abortion is unmarried, in the United States 85 percent are unmarried according to the national Centers for Disease Control. The corollary social movement to sexual activity as a personal choice has been the "necessity" of abortion to deal with the reality of "unwanted" children produced by exercising this new freedom.

> In these and other ways, the costs of sexual activity outside of God's plan are staggering.

In these and other ways, the costs of sexual activity outside of God's plan are staggering. Far from being an appropriate tool of adolescent self-exploration and amusement or adult recreation, sexual activity outside of marriage results in massive physical, emotional, relational, and socioeconomic consequences despite every "safe sex" measure that can be recommended to mitigate some of the risks. By the way, rather than prudish moralizing, this is a urologist speaking after decades of clinical experience. If you really let the above statistics sink in, it will become evident that just one predictable consequence of sexual activity—pregnancy—has been the rallying cry to kill more human beings in the last forty years than have been killed by all the wars in human history. Over 20 percent of the earth's population has been killed by abortion during my lifetime—again, 1.72 billion people.

Then there is the individual cost. If, as God says, offering ourselves for sexual activity actually alters who we are, and if we are not to offer our most precious of all possessions, our very identity, on the street like an inexpensive commodity—as Proverbs says, like a loaf of bread—what if we do take this casual approach to our own lives? What value do we place on ourselves? On our being, our nature and identity? No wonder depression is a rapidly growing phenomenon over the last sixty years. And if this is represents the true value of human life, made in the image of God—worth little if anything, to be given to passing strangers at no cost—is it any surprise that human trafficking, the buying and selling of human beings to serve the sexual appetites of others, is sharply on the rise at the same time? Or rape? While one might argue the difference between "consensual" and intercourse via violence or enslavement, all of these make essentially the same statement: I, as a human being made in the image of God, am merely a commodity—to be given, bought, sold, or taken by force. This is not how God sees us, nor how we should see each other, nor how we should see ourselves.

Sexual activity outside of God's plan therefore represents the most devastating war that has ever been waged against the human race. Who is the general spearheading this war? Termed the "father of lies," here we see some of his most powerful work in action.

IS CONFINING SEX TO MARRIAGE EVEN POSSIBLE IN THE REAL WORLD?

Another question often posed is whether God's command of chastity, and therefore of virginity until the time one weds, is even possible. Would not people simply fall dead on the streets due to this deficiency, or kill themselves in vast numbers if they could not have sex when they wanted? The assertion is made that people have "always" had intercourse sans marriage in a way that reflects our current cultural standards for sexual behavior. This behavior was simply not acknowledged by past generations. It was kept a secret.

When I reference the dramatic shifts seen during my lifetime, here is one of the most significant: until the 1960s the cultural expectation was that people be virgins at marriage. There are virtually no data on virginity at the time of marriage in the 1950s and before because, until this time, virginity would be assumed for the vast majority of people. But this, again, is not what the social scientists are asserting. Instead, they are asserting that no sane person could believe that this kind of self-control was ever seen in all of human history. I strongly disagree with this assertion; this is an important issue for all of us to understand. Does God require something of us that is literally impossible, or if possible completely undesirable? I am a physician whose scope of practice included fertility and infertility, so my medical knowledge base includes this area. Please indulge me while I demonstrate with statistics why the assertion of social scientists—that wide-spread virginity has never been and can never be—is simply wrong.

The assertion most common in the social science realm today is that the percentage of virgins at the time of marriage has always been similar to the 3 percent of marriages today in which both partners are virgins (although, as noted, there are almost no statistics available to cite pre-1950s). It would be interesting to see where they obtained subjects to sample for this 3 percent result, as this is out of sync with other current statistics on virginity, which show much higher rates than this for males and females in teenage and adulthood. Rather than speculation rooted in their desire to "prove" that almost no one in history has ever really taken abstinence till marriage seriously, let me point to a few statistics cited by the Guttmacher Institute (associated with Planned Parenthood)[7]. Teen pregnancy rates in the 1950s were higher than current rates because most people married before 20 years of age. Thus, around 9 percent of teens became pregnant per year, but in only 12 percent of these pregnancies was the mother unmarried. Thus, 12 percent of 9 percent of pregnant females means around 1 percent of teens were *pregnant but not married* in a given year. We can get a pretty accurate estimate for the frequency of

> Does God require something of us that is literally impossible, or if possible completely undesirable? I am a physician whose scope of practice included fertility and infertility, so my medical knowledge base includes this area.

intercourse among unmarried teens from these figures. How can we do this?

A STATISTICAL LOOK AT TEENAGE SEXUAL ACTIVITY IN THE 1950S

The birth control pill had not been developed, and other less effective measures like condoms were generally also not available to teens. Given the fertility rate of teen females, in whom having unprotected intercourse results in a *20 percent rate of pregnancy per month*, if "everyone" were having premarital intercourse, far more than around 1 percent per year of females would be conceiving, right? In contrast, in 2000, according to Guttmacher,[8] 5 percent of teens became pregnant per year, despite this group having access to vastly more effective means of birth control. Eighty percent of these were unmarried (four of every five), so for the most part the contraceptive failure—which is a good deal lower than 20 percent per month for unprotected intercourse—rate led to 4 percent of teens becoming pregnant per year. To say that, therefore, the rate of sexual activity in these two groups—1950 versus 2000—was comparable means that one is not very good at math. For unmarried teens in the 1950s to have only a 1 percent pregnancy rate per year (that is a rate of 0.8 percent per month), given the 20 percent rate of pregnancy per month for unprotected intercourse, and given the fact that intercourse in the 1950s would have almost always been unprotected, there simply must have been vastly fewer unmarried people having intercourse in that era. The best estimate would be obtained by multiplying 0.8 percent by 5, assuming that one-fifth of people who were having intercourse got pregnant per month. Five times this number would be the number of people having intercourse with any frequency. And, as we know, once may be enough. This would suggest that, looking at monthly figures, around 4 percent of teen couples had premarital intercourse in any given month, or 5 percent at any time during the year if one looks at the yearly rates. This, again, squares much better with reported rates of virginity in high school students, male and female, in the 1960s when social scientists began asking this question.

A few months of unprotected intercourse would be expected to impregnate about half the females. To offer still more weight to this, engaging in unprotected intercourse for a year without producing a pregnancy is the clinical definition of *infertility*, and the vast majority of these people were certainly not infertile. Thus, what percentage of these people were having intercourse outside of marriage? In the absence of data we do not know the precise answer. What we do know is that current estimates for pre-1960 teenage sexual activity thrown around by social scientists on the Internet are medically implausible. These appear to be more about marketing recreational sex to our rising generations than an exercise true social science.

THE CONSEQUENCES OF DEPARTING FROM GOD

> In addition to the actions, please note the resulting frustration, contention, and lack of fulfillment noted in people who follow these deceptions.

In Romans chapter one God takes us through a sequence of steps that individuals, and therefore whole societies, take after they choose a path for living that is not God's. Let's look at this passage in its entirety, for it clearly describes the shifting paradigm, the progressive changes of behavior, and the consequences we see all around us. In addition to the actions, please note the resulting frustration, contention, and lack of fulfillment noted in people who follow these deceptions. Then note the association between this progression of sexual behaviors and the progression to behavior that is distinctly destructive and criminal, behaviors now reasonable in the misshaped minds and hearts of the perpetrators as a logical extension of lies they have embraced.

The wrath of God is being revealed from heaven against all the godlessness and wickedness of people who suppress the truth by their wickedness, since what may be known about God is plain to them, because God has made it plain to them. For since the creation of the world God's invisible qualities—his eternal power and divine nature—have been clearly seen, being understood from what has been made, so that people are without excuse. For although they knew God, they neither glorified him as God nor gave thanks to him, but their thinking became futile and their foolish hearts were darkened. Although they claimed to be wise, they became fools and exchanged the glory of the immortal God for images made to look like a mortal human being and birds and animals and reptiles. Therefore God gave them over to the sinful desires of their hearts, to sexual impurity for the degrading of their bodies with one an- other. They exchanged the truth of God for a lie, and worshipped and served created things rather than the Creator—who is forever praised. Amen. Because of this, God gave them over to shameful lusts. Even their women exchanged natural sexual relations for unnatural ones. In the same way the men also abandoned natural relations with women and were inflamed with lust for one another. Men committed shameful acts with other men, and received in themselves the due penalty for their error.
ROMANS 1:18-27

The passage continues (verses 28-32) by drawing the additional connection between denying God and other sorts of evil and destruc- tive behaviors.

Furthermore, just as they did not think it worthwhile to retain the knowledge of God, so God gave them over to a depraved mind, so that they do what ought not to be done. They have become filled with every kind of wickedness, evil, greed and depravity. They are full of envy, murder, strife, deceit and malice. They are gossips, slanderers, God-haters, insolent, arrogant and boastful; they invent ways of doing evil; they disobey their parents; they have no under-

standing, no fidelity, no love, no mercy. Although they know God's righteous decree that those who do such things deserve death, they not only continue to do these very things, but also approve of those who practice them.

This is the world we live in. This is the world that has trained and influenced each of us. This is the world influencing our children, and it will happily raise them if we do not intercede. This is the world we must depart from in principle and practice if we are to have the best marriage and most successful families. The passage above describes the Roman Empire at the time Christ walked the earth, and our current society is being transformed to resemble it once more. God's plan worked then, and it will work now if tried.

CHAPTER THIRTEEN

The Covenant of Marriage in Summary

Where your treasure is, there your heart will be also.
MATTHEW 6:21

The Covenant of Marriage is, at first impression, a very simple thing. The simplistic way God introduces this topic assumes a lot—for instance, that we already understand what the word covenant means. The passage in Genesis that introduces covenant is only a few lines long, and it does not even use this term. The first time the term covenant is applied to marriage is in the last book of the Old Testament, Malachi, though it was always clear from the nature of this relationship that marriage is a form of covenant. The rest of God's counsel on marriage is scattered in bits and pieces throughout Scripture. The fundamental reality, one flesh, seems straightforward enough, though this concept is obviously subject to misinterpretation. As with many things of God, though, as we examine these things or try to live them, we find beneath the apparent simplicity vast complexity and unexpected power.

Covenant is about total transformation. Our beings are transformed at the deepest level, and joined. We want unity and union; now we have it. This one move removes the basis for most interpersonal conflict in marriage, and it inserts the most compelling reason of all to love each other. Our understanding of the nature of the relationship must be transformed from what we can perceive or from cultural understandings to God's original definition and intent. Our understanding of love and what it means to love is transformed by simply being in the relationship, and by God's educational process. The process of growth and transformation inherent in this relationship reaches into every corner, every aspect of our lives and persons, extending the immediate transformation of nature over time into comprehensive character change. This growth and transformation of character, then, builds a much different life than would have been built by the person otherwise, a life fashioned after God's plan, one built to accomplish His loving purposes for self, family, community, and world.

Covenant is about total commitment, about being totally invested. As noted in Matthew 6:21 above, our hearts follow our investment of ourselves. If we are totally invested in our husband or wife, if we are totally committed to God's plan to build our marriage to its potential, our hearts will grow to completely, wholeheartedly love the other person, and our heart

> Through faithfulness to covenant our lives and hearts are built around the one who is already in us, and we in them.

for our marriage and family will continue to grow for the rest of our lives. In covenant, our husband or wife immediately becomes our life. Through faithfulness to covenant our lives and hearts are built around the one who is already in us, and we in them.

Covenant is about taking full responsibility. Each partner in covenant is charged with taking responsibility for every need of the other, for their global well-being. It requires a training process coupled with proper character development to produce a highly responsible person, one who recognizes their obligation for personal conduct as well as caring for whoever or whatever is placed in their charge. *"Those who are faithful in little things are faithful with much."* When responsible spouses are given the next level of responsibility—children—they recognize and fulfill their responsibility to raise those children properly. Absent this developmental process, the raising of children is de facto delegated to media, peers, and schools, with the results we are now seeing on all sides. But when taking on increasing responsibility becomes a way of life—which is God's intention—how might God be able to use such a person?

What has surprised me most, as Holley and I aggressively pursued this course—as we learned God's definition of love and learned to apply it in a growing array of ways across the relationship; as we learned how to learn, and learned how to grow; as we together applied the process of transformation inherent in this relationship—is that this approach works even better than we hoped! We did not give God enough credit initially even though we were committed to Him. We did not understand how beneficial all of this would be as we lived out our covenant commitments to each other. We did not realize the things that were within us, waiting to be brought forth at the right time, which could only have developed in the relationship environment already built by God's plan.

Then we watched God, time after time, match developing things in one or both of us with new opportunities—new things to build— which led to even more lessons and more life change, which led to yet more opportunities. We cannot begin to detail all of this in a book. All of this flowed directly from two things: a correct definition of covenant, and everything that flows from this definition. This understanding congealed into a logical series of steps to build our marriage, a plan that flowed naturally from the definition of this relationship and what is required to implement this understanding. From this plan a marriage grew that I would not trade with anyone, although it is one we do want to give away to others. Thus, this book was written.

Why is everything in this book not common knowledge in our culture, as it was for the most part when the Scriptures were written? The understanding that informed this book series was rediscovered by H. Clay Trumbull, a highly respected Christian leader and writer, and conveyed through his book published in 1885, *The Blood Covenant*. I suspect one reason Trumbull's well-researched treatise on covenant was not more enthusiastically embraced by the theologians of his day, in addition to Satan's obvious motivation to suppress this information, was the naturalistic bent that was sweeping not only academia but the theological world in the late 1800s.

In past centuries the best and brightest scientists saw no problem juxtaposing the realm of science and the visible natural world with a supernatural realm. There is no inherent contradiction between these two realms, and there is much evidence that things beyond the physical realm exist. However, with increasing fervor since the mid-1800s, philosophers and scientists have asserted that the physical realm is all there is, period. This leaves them with no satisfying explanation for many things that impact our lives and world. And among theologians there arose a similar notion, and this left many trying to reconcile the miracles recorded in Scripture with a "natural" explanation, leading many to simply discard the parts of Scripture that did not fit their new preconceptions.

Into this world was born an excellent book on covenant. This topic, however, speaks of something that is more of the spiritual realm than the natural. The bond of covenant is not easily observed or measured; God's revelation, with words properly defined, is required to understand it. Trumbull's work redefined the word *covenant*, and in doing so went up against the already well entrenched "modern" view of covenant as a contract. I suspect that few in Christian academia were anxious to champion this work given the shifting tide of thought among their peers, and far fewer would do so today. One could make the same observation about other topics, like the indwelling Holy Spirit or the virgin birth. How much academic effort has gone toward understanding these remarkably important realities in the last century and a half?

While trends of thought may change, cultures come and go, nations and empires rise and fall, and millennia slowly tick by, God, His Word, and His plan do not change. He is there to be trusted and loved always, and He blesses those who do so. Marriage is vastly more durable than any other social institution in history, precisely because it perfectly reflects God's creation and plan. Though this plan is often implemented imperfectly, its power is such that it survives even human ignorance and ineptitude, and the institution has maintained its central role in human civilization for six thousand years.

God has left detailed instructions to build this relationship to full potential, and He has left them where we can find them if we care to look. We have taken a look at these instructions in the way a book of this length allows. In marriage we are not dealing with something new, untried, or of an uncertain outcome. I believe we are dealing with the heart of God's plan for humanity from the beginning, along with the other form of covenant we will examine in the next volume in this series.

May God richly bless you as you take His plan and implement it in your marriage and life.

ENDNOTES

CHAPTER FOUR

1. Shaunti Feldhahn, The Good News About Marriage, (Multnomah Press, 2014), cited on shaunti.com. Accessed May, 2019.

CHAPTER SIX

2. Wedding Paper Divas. From WeddingPaperDivas.Nearlyweds. com. Accesssed May, 2019.

CHAPTER SEVEN

3. I Can Only Imagine, Erwin Brothers Entertainment, 2018

CHAPTER TWELVE

4. The Bad Touch, Bloodhound Gang, (Geffen, Santa Monica, Ca., Jimmy Pop), 1999.

5. guttmacher.org/statistics, World Abortion Statistics-Data by Country. Accessed May, 2019

6. lifesitenews.com, 1.72 billion abortions worldwide in the last 40 years, April 1, 2013.

7. Guttmacher Institute, guttmacher.org., Teen Pregnancy: Trends and Lessons Learned, Heather Boonstra, February 1, 2002. Accessed May 2019.

8. Ibid.

Printed in the USA
CPSIA information can be obtained
at www.ICGtesting.com
JSHW012048140824
68134JS00035B/3316

9 781949 572520